P A N D O R A

Discovering
women's history

Deirdre Beddoe is one of Wales's leading feminist historians. She has taught in secondary school, is an experienced lecturer in women's studies to adult, extra-mural and degree students, and is Senior Lecturer in History and Art History at the Polytechnic of Wales, Pontypridd. Deirdre Beddoe is the author of *Social Life in Seventeenth-Century Wales*, and of *Welsh Convict Women*, the story of the women from Wales who sailed as convicts to the penal colonies of Australia.

Cover Illustrator Christine McCauley is a painter, illustrator and teacher who lives in London. She has done graphics work for *Spare Rib* since it was founded and has illustrated book jackets for The Women's Press.

Discovering women's history

A practical manual

Deirdre Beddoe

P A N D O R A   P R E S S

London, Boston, Melbourne and Henley

To Jen with love

First published in 1983
by Pandora Press
(Routledge & Kegan Paul plc)
39 Store Street, London WC1E 7DD,
9 Park Street, Boston, Mass. 02108, USA,
296 Beaconsfield Parade, Middle Park,
Melbourne, 3206, Australia and
Broadway House, Newtown Road,
Henley-on-Thames, Oxon RG9 1EN
Photoset in 10 on 11½ Century Schoolbook by
Kelly Typesetting Ltd, Bradford-on-Avon, Wiltshire
and printed in Great Britain by
Cox & Wyman Ltd, Reading

Library of Congress Cataloging in Publication Data

Beddoe, Deirdre.

Discovering women's history.
Includes bibliographies and index.
1. Women–History. 2. Women–History–Research.
I. Title.
HQ1121.B37 1983   305.4'09   83–8131

ISBN 0–86358–008–4

Contents

Illustrations

Plates

Preface

I have been able to write this book only because I have had the help and support of many people. I want to record my special thanks to Jennifer L. Homer, Katie Durbin, Anne Jones, Arrol Evans and Sheila Owen Jones. Friends and experts in their fields have read and advised me upon various chapters in this book and I wish to thank them. They are Chris Weedon (Chapter 2), Anna Davin (Chapter 3), Angela John (Chapter 4) and Stevi Jackson (Chapters 5 and 6). I also wish to thank Philippa Brewster of Pandora/Routledge & Kegan Paul with whom I have enjoyed working.

Many people have given generously of their time in the oral history programme on which this book draws. I wish to thank Eileen Hannaford, John Howells and Phil Wade for their help and to thank Nora Withers, Bella Hannaford, Alice Howells, Katie and Lal, Bessie, Olive London-Ager and Katie and Effie MacDougal for contributing so willingly.

The women of Penarth Women's History Group deserve a special mention for working so enthusiastically on our local women's history project. I have drawn greatly upon my experience of working with them.

Individuals have made material available to me. I should like to thank Margaret Hind for lending me her mother's account book and Carey Smith for lending me her collection of old women's magazines. Many archivists, librarians and museum curators have given me great assistance. They are too numerous to mention them all but I should particularly like to thank Elspeth King of The People's Palace, Glasgow, P. A. Goodchild of Cadbury Schweppes at Somerdale, David Doughan and Catherine Ireland of the Fawcett Society Library, the staff of the National Library of Wales and of the Polytechnic of Wales Library and the archivists and staff of the Bristol, Birmingham, Glamorgan and the Greater London Council Record Offices.

Deirdre Beddoe
Penarth

Acknowledgments

The author and publishers would like to thank the following for permission to reproduce photographs in this book. The Tate Gallery, London, for plate 1; *Punch* for plate 2; the Greater London Council Photographic Collection for plates 3 and 4; J. L. Homer for plate 5; the People's Palace Museum, Glasgow, for plates 7 and 8; Wolf Suschitzky for plate 12; the National Museum of Labour History, London, for plate 15; the Museum of London for plate 16.

Introduction

This book is a guide for people who wish to find out about the lives of women in the past. I hope it will be of use to those who have time only to sit and read books on women's history; for them I include reading lists of material in print. However, this is essentially a practical guide for those whose curiosity drives them (and whose time and energy enables them) to proceed further. It is intended as a manual for students of women's history who are prepared to venture into attics, old people's parlours, cinemas, art galleries, museums, libraries and record offices in their quest for a history of ordinary women. I hope that it will prove helpful both to individuals and to Women's Studies groups. It is perfectly feasible for an individual to embark on a piece of research, though I think it is much more fun for a small group to launch an inquiry.

I have not written this book for professional historians. The past belongs to us all and we are all entitled to find out about it. Why should an investigation of your grandmother's lifestyle be left to some university don, who probably would never bother with it anyway? There is a great mystique about historical research and therefore people lack confidence in tackling it. Fortunately this mystique is beginning to wither and even primary schoolchildren conduct their own researches into local history. I was incredibly impressed by the work of nine-year-old London girls and boys, who, under the guidance of an imaginative student teacher, interviewed their grandmothers and consequently produced first-rate oral history. It is my aim to encourage people, particularly women, who have not done anything like this before, to 'have a go'. Would-be investigators should not allow themselves to be overawed by stereotyped notions of historical research. The expression should not conjure up visions of learned, elderly gentlemen arguing interpretations in a senior common room. We are far better off visualizing the nine-year-old

girl asking her gran what things were like in 'the olden days'
and we have a far more comprehensive and valuable history
when the 'ordinary lives' of people are included in the record.

The art, or knack, of selecting a good piece of research,
i.e. a project which is interesting and which holds the
enthusiasm of the researcher or researchers so that it gets
completed, is to select a piece of work which is manageable. If
one agrees at the outset to impose certain limitations on the
investigation then there should not be too many difficulties.
For the non-professional historian I think that it is necessary
to suggest limitations of time, space and scale. It seems
sensible to restrict inquiries to the nineteenth and twentieth
centuries − to go back further than the eighteenth century
brings the researcher up against problems of handwriting
which may prove a deterrent. In fact palaeography, or old
handwriting, is not always an insurmountable barrier and
there may be occasions when curiosity impels a student to
unravel the twirls of a seventeenth-century hand. The
sources indicated in this book cover the period from c. 1800 to
1945. A limitation in area is again a sensible step. In one
sense all history is local history and what is needed is to build
up more and more local studies of women's lives. Women
probably more than any other group have been, and still are,
the subject of sweeping generalizations; for example, historians make statements which lump together all married
women in the nation. How can they generalize about this
group, without regard to where they lived? Can one generalize about 'married women' in central London, Merioneth-
shire or Dundee? I think not. Local contributions are vital to
reveal the full range of British women's experiences both
inside and outside the home. If a group of people in Durham
undertook a piece of research into the lives of women in a
mining community, they would be performing a very useful
service. If a similar group in South Wales did the same thing,
it would then be possible to examine the points of similarity
and difference between the women's experiences. We cannot
know what these are unless and until the work is done. It is
obviously far more practical to concentrate on one's own
home area; records are held locally and the older people, with
their memories of the past, are on hand to contribute. There is

a great fascination in looking at the past in the area one knows and understands well. It is right to dig where you stand. As for scale, that too is crucial. It would be off-putting to try and write a history of women in say Bermondsey or Kidderminster throughout the ages, but 'between the wars' is not unreasonable. Actually even a town or borough may prove rather big and it may be more manageable to choose a street, a factory or a shop.

Clearly, the sort of history and historical investigation which I wish to encourage is not an old-type school view of history. It is necessary for many people consciously to break away from the notion that history is something to be learned. Most of us have been conditioned to believe that there is a concrete body of facts, an inviolable entity, that somehow *is* history. In school we were led to believe that history was the Lancastrians and Yorkists, the Tudors and Stuarts and the dull Hanoverians. If we spent a year, a term or perhaps a week on each of these we had *done* history. It was all wrapped up. What most of us were not conscious of was that this package had been *selected* for us. History is, in fact, what it is selected to be. Past selection procedures for a long time omitted the history of the working people. In this century a great deal has been done to redress the class imbalance of history as far as working *men* were concerned. Social and labour historians concerned themselves with miners, iron workers, quarrymen, printers, etc., and the struggle of organized labour. But women – somehow invisible – remained beyond the pale. It is only very recently that women, newly conscious of the deficiencies and inequalities of the present, have begun to look to their past to seek explanations of the present, and hopefully to seek roads to alternative futures. But when the new generation of feminists turned to the study of their history they found it had not been written. The recovery of the past is part of the current struggle. Yet seeking for explanations to the present is by no means the only reason for looking to the past. Investigating the lives of women in other periods is in its own right a valid pursuit. It is also a fascinating pursuit and one which brings with it all the excitement and exhilaration of discovering something new.

I have organized this book in what I hope will prove a

useful way. I begin by posing the question 'Why should we study women's history?' – and I go on to present some of the arguments for doing so. Thereafter, the book is essentially a practical guide to the sources of women's history (c. 1800–1945). I have organized the guide to the sources around certain key topics which I regard as essential to a reconstruction of women's lives in the past. My selection is images of women; education; waged work; family and home life; sexuality and birth control; political activity. It is not an exhaustive list but it does cover many of the most important facets of women's lives. Each chapter follows approximately the same format (with the exception of Chapter 2 on Images). This is as follows: an introductory survey aimed at providing a factual background (by noting any particular developments related to a topic, e.g. legislation) and at *suggesting* certain approaches to a topic; a suggested basic list of questions which may form a starting point for an investigation; a short bibliography of useful publications; then a review of some of the sources (e.g. printed, record, oral, photographic) and examples taken from these sources to indicate the sort of information which may be learned from them. Finally, I think it is vital that the findings of individuals or local groups should be made known and shared: the last chapter of this book is devoted to ways of doing this.

Chapter one

Why should we study women's history?

In this chapter I should like to pose and to attempt to answer the question, 'Why should we study women's history?' I think it is a relevant question to ask at the beginning of this book, which is, after all, asking people to take on a considerable amount of work. I should like to answer this question firstly in a general way – by looking at the relevance of a study of the past to women who are involved in attempts to change the position of women in present-day society and also by demonstrating the inherent interest and importance of women's history as a subject of academic study at all levels – in schools, colleges and universities. For this purpose I wish to take a broad view of women's history and not to confine myself strictly to the period covered by the research guide. Secondly, I should like to answer the question specifically from the viewpoint of people who are considering embarking upon local research into women's history. However, I should like to do more than list reasons why people should study and research women's history. I want to suggest a positive programme of action for the future. Consequently, I shall look briefly at the current state of women's history in Britain and then proceed to suggest what I see as the way forward for women's history. I think that it is important to outline such a scheme not only in order that local groups and individuals can see how they fit into the whole operation of the study and research of women's history, but also that they should see how extremely important their role is.

To me the most exciting development in historical investigation in recent years has been the realization that women have a history too. For too long the history of half the human race has been ignored: the absurdity of speaking and writing about 'people's history', whilst leaving half the people out, is quite patent. Nevertheless one is frequently asked 'Why study women's history?' Is it worth bothering about? Wasn't it all the same?

We need to know our past to understand our present. The present is a product of the past: we are moulded and conditioned by a past of which we are alarmingly ignorant. To explain the subordinate position of women in society, the narrowly defined female role, the attitudes of men towards women, the low esteem in which women hold themselves, etc., we need to look backwards to the origins and development of these ills. If we seek to understand the workings of our present patriarchal system, it is an aid to observe the more overt patriarchy of the nineteenth century in operation. If we take specific examples of the past illuminating (or darkening) the present, we can consider, for example, the present continuing fight for equal pay. By looking back to an earlier stage of industrial society, perhaps we can gain some clearer understanding of why women's work has been evaluated as worth less than men's. Again, if we consider education in the twentieth century, we see that it is still sexist and dogged by gender-role stereotyping. In this case too, a study of women's position and carefully proscribed role in previous times will go a long way towards an explanation.

Not only can the past explain the present, but a knowledge of the past can also prove a source of strength, encouragement and admonition to women engaged in current initiatives for change. From a study of ancient societies we can question the notion that patriarchy was the only organizational style ever known.[1] We can study other societies in which women had a far greater control over their own bodies than within patriarchal capitalism: abortion was not considered a crime until the early church made it so.[2] Closer to our own time, we can look to the early twentieth-century suffrage movement, so full of promise and enthusiasm and ask where did it go wrong? Can political solutions cure social injustices? Were the suffragettes too narrow in the changes which they demanded? What good was the vote without a social and a sexual revolution? Or did the suffragettes want more than the vote? There is much to find out.

There is a whole range of utilitarian reasons for studying women's history and the parallels with other oppressed groups like the blacks, the American Indians and the Irish are obvious. A knowledge of a common history can prove a unifying force and women should be aware of its potential. But propaganda and polemics aside, in its own right the subject has a tremendous amount to offer. The study of women's history presents an exciting challenge to the research historian, the student of history and the interested reader alike. The fact that the historical sources are not always obvious or conventional stimulates the investigator to look for and use new sources. Novels, hymn books, songs, criminal records, myths, old wives' tales, folk remedies, rituals, women's magazines and oral testimony need scrutiny as well as do such traditional historical materials as parish registers, census returns and Parliamentary Papers. Both female historians and students, given the strong incentive to discover their *own* past and to dig out the roots of many current issues, are beginning to take up the search. It is challenging to test received truths and to hold up to the light many generalizations, which have served as substitutes for conclusions based on well researched fact. The attempt to retrieve the history of women, though a massive task, is an absorbing and rewarding one.

As to the notion that women's history is not worth bothering about because the lives of women have somehow always been the *same*, this is, at best, based on sheer ignorance. No one writes off the history of men, from the Old Stone Age to the twentieth century, in this way and it would be just as ludicrous to do so. Women have, at different times and in different circumstances, faced varying problems and have reacted to them in diverse ways. One cannot simply lift out of context women from medieval Europe, Puritan England and World War II America and treat them as some a-historical caste, transcending time and place, and sharing the same difficulties, pursuits and thought patterns. The history of women in each age needs to be researched and studied as meticulously as the history of men.

Very probably, part of the reason why the history of women has been shelved as monotonous and uniform is its close identification with domestic chores and with childcare. The housewives' fight against dirt and dust, it is argued, can not have changed very much between the Middle Ages and the Industrial Revolution and when change did come about, it was, of course, the gift of a benevolent male technology, providing vacuum cleaners and dishwashers. Similarly, childcare is regarded as having always been basically the same, regardless of the demands of society on particular households. This whole view needs drastic reappraisal. Firstly, women's history is not exclusively domestic, any more than men's history can be seen as being exclusively political. However, since a large proportion of the lives of many women has been spent in the domestic sphere, it is worthy of study. Secondly, why is any history concerned with domestic affairs regarded as *ipso facto* rather dull? The elderly Menagier of Paris, a fifteenth-century French bourgeois, gave to his teenage bride a fascinating book advising her how to catch fleas in their bedroom, to grow fruit and to hire farm hands.[3] I have read much duller political source material! As to the accepted truth that domestic appliances have improved women's lives, if not *liberated* women, this certainly needs questioning. The omission of childcare and related aspects of family life, as an object of study, is even more serious, not only for the study of women's history but also for the study of people's history. The very obvious link between the private world of the home and the public world of affairs makes the neglect of this all the more surprising.[4] All these 'servile' occupations, cleaning, cooking and propagating the species, have been omitted from the grand catalogue of academic history, as the subject is at present defined. The total redefinition of history to include many of the everyday experiences of women in the past, (insignificant though they may be, if measured in terms of power politics) is not least of the tasks facing feminist historians.

Why should it be necessary in the 1980s to be making a plea for women's history? Why has the history of such a large proportion of the population been so neglected for so long? There are, of course, some who would deny this hypothesis altogether. They usually list half a dozen women 'worthies' who figure in history text books. These invariably include Joan of Arc, Elizabeth I, Elizabeth Fry, Florence Nightingale and Mrs Pankhurst i.e. a saint, a queen, two near angels and a married woman – a truly representative cross-section of women! Those who would cite these names to mollify the less easily satisfied of us are themselves usually unaware of what a true group of deviants they have cited. All of these named women 'worthies' have broken through the female stereotype of their own day and have reached the pages of the history books because they made their marks in men's fields . . . warfare, government, prison administration, medicine and parliamentary politics respectively.

Marginally more aware historians consider that they *cover* women's history if, in a year's course on modern Britain, they give the odd few lectures on women's suffrage. Again, this view only attributes a history to women when they enter traditionally male spheres. But women's history is not the history of a few great names. I intend, for the purposes of this book, to define women's history as the history of most women, i.e. the women of the working class and of the middle class. It is the history of this massive group which has been most neglected. Where does the blame lie? With the dearth of conventional historical sources? Possibly, in part, but I have already noted how feminist historians are imaginatively overcoming this obstacle. I suggest the blame lies squarely with historians. Most historians are male, middle-class, university graduates. They are not concerned primarily with the history of the women who clean their studies or do their wives' harder labour at home. Historians are the products of their own culture and society: most are totally unaware of their culturally determined prejudices and values. They reflect the value system of our society. History, as written and taught for most of this century, has been as class ridden as our society. Our history has been, and often still is, the history of the monarchy, the aristocracy and the ruling elite. Similarly, history has been, and continues to be, as male dominated as our society: it is the history of men and male affairs . . . wars, diplomacy, politics and commerce. Whether male historians' complicity in this conspiracy to rob women of their history is witting or not is not the central question here. What matters now is to recognize the historical selection process which operates and to reject it.

In fact, for some years significant advances have been

made to correct the class imbalance in the study of history. The maturation of social history into a respectable field, with its emphasis on the lives of the 'lower orders', has gone some way towards writing the masses into history. But how, if at all, has this development affected the sex imbalance of historical studies? The answer must be hardly at all. Sexism seems to be far more deeply rooted than class hostility and far less easy to eradicate – after all, the present arrangement suits many men of all classes. Social history is more concerned with male struggles for political representation and conflicts between male workers and male employers than it is with women workers in the home or outside it. The teaching of history in schools and universities still presents students with an almost exclusively masculine view of history. Small wonder school pupils think history *is* Old Stone Age Man. King John and his Barons, or Wellington at Waterloo. Overtly sexist textbooks hide women's history from view. To test the truth of this, simply choose any school text book and compare the number of references to men and women. One very widely used secondary school textbook has unashamedly altered a medieval illustration of a woman catching rabbits to one of a little man, catching rabbits.[5] It is terribly dangerous to tamper with the past like this and to impose twentieth-century sex stereotyping on earlier societies. In schools, class exercises reinforce the sex roles: girls are expected to be interested in costume and boys in the navy: boys are told to write on a day in the life of a Viking/ Explorer/Crusader and girls about his wife!

Given the practical and academic reasons for the study of women's history, are there any further particular reasons why local groups and individuals should undertake the study of women's history in their own localities? I believe that there are many pressing reasons for doing so.

There is a clear need for many specific local investigations in order to try to establish what was the reality of women's lives at home and in outside employment in various parts of the country. We need to try and assess the impact of various economic, political and social changes on women's lives in different parts of Britain so that we can see any regional variations. Only by doing this work can we challenge, or verify, much-vaunted generalizations, such as – 'married women did not go out to work', 'the man was always the breadwinner', 'birth control was generally available after Marie Stopes', 'women never went into pubs – at least, not nice women', and 'women had all the real power in the family'. Unless local studies are undertaken, particularly oral studies, information will be irrevocably lost. There is a great urgency. I think too that a study of women's history within one's own locality can establish a sense of continuity with the past. It may turn out to be a very revealing and encouraging experience by demonstrating the strength and activity of women in the community in the past. It can certainly be fun. It is a great pleasure to come up with information long since lost and, indeed, it can be very rewarding to work as a team with other people: it is good to have the support and interest of other people involved in a project. Finally, the pursuit of local history which will involve the interviewing of older women or consulting with them, can be a very good inter-generational community exercise. It can bring younger researchers and older women into contact for their mutual enlightenment and pleasure. It is certainly a good idea to involve these contributors in any end product of the project (See Chapter 8.)

Before turning to a programme of positive action for the future, I think it is useful to note briefly the current state of women's history in Britain.

Firstly, it should be pointed out that the very fact that I can be writing about women's history in Britain at all is a consequence of the existence of the women's movement. The main incentive to the investigation of women's history has been the women's movement. The awakening of female consciousness to the oppression of women in our society has led, not only to campaigns to bring about practical change, for example, in the law, in health, work, etc., but also to a serious review of academic courses. The teaching of literature (English, American or European), psychology, history, art history, sociology and other subjects was found to minimize or ignore women's contribution. The redress of this imbalance in a wide range of subjects is but one of the arenas in which the women's struggle is taking place and most women,

engaged in this academic reappraisal, are in little doubt of
how central their efforts are to the main fight.

What has been and is being done now in the investigation of women's history? Of course, there are books on
women's history written in the past, although most of these
concentrate either on women acting within organizations,
especially for suffrage, or are biographies of distinguished
women. A few older works on British women rise far above
the average. Of these I would mention Alice Clark's, *Working
Life of Women in the Seventeenth Century*, (1919, reprinted
1982)[6] which deals with the impact of early capitalism on
female workers and Ivy Pinchbeck's *Women Workers in the
Industrial Revolution* (1930, reprinted 1969).[7] These two
excellent works, however, were not followed up by a spate of
similar studies. It was to be another forty years before a
renewed and sustained curiosity about women's history
emerged. Amongst written work, emanating from this later
period, I think Anna Davin's essay on 'Women and History' in
The Body Politic (1972)[8] was perceptive and thought-provok-
ing and Sheila Rowbotham's survey, *Hidden from History*
(1973)[9] was the first step in the right direction towards
making women's history widely and easily available. These
are being followed by what is still a relatively small number
of monographs dealing with specific aspects of women's
history – women in Stuart England and America, women's
work in nineteenth-century London and in Victorian coalmines, the struggle of Northern English working-class
women for the vote, the position of women in Nazi society
etc.[10] Another feature of recent years has been the reprinting
of older source material e.g. Olive Schreiner's, *Women and
Labour* (1911),[11] the writings of Vera Brittain[12] and source
material on the lives, home conditions and health of working-
class women in Britain from c. 1910 to 1939.[13] Yet another
development of the period from the mid-1970s onwards has
been the emergence of journals such as *Feminist Review,
Feminist Studies* and *Women's Studies International Quarterly* which are wholly devoted to feminist scholarship – including feminist history, and *History Workshop*, which deals
with a wide range of topics, chiefly relating to working-class
history, and which has a commitment to women's history.

Finally, in terms of academic research and written work, it should be noted that an increasingly large number of theses for higher degrees are dealing with aspects of women's history.

As to the teaching of women's history, here too encouraging developments are taking place. Women's Studies courses, run by Local Education Authorities, the Workers' Educational Association or University Extra Mural Departments offer an important channel for the transmission of ideas and information about women's history. The number of full time higher education courses dealing with women's history has risen significantly.[14] However, often the subject of women is not treated as central to historical studies but is placed within an interdisciplinary course or in a course dealing, for example, with minorities! It seems to be departments of sociology or other newer disciplines, which are prepared to give the study of women's position, past and present, active consideration.

Traditional departments of history, whilst often progressive about social or labour history, remain staidly conservative on women and most do not offer the study of women either as separate options or within existing courses. I have no accurate picture of the progress in schools. This would be an interesting piece of investigation for someone to take up. One strongly suspects that if public examinations are any indication then the subject of women's history is largely ignored.

Finally, another indication of the interest which exists in women's studies is the existence of the Women's Research and Resources Centre, a voluntary body set up in the 1970s. Among other things, it acts as a clearing house for information on women's studies. The emergence of a Feminist History Group within the WRRC and its regular and continued operation is further evidence of the enthusiasm which exists for women's history. That particular group is London based but there are other Feminist History Groups (or women's history groups) in other major cities, e.g. Manchester and Birmingham.

What needs to be done now to further the cause of women's history? I think we must advance on three fronts, if we can permit military metaphors in women's history.

Firstly, the work of research, of actually finding out about the past, must be tackled. This is an enormous task and it needs a very large group of committed people. Obviously, academic research is vital in this field and interested students must be encouraged to take it up. But the study and writing of history should not be seen as an elitist, professional concern. The fact that it has been so, has merely divorced ordinary women and men from their past! There is no reason why interested individuals and groups, such as women's study groups, local history groups or community centre groups should not take up the search and make a contribution to women's history. Local community organizations are increasingly doing just this – by producing booklets, by making transcripts of the recollections of older people and by collecting old photographs. Committing to permanent record the experiences of working women, which may otherwise have gone totally unrecorded, is a vital piece of work. There are obstacles to tackling this task but the puprose of this book is to give some guidelines on how it can be done – by pointing out sources, by indicating ways in which the findings can be evaluated and analysed and by suggesting a variety of ways of presenting the newly retrieved information.

Secondly, there is a great need for books. The teacher and student of women's history require both books dealing with fairly broad sweeps of women's history and others dealing with very specific aspects. Until a wide range of such material is published, the development of this subject, below postgraduate level, will be seriously curtailed.

Thirdly, pressure should be exerted to include the history of women within history courses at all educational levels. Pupils and students should question the sexist bias of their courses. In higher education in particular, where institutions vie to attract students, course planners are increasingly sensitive to student demands. If sufficient people ask for courses the demand will be met.

If we proceed in the above ways we will begin to meet the challenge of women's history. A great part of the joy of the enterprise is that we will be embarking upon new history.

NOTES

1 See, for example, E. Gould Davies, *The First Sex*, New York, Putnam, 1971, chapter 4.
2 Ibid., p. 200.
3 E. Power, *Medieval People*, London, Methuen, 1924, pp. 85–110.
4 Adolf Hitler states clearly the link between the world of the home and the state, within patriarchal society.

> If we say the world of the man is the state, the world of the man is his commitment, his struggle on behalf of the community, we could then perhaps say that the world of the woman is a smaller world. For her world is her husband, her family, her children and her home. But where would the big world be if no-one wanted to look after the small world? How could the big world continue to exist, if there was no-one to make the task of caring for the small world at the centre of their lives? No, the big world rests upon this small world! The big world cannot survive if the small world is not secure.

(Adolf Hitler, speech to the National Socialist Women's Organization, Nuremberg Party Rally, 8 September 1934. Cited T. Mason, 'Women in Germany 1925–1940', *History Workshop*, vol. 1, 1976.

5 This came to my attention through K. Davies's article, 'History is about chaps', *Times Educational Supplement*, 29 November 1974. The offending illustration is by R. C. Sherriff in *A Portrait of Britain in the Middle Ages 1066–1485*.
6 A. Clark, *Working Life of Women in the Seventeenth Century*, 1919, republished, London, Routledge & Kegan Paul, 1982.
7 I. Pinchbeck, *Women Workers in the Industrial Revolution 1750–1850*. 1930, republished London, Virago, 1981.
8 Anna Davin, 'Women and history', in M. Wandor (ed.), *The Body Politic*, London, Stage 1, 1972.
9 S. Rowbotham, *Hidden from History: Three Hundred Years of Oppression and the Fight against It*, London, Pluto, 1973.
10 R. Thompson, *Women in Stuart England and America: A Comparative Study*, London, Routledge & Kegan Paul, 1974; S. Alexander, 'Women's work in nineteenth century London', in J. Mitchell and A. Oakley (eds), *The Rights and Wrongs of Women*, Harmondsworth, Penguin, 1976; A. John, *By the Sweat of their Brow: Women Workers at Victorian Coalmines*, London, Croom Helm, 1980; J. Liddington and J. Norris, *One Hand Tied Behind Us: The Rise of the Women's Suffrage Movement*, London, Virago, 1978; J. Stephenson, *Women in Nazi Society*, London, Croom Helm, 1975.

16   Why should we study women's history?

11 O. Schreiner, *Women and Labour*, London, 1915, reprinted
    London, Virago, 1978.
12 V. Brittain, *Testament of Youth*, London, 1933, reprinted
    London, Virago, 1978; *Testament of Friendship*, London, 1940,
    reprinted London, Virago, 1980; *Testament of Experience*,
    London, 1957, reprinted London, Virago, 1980.
13 M. Llewelyn Davies, *Life as We Have Known It by Co-operative
    Working Women*, London, 1931, reprinted London, Virago, 1977;
    M. Llewelyn Davies (ed.), *Maternity: Letters from Working
    Women*, London, 1915, reprinted London, Virago, 1978; M.
    Pember Reeves, *Round About A Pound A Week*, London, 1913,
    reprinted London, Virago, 1979; M. Spring Rice, *Working Class
    Wives*, London, 1939, reprinted London, Virago, 1981.
14 For information on the availability of women's studies courses in
    Britain, see *Women's Studies Courses in the U.K.*, WRRC, 1981.

Chapter two

The changing image

Many women in present-day society are very conscious that the media projects certain stereotyped images of women. It is important to recognize that this is nothing new: when we look at the past we see that each age has projected particular images or dominant stereotypes, to which women were persuaded or coerced to conform. In this chapter I propose firstly to show why these images are so very important. Secondly, at much greater length, I shall survey the changing image of women in Britain from about the middle of the nineteenth century to the end of the Second World War – looking particularly, where possible, at who devised these images, at the agencies through which they were projected and reinforced and asking why one image gave way to another: brief allusions will be made to the reality of women's lives – in counterpoint to the media images – but these references to reality must necessarily be brief and I shall leave the historical sources, outlined in later chapters, to reveal the real contrast. Thirdly, I should like to suggest a schedule of practical work, which can be undertaken on either of two levels: it can be as undemanding as sitting back and reading old copies of *Woman* and *Woman's Own* and watching old films on television or, on the other hand, it can involve an attempt to assess what were, for the most part, national images on the lives and imaginations of women in various parts of Britain.

Images are immensely important. I am very aware of their role in present-day society and I believe that although many women in the past were not conscious of the coercive power of images and stereotyped models, their lives were greatly shaped and influenced by contemporary images of femininity and the female role. In both the present and the past women are and have been subjected to the power of media images. The agencies of the media may vary, but the idea and the effect is the same. This continuity is important: it can be very helpful. We can, by considering our own experiences of the impact of media images upon our own lives, reach some understanding of their impact on the lives of women in the past.

In my view, images are all important. They tell us what to be and we are made to feel uncomfortable if we do not conform. We are made to feel deeply anxious if we break the rules. No belief is more entrenched in our society than the belief that men and women are fundamentally different beings and that there is an appropriate mode of behaviour and appearance for each sex. Society is threatened by people who challenge this. Women should not do 'men's jobs', wear 'men's clothes', 'think like men', etc. Worse still, men should not do 'women's jobs', wear 'women's clothes', 'think like women,' etc. Women are made to feel anxious and guilty if their behaviour is interpreted as being 'unfeminine'. Men are similarly afraid of being thought 'unmanly'. In the eyes of society men who emulate 'female behaviour' are the most menacing of all. They reject masculinity and by so doing reject the whole system. Women who step outside the sex boundaries are a similar, if not quite so serious, threat. We, women and men, are kept in line by fear. We have been taught our role from babyhood: one is a little girl, with all that that involves, before one is an individual human being. We identify with sex-determined role-images. We are frightened to reject them. We fear that in rejecting the images of femininity, we will cease to exist. Society has made us believe that our only existence is as a role image. But what can happen to women who turn their backs on the role image? They cannot literally cease to be women. They *are* women – with women's bodies. The tragedy is that women have been made to conform to shallow and stupid, externally imposed images of femininity. They are told that in order *to be women* they must be/do certain things. So artificial and inadequate are the images of femininity held up to them to copy, that these images have constantly to be changed and revised. It is an enormous confidence trick and most women have still not realized this.

John Berger understands the mechanism of images very

well, and is also aware of the ways in which men have dominated women. His remarks are very pertinent. He writes,

> To be born a woman has been to be born within an allotted and confined space into the keeping of men. The social presence of women has developed as a result of their ingenuity in living under such tutelage within such a limited space. But this has been at the cost of women's self being split into two. A woman must continually watch herself. She is almost continually accompanied by her own image of herself. Whilst she is walking across a room or whilst she is weeping at the death of her father, she can scarcely avoid envisaging herself, walking and weeping. From earliest childhood she has been taught and persuaded to survey herself continually.[1]

All around her – from the TV set, the advertising hoarding, the cinema screen or, in an earlier age, from sermon, hymn, poem and manual of behaviour – she is told what to be and how to see herself. When we see the smiling white face of the housewife beam at us from the advertisement, the rest of us feel out of step. Among the rest of us are black women, gay women, unmarried women with children, women engineers, artists, musicians, farmers etc. The real live housewife feels no less out of step.

In the light of present-day women's first-hand knowledge of the power of images and from the vantage point of a consciousness of the process, it is clearly important to examine past images of women. By so doing we shall see how society viewed women and how women were encouraged to view themselves. There is a further important reason for examining these past images. They are not static: they are subject to change. In the following survey of images from the mid-nineteenth to the mid-twentieth century we see one dominant image give way to another in order to suit the changing needs of the nation and/or of capitalist industry. In seeing this, we see what nonsense it is to talk of a 'natural', unchanging concept of femininity. Femininity has been defined and constructed in each age to suit factors which have little to do with women's best interests. Finally we should note that time or historical studies has a propensity to flatten. If our own experience is anything to go by, each age was probably subjected to a variety of sometimes conflicting images. Today we are subjected to a spectrum of images, ranging from the housewife to the sex-bomb. We would probably be naive to think that women in the past were only presented with the single image, to which history has given prominence.

Of all the stereotyped images the Perfect Lady is probably the best known. 'Throughout the Victorian period', writes Martha Vicinus, 'the Perfect Lady as an ideal of femininity was tenacious and all pervasive.'[2] The model certainly held considerable sway from about the time of the Queen's accession in 1837 until the 1870s. Its influence was to persist much later but the essential background to the emergence of the Perfect Lady is what may be termed the rise of the domestic ideology in the early nineteenth century. Catherine Hall is one of the best exponents of this theory.[3] She examined certain developments affecting women's lives in Britain from the 1780s to c.1850 and she concentrated particularly on one urban centre, Birmingham. She looked at the anxiety of the English middle classes regarding the stability of English society: the French Revolution of the 1790s had greatly alarmed them and they feared the possibility of a similar revolution in England – unless society was stabilized. One of the chief ways that the English middle classes, particularly those associated with the evangelical wing of the Anglican church, sought to bring about such stability was through strengthening the idea and role of the family. They advocated a bourgeois view of the family – male breadwinner, dependent, home-based wife and dependent children. The old, pre-industrialized family, living on and in the productive unit of the farm and with all its members contributing to some aspect of production had all but disappeared and it was to be replaced by this new version. It was this version that the middle class advocated not only for itself but also for the aristocratic level of society above it and for the working classes below it. Within the family the wife was to be the centre of the home – the perfect wife, the perfect mother and the perfect lady. Hers was the private domain: her husband's the public. The message and image were widely projected from the pulpit, in religious tracts, in poems, in magazines, in paintings and in manuals on the behaviour of women. From looking at some of these sources I gained the following impression of the Perfect Lady.

The Perfect Lady had to grasp a few essentials if she was ever to succeed. Above all she was to acknowledge and inwardly assimilate the fact that she was inferior to men. Mrs Sarah Stickney Ellis, best-selling authoress and mid-century pundit, put the message succinctly when she wrote, 'As women, then, the first thing of importance is to be content to be inferior to men – inferior in mental power, in the same proportion that you are in bodily strength.'[4] The young girl would be educated in her role of service to the male until she developed, 'a sort of knee-jerk submissiveness, an automatic Pavlovian response of homage and obedience to anything in trousers.'[5] In childhood she could practice her submissive and servile role upon her demanding brothers.[6] A sister should studiously consult her brother's whims and her aim should be to please him. Mrs Ellis was not writing of a brother and sister sharing their childhood leisure hours nor indeed of the sister participating in the young man's superior intellectual pursuits. She makes this quite clear,

If, again, they read some interesting volume together, if she lends her willing sympathy, and blends her feelings with his, entering into all the trains of thought and recollection which two congenial minds are capable of awakening in each other; and if, after the book is closed, he goes up into his chamber late on the Saturday night, and finds his linen unaired, buttonless, and unattended to, with the gloves he had ten times asked to have mended, remaining untouched, where he had left them: he soon loses the impression of the social hour he had been spending and wishes, that, instead of an idle sister, he had a faithful and industrious wife.[7]

As for the Victorian woman who really could not dupe herself into believing that she was inferior to man, there was always the persuasive doctrine of 'separate spheres', so unctuously expounded by the art critic John Ruskin. In a lecture delivered to the bourgeois matrons and burghers of

Manchester in 1864, and later printed under the precious and obscure title *Sesames and Lilies*, Ruskin shied away from the reality that man ruled and women were his subjects.[8] He would not countenance, 'the idea that woman is only the shadow and attendant image of her lord owing him a thoughtless servile obedience'.[9] She was, according to Ruskin, man's complement and helpmeet. Man was the doer of deeds and the great function of woman was to praise. So much for 'separate but equal', an insidious doctrine designed to subvert women from seeking change.

Marriage was the highest goal of the young woman. Indeed, the Perfect Lady was a married lady – the single woman was to be pitied or derided. The price of actually winning the sacred name of wife was high. On marriage a woman's property became her husband's.[10] Within marriage her role was to procreate and thereby provide her husband with legitimate male offspring to whom he could pass on his property. The birth of her children elevated her yet further to the divine heights of motherhood, 'a high and holy office'.[11] Little was done to prepare the young bride for 'the shock of the marriage bed.' A popular manual for married women entitled *The Child: its Origin and Development*, referred to sexual intercourse as a 'sacrifice' and as a necessary ordeal. The Perfect Lady would feel no sexual impulses nor would she enjoy any pleasure from the act. Only lascivious and immoral women actually enjoyed sex. Rees's *Encyclopaedia* actually stated, 'That a mucuous fluid is sometimes formed in coition from the internal organs and vagina is undoubted; but this only happens in lascivious women, or such as live luxuriously.'[12] If the Perfect Lady began to find sex enjoyable then she became anxious that her base and animal nature was coming to the fore. Sexual enjoyment, it was feared, would lead to promiscuity and even adultery and the adulteress, no matter what her circumstances, was in the eyes of Victorian society a prostitute. The feckless wife, found in adultery in scene 1 of Augustus Egg's cycle of paintings, *Past and Present*, became by scene 3, the pregnant prostitute underneath a London bridge. Such moralizing, such threats and the dread of successive pregnancies kept the Perfect Lady pure.

The proper sphere of the Perfect Lady was, of course, the home. It was she who converted mere bricks and mortar into that bastion of Victorian cosiness, 'the home'. As the gushing Ruskin wrote,

> This is the true nature of home – it is the place of peace; the shelter, not only from all injury, but from all terror, doubt, and division. In so far as it is not this, it is not home; . . . And wherever a true wife comes, this home is always round her. The stars only may be over her head, the glow-worm in the night-cold grass may be the only fire at her foot, but home is wherever she is; and for a noble woman it stretches far round her, better than ceiled with cedar or painted with vermilion, shedding its quiet light far for those who else were homeless.[13]

The outside world was a wicked place, full of terrors. Newly industrialized Britain, with its ugly manufacturing towns, coalmines, iron-works and cotton mills, was scarred by poverty, squalor, disease and crime. Small wonder the Victorian businessman, whose materialist greed was responsible for the creation of the outside world, sought refuge close to his own warm hearth. In Dickens's *Great Expectations* (1861) Mr Wemmick literally had a drawbridge separating his home from the world of work. Within the home the male willingly submitted to the devoted ministration of his dear wife – the angel in his home. She was totally untainted by the grimy realities of industrial capitalism. If the outside world was dark, discordant and evil, the angel in the home brought light and harmony to the secure home world. The sentimental poet, Coventry Patmore, saw well the beneficial light radiating from the angel-mother,

> For something that abode endued, with temple
> like repose, an air
> Of life's kind purposes pursued
> With order'd freedom sweet and fair
> A tent pitch'd in a world not right,
> It seem'd whose inmates every one
> On tranquil faces bore the light
> Of duties beautifully done.[14]

The title of the poem is 'Angel in the Home'. Victorian magazines for women, many of them with the word 'Home' in the title, glorified the domestic role and reinforced the dominant female image. Paintings on show at the Academy did the same. George Elgar Hicks's painting *Woman's Mission: Companion of Manhood*, exhibited at the Royal Academy in 1863, projects the ideology of woman's place beautifully.[15] In it the loving wife comforts her grief stricken husband, in whose hand is held a black-bordered letter. The painting demonstrates not only this specific act of comfort, but the wife's general concern for her husband is shown in the neat room, clean table-cloth, shining cutlery and crockery and in the vase of flowers on the mantel. The wife herself is modestly and neatly attired, as befits a dedicated wife and homemaker.

The image which we have of the Perfect Lady depicts her as idle. Her husband's new prosperity, earned in the wicked outside world, enabled him to support an idle wife. She depended upon servants to run her household – to shop, cook and clean. She was mother only at set times of the day whilst a nurse and governess carried on the full-time role of child-rearing. Perhaps it was just as well that these trusty helpers were at hand since another feature of the stereotype is that she was delicate and often indisposed. The Perfect Lady was, as Lorna Duffin labels her, 'The Conspicuous Consumptive'.[16]

In addition to her physical disabilities the Perfect Lady was an intellectual cripple. She was not required to be clever: indeed, cleverness was a most undesirable and unfeminine characteristic. A modest ignorance was what was called for. Mrs Ellis counselled the young women not to inquire deeply into science 'lest you should sacrifice any portion of your feminine delicacy'. Fortunately, 'it has been accorded by man to his feebler sister, that it should not be necessary for her to talk much, even on his favourite topics, in order to gain favour. An attentive listener is generally all that he requires.'[17] Intellectually, just as sexually, the Perfect Lady was of stunted growth. She was always an innocent child and a legal minor. The following comment by a gentleman to his male companion on the object of his desires, Beatrice, comes from a story in a widely read magazine,

In some things she is as ignorant as a child, but hers is a blessed ignorance. . . . Between us no worldly questions are discussed; this is an idyll, Phil, a thing not of this earth, earthy. Little Beattie's mind is more eager to watch the flight of swallows or inquire into the growth of her roses than to learn the distinction of pounds, shillings and pence, and I would not have her different.[18]

One might be forgiven for thinking little Beattie got it right and it is the male stereotype that needs questioning. Indeed it does – but that is another story.

The role of Perfect Lady was widely advocated. Both male and female writers, secular and clerical, sang its praises. But how representative of nineteenth-century British womanhood was this stereotype?

The existence of Perfect Ladies presupposes the availability of servants and of a plentiful supply of money, provided by the working husbands, to create that cosy sanctuary, the home. But, obviously, the vast majority of women in Britain belonged to the working class. In trying actually to find Perfect Ladies one has therefore to look to the middle and upper classes – so we are already dealing with a fairly small minority. Mrs Ellis aimed her books specifically at the middle classes, but if we look closely at the middle classes some major flaws occur in the notion that Perfect Ladies predominated there.

Patricia Branca, in an interesting article entitled, 'Image and Reality, The Myth of the Idle Victorian Woman',[19] looked at the economic realities of middle-class life. Quite simply, the great majority of middle-class families had insufficient income to employ a legion of cooks, maids, nannies and governesses. The lot of the middle-class woman, as portrayed by Branca, was often one of hard work and of making ends meet, whilst helped in the house often only by a single young maid-of-all work. If most middle-class women could not afford idleness or other trappings of the Perfect Lady stereotype, there were those, who could afford it, who found the prospect intolerable. Charlotte Brontë's fictional heroine, Shirley Keeldar, spoke with anger against the inactive role in which she was cast:

'Caroline,' demanded Miss Keeldar, abruptly, 'don't you wish you had a profession – a trade?'

'I wish it fifty times a-day. As it is, I often wonder what I came into the world for. I long to have something absorbing and compulsory to fill my head and hands, and to occupy my thoughts.'

'Can labour alone make a human being happy?'

'No; but it can give varieties of pain, and prevent us from breaking our hearts with a single tyrant master-torture. Besides, successful labour has its recompense; a vacant, weary, lonely, hopeless life has none.'[20]

Real life women, like Florence Nightingale, became ill through boredom and an absence of any sense of purpose in their lives. She had cried out in anguish against the intellectual starvation of women.

To have no food for our heads, no food for our hearts, no food for our activity, is that nothing? If we have no food for the body, how do we cry out, how all the world hears of it, how all the newspapers talk of it, with a paragraph headed in great capital letters, Death from Starvation! But suppose one were to put a paragraph in *The Times*, Death of Thought from Starvation, or Death of Moral Activity from Starvation, how people would stare, how they would laugh and wonder![21]

In reality, one has doubts too, whether many women indulged in the hypersensitivity with which the Perfect Lady is usually accredited. Ill health among lower middle-class women was far more likely to arise from overwork and from non-stop child-bearing than from inertia. Yet this sickly facet of the Perfect Lady stereotype is important. Many novels bear testimony to this invalid image and one thinks of Elizabeth Barrett Browning kept as an imprisoned invalid by a possessive father. This view of women as consumptive weaklings could not have been projected without the active support of the medical profession. Lorna Duffin has shown how the medical profession attempted to exert social controls over women's lives by producing medical arguments in favour of the 'traditional' female role.[22] Medical practitioners' views on the health of women actually differed enormously according to class. Working-class women were not dubbed as delicate invalids! As Duffin puts it, women, according to class were either sick or sickening. Middle-class women were regarded as inherently sick if they tried to step outside their prescribed role; working-class women, on the other hand, were themselves health hazards, who harboured the germs of cholera, typhoid and venereal disease, and who bore numerous unfit and inferior working-class babies. The operation of a dual standard between the women of the middle and the working class is quite striking. The latter were expected to be strong – strong enough to carry coal in the mines, to lug heavy bricks and chains and to work the land. When it came to bearing large families even middle-class women were expected to be strong.

Other aspects of the stereotype are harder to test – e.g. the question of repressed sexuality. If indeed this does contain a large element of truth, then it may go some way to explaining why many women channelled their passions into evangelical religion and into literally 'adoring' Jesus.

In summing up the Perfect Lady, it must be restated that in many respects she represents only a very small minority. But how important was her influence? As the nineteenth century progressed, rising living standards led to a rise in social aspirations among the lower middle class and the better-off working class. The idea of the wife at home to look after house and family became increasingly desirable. This copy of the Perfect Lady could not afford servants or idleness but she could be respectable, chaste and virtuous. Women who did not live up to these standards would be cast off by affronted husbands and be socially ostracized. It is, incidentally, in this diluted version or this imperfect copy of the Perfect Lady that one sees the prototype of the later housewife, and in this legacy the Perfect Lady was to continue to exert influence. Given the hold the image held over people's minds, how did it come to be challenged?

The really important and exciting point is that the Perfect Lady stereotype was rejected by women – by women who felt themselves suffocated by this cloying stereotype.

Women themselves launched the attack on the inactivity and economic dependence which was expected of them. They demanded control over property, economic independence, admission to education, entry into the professions, wider job opportunities, the vote and freedom to think and act for themselves. Given the social attitudes of the period and the patriarchal nature of the establishment, their demands were not only amazing but they also required great bravery to pursue. We should be prepared to acknowledge the role played by a courageous minority in bringing about this change but we should also note that there were economic and social factors which played a part. Historians have suggested a variety of theories, based upon certain major developments, to explain the emergence of feminism in the late nineteenth century. Some put it down to the breaking up of the old productive family unit, consequent upon industrialization, which left single women redundant. Others pursue the sex ratio theory, showing that a 'surplus' female population existed in this period and stating that these surplus, unsupported spinsters broke down the barriers to entry into the professions. There may be an element of truth in both theories but objections can be raised to them as a stimulus to the growth of feminism.[23] One further factor, however, which I regard as of paramount importance is social class.

The nineteenth century saw the emergence of a distinct middle class. This class greatly expanded in the course of the century – due to new opportunities arising from the growth of industry, trade, commerce and the professions. The growth of this class meant the existence of increasing numbers of women, married and unmarried, whose pattern of life was unlike that of women in the past. These women were not gainfully occupied, as they would have been in earlier farming communities and yet they were imbued with middle-class male values. They believed that merit is based on hard work and usefulness. Many of their old outlets for these women were closing. Increasing professionalization closed medicine, secondary teaching and even philanthropy to women. It is precisely this group of middle-class women, who, dissatisfied with their lot as defined for the Perfect Lady, sought to redefine women's social position. This group provided the overwhelming majority of feminists or New Women. It was these bourgeois women whom John Stuart Mill had in mind when he pleaded for equality of the sexes in *The Subjection of Women* in 1869 and it was they who took up the challenge.

The feminists who broke down the old stereotypes of the Perfect Lady were themselves to be slotted into a new pigeon hole and labelled with a new sticker – that of New Woman. The new image was again not of women's making! This new stereotyped image was very different from its predecessor. Whereas the title Perfect Lady infers approval, respect and even reverence, the epithet New Woman denotes disapproval and ridicule. Any stereotype, by its generalized nature, although influential, is likely to be unrepresentative and inaccurate: the New Woman is no exception.

The pages of *Punch*, a journal renowned for its anti-feminism, provide us with the popular caricature of the New Woman. Her aspirations to education were derided in that magazine throughout the 1890s. *Punch* printed many cautionary gems of verse such as,

Advice to Girl Graduates

Dress well, sweet Maid, and let who will be *clever*.
Don't study all day long
Or else you'll find,
When others girls get married,
You'll sing a different song.[24]

Punch made the SAFE PREDICTION that, 'The New Woman of this decade [the 1890's] will be the OLD MAID of the next'.[25] The entry of women into the professions was similarly a great joke. When the first woman barrister took the oath in Paris in 1900 *Punch* commented, 'Welcome bar maid'.[26] The New Woman was lampooned and shown in a variety of unladylike, and therefore hilarious, postures – such as playing golf, or riding bicycles. Women's costume was in fact somewhat anachronistic: although the New Woman wore the new tailor-made outfit with shirt blouse, collar and tie and pork pie hat, many enlightened women still restricted their waists with very tight belts. Skirt lengths remained inconveniently long. As for women's claim for the vote, *Punch* was similarly biting. All its suffragettes are uniformly

old, ugly, butch and bespectacled. In short, there was a deep-
seated and anxious male hostility displayed towards the New
Woman.

In literature, she was more sensitively portrayed but
still the warning was there. No good would come of these
antics. Sue Bridehead in Thomas Hardy's novel, *Jude the
Obscure*, is sometimes acknowledged as:

> The first delineation in fiction of the women who was
> coming to notice in her thousands every year – the
> woman of the feminist movement, the slight pale
> 'bachelor' girl – the intellectualized emancipated bundle
> of nerves that modern conditions were producing,
> mainly in the cities as yet; who does not recognize the
> necessity for most of her sex to follow marriage as a
> profession, and boast themselves as superior people
> because they are licensed to be loved on the premises.[27]

There was to be no happiness for poor Sue, who recoiled from
marriage to the good man, Jude: her children died horribly
and she broke down. Similarly, George Gissing's depiction of
spinsters supporting themselves in *The Odd Women* (1892)
showed the unhappiness to which their course had led them.
It is, however, often in less elevated literary genres that the
confident and successful New Woman appears. Female detec-
tives like the astute Miss Loveday Brooke or Miss Dora Myrl
cut dashing figures in the late nineteenth century. Note Miss
Myrl's superlative confidence, as singlehandedly she steals
up upon a thief, whom she has tracked down. She comes upon
him at the very moment when he is retrieving the stolen loot
– which, incidentally, he has stolen from a strapping young
man.

> 'Good morning, Mr. McCrowder!' she cried sharply. The
> man started, and turned and saw a girl half a dozen yards
> off standing clearly in the sunlight, with a mocking smile
> on her face.
>> His lips growled out a curse; his right hand left the
> bags and stole to his side pocket.
>> 'Stop that!' The command came clear and sharp.
>> 'Throw up your hands!' He looked again. The sunlight

glinted on the barrel of a revolver, pointed straight at his head, with a steady hand.

'Up with your hands, or I fire', and his hands went up over his head. . . .[28]

The image with which we are most frequently presented of the New Woman is cruel, mocking and hostile. What of the real-life New Women? Who were they and what did they want? As was to be expected, they were mainly fairly well off, with sufficient resources for new activities; many came from the upper middle class. They sought education, economic independence and equal legal and political rights. Many aspects of these struggles are touched upon in the introductory sections to subsequent chapters and it is not necessary to duplicate the information here. I would simply say that these women fought determined and hard campaigns, over many years, on all these fronts. *Punch*, it would seem, was right about them in one respect – many New Women of the turn of the century were to become the next generation of old maids. The price exacted of many of them for professional success was often celibacy.

In August 1914 the First World War broke out and by 1915 women were employed in their thousands making munitions, tanks and aircraft. They took over men's jobs in heavy industry and in offices, on the railways and on trams. Women's new role demanded a new image. Magazines, posters, films and paintings depicted the new desirable stereotype. She was 'the girl behind the man behind the gun' – the 'munitionette', the VAD or the landgirl. Propaganda films deplored the old pre-war life of idleness of the middle-class woman and praised the rigours of life in the land army. But an analysis of war posters and a comparison between British, American and German depictions of women is revealing.[29] The Americans frequently use a sexy female in recruitment posters. 'I want you for the Navy', drawls a smiling, windswept blonde in a male naval uniform in a Howard Christie poster. The implication is that she will strip that uniform off for the recruit. French, Russian and British posters show women engaged in industrial and agricultural production for the war effort, but another familiar figure in

British war posters is the woman in the home. 'Women of
Britain Say Go', is the clear message. Men must protect
home-bound women. Other posters, British and Imperial,
depict woman as the mother – not wasting bread (the flour for
which sailors have risked their lives to import), or in prayer
with her tiny child – 'God bless dear Daddy who is fighting
the Hun and send him Help'. The munitionette or VAD was
just fine for an emergency but the last listed posters reflect
women's expected role in normal peacetime society.

Employment, on trams and buses, in factories, on farms
and indeed on service in France, for the first time, took many
girls away from their sheltered home environment. It meant
in many instances, despite strict regulations, far greater
freedom. Young women enjoyed a new financial independence and control over their own lives. These girls and
women ate in restaurants alone or with only a female friend
and they went unaccompanied to cinemas and dance halls.
Clothes were changed dramatically. The Edwardian New
Woman wore floor-length skirts. The wartime girl wore short
skirts – a clear foot off the ground – and she even wore slacks;
some wore make-up and smoked cigarettes. Many accusa-
tions of female immorality were made (note not of male) and
the illegitimacy rate rose, as one would expect when men
were being sent to die at the front.

In 1918 the Great War ended, leaving behind the old
Edwardian world for ever. The immediate post-war period
displayed some encouraging signs for women – in politics
with the granting of the vote and in education with the
admission of women to degrees at Oxford. Things appeared to
be looking up. Shorter skirts and long loose jumpers gave
women a new physical freedom and comfort, whilst the new
short hair cuts – shingles, bobs, bingles and Eton crops –
released them from the daily chore of hair brushing. Working-class girls now spurned domestic service with its repres-
sive discipline, long hours and poor pay. Popular fiction
depicted independent young women who succeeded.
Tuppence, the female half of Agatha Christie's detective
team of Tommy and Tuppence, was altogether more inven-
tive and daring than the plodding Tommy. Lady Eileen
Brent, known to her friends and society in general as Bundle,

as another of Christie's daring heroines of the period. Bundle
as quite prepared to hide in a cupboard in the very room
here mysterious masked men met in a sordid night haunt,
nd she was not afraid to track down killers and foreign
gents.[30] The cinema screen, the new potent medium which
eflected and reinforced the image, now rejected its early
odels, i.e. the two absurd polarities of sweet-child Mary
ickford and the crudely sexy kohl-eyed vamp, Theda Bara.
the Twenties Hollywood made films depicting 'flappers'
nocking back cocktails and puffing at cigarettes – but main-
aining their moral purity. The working girl featured fre-
uently in such movies as *The Girl from Woolworths* – 1929
hop assistant), *Her Winning Way* – 1921 (housemaid) or
ittle Mickey Crogan – 1927 (factory worker). Women's
agazines encouraged their readers to take advantage of the
ider opportunities afforded them by the war. *The Lady's
ompanion* (20 January 1920) urged women 'to get out of the
roove'. The war, it said, had been a golden opportunity for
omen and their experiences in France or on the land had
abled them to break out of the dull groove. The careers
dvice column of the same issue was devoted to women in
gineering. The title was 'The Girl Engineer' and the item
uggested that engineering, for which women had shown
uch aptitude during the war, was a very good field of
mployment for women! In the 24 November 1924 issue of
his largely working-class/lower middle-class magazine, the
ditorial proclaimed proudly the following catalogue of suc-
esses: the Ministry of Health had entrusted a woman with
roducing a major medical report, a woman was now in
large of the reptile department of London Zoological
ardens, Colchester had its second lady mayor in succession
nd a woman was representing Rumania at the League of
ations; 'really there seems no end to our success'.

But such optimism was ill-founded. The speed by which
omen had appeared in industry during the war was sur-
assed by the speed with which they vanished from it. When
e war ended the women were dismissed and their jobs were
stored to men. By March 1919 more than ½ million women
ere claiming unemployment donation – far more than men,
cluding demobilized soldiers. But, by November 1919 the

number of women claimants had dropped to 60,000. Wher
had they gone? They had not found jobs, but quietly and wit
scarcely a finger raised on their behalf, they had gone back t
the home.

In the post-war era women were again persuaded tha
their place was in the home. The very same issue of *Th
Lady's Companion* which I cited above, i.e. 24 Novembe
1924, that had tabulated women's achievements, in its fictio
pages advocated marriage as a woman's goal. It containe
two very similar stories. The heroine of the first tale is
career photographer, who has been sent on a sea cruise t
arctic waters to photograph the northern lights for a maga
zine feature. Throughout the trip she was pursued by a hand
some playboy, who tempts her with invitations to dinner an
strolls around the deck. Not without regret, she puts he
photographs first. The idle layabout interpreted her refusal
as a brush-off. It is only, when, somewhat ruefully, sh
returned to her office that she discovered that the handsom
pleasure-seeker was the magazine's new owner, and he dis
covered that she, whom he thought merely an amateur, wa
his employee! Joy, happiness and wedding bells! The ver
same issue of the magazine ran another story which told th
tale of a young woman who was trying to work in busines
and be a wife. It was, according to this short story, an impos
sible combination in 1924 and it ended triumphantly wit
her getting the sack from her secretarial post and rejoicing i
the thought that now she could go shopping in the mornin
like the other wives.

The reality of the 1920s is that feminism was in retrea
The great mass movement of the suffrage campaign had bee
tamed into a Campaign for Equal Citizenship and only a fe
individuals still carried on the struggle for feminist reform:
The mood of the times, one might go as far as to say, wa
anti-feminist.

The Housewife was the dominant stereotyped imag
throughout the 1930s. Women's magazines of the perio
indicate that the great majority of British women were stay
at-home housewives, preoccupied with finding new recipe
and dress patterns, experimenting with make-up, when ne
lolling about reading romantic short stories. The actua

agazines would appear dowdy to us now; they were printed
sepia paper with no coloured illustrations. The following is
ypical contents list from *Woman's Own*.

November 1932

Listen In (gossip column).

Short story: 'The Pretty Woman Next Door'. (Harold and
Edna have a new neighbour, a pretty young widow,
named Daphne. Edna suspects that Harold has fallen for
Daphne and her suspicions are fired by Harold's absences
from home. In fact, Harold has lost his job but with
Daphne's help he finds an even better one.)

Housewives Get Together (household hints).

Party Styles (dressmaking article).

Serial: 'From this Day Forward' (powerful Ruby M. Ayres
romantic drama).

Should a Wife Make-Up? (Item on post-marital beauty,
giving remarkably detailed advice on how a wife should
persuade her husband to allow her to wear make-up. She
should never, of course, make up in front of him.)

Making table mats.

Making Christmas presents.

Women Who Have No Homes (a serious discussion of the
growing problem of female homelessness).

Baby Clothes.

Furnishing.

'I Was Jealous of His Friends' (true confession).

Food for Growing Children.

'Hats and Husbands', by Meg Arnold. (The story of Phil, a
discontented young housewife, who hankers after the
excitement of her maiden-life as a milliner. She returns
to work for a rush-job and is punished by a series of
domestic disasters – including her husband being taken
ill. She throws up the job immediately since 'What is
anybody's hat compared to the chance of looking after
you?')

Competition for Husbands: the prize is a kitchen cabinet
'for her'.

How to Feed Your Baby.

Knitting Pattern

Problem Page (Mrs Eyles's advice column).

These magazines assert that a woman's world is almo
exclusively domestic. The one serious note and indicati
that there was a nasty outside world, comes in the excelle
article on homelessness. Other issues taught women how
make rag-dolls, boys' clothes, a shawl for granny and ar
ficial flowers. There was also an emphasis on healı
Woman's Own of 31 December 1932 urged housewives to gi
up ten minutes a day to exercise: exercise would overco
that major problem of the house-tied woman, 'Nerves'. T
item reads –

> Few housewives realize what powers they possess and
> how much depends on them; how they have within their
> grasp to make or mar the lives of everyone within the
> household. They are the pivot – the centre around which
> this small organization works and when it is out of gear
> everything is affected.
>   A few simple hints will help restore the housewife
> again to an harmonious frame of mind and keep her fit
> and cheery. There is no reason why she should not be as
> charming and attractive as she was before her marriage,
> in spite of the added responsibility and if she takes this
> nervy condition in hand in its early stages, she will
> prevent disaster in the future not only from the point of
> view of her own health, but because she is risking some-
> thing none of us like to lose – the power to keep her
> husband.

Apart from the perennial problem of nerves, other issu
prompted readers to write in for the guidance of Mrs Eyl
Her answers were practical, helpful and unprudish. To t
real-life working housewife, who complained that her hu
band did no housework, Mrs Eyles replied, 'Your work in t
home is worth money too, so unless he pulls with you he is n
really paying half at all' (5 November 1932). In reply to t
worried young wife who did not like sex, Mrs Eyles recoı
mended a good sex manual. Freud's writings were by n
becoming widely known and it was beginning to be admitt
that women were sexual creatures. In fact, Lady Rhond
complained that middle-class housewives were obsessed wi
sex! This seems an extreme statement, however; in fa

many women remained sexually ignorant. Romance, rather than sex, was the great subject of the women's magazines.

Magazines told women that they should strive to be attractive and well-dressed, that they should furnish their houses tastefully, dress their children in hand-made clothes and that they should constantly be tempting their families with new dishes. It was a dream world and George Orwell realized this. Looking at *Peg's Paper* and the *Oracle*, he wrote, 'It is a pure fantasy world. It is the same fantasy all the time; pretending to be richer than you are.'[31] The chief impression that one carries away from all these stories, noted Orwell, is of a 'frightful, overwhelming refinement'. Indeed the characters appear quintessentially middle-class – in their habits, dress and speech. Mary Grieve, editor of *Woman*, emphasized the magazine's policy of not offending working-class women. There were to be no casual references to bathrooms, telephones or holidays abroad.[32] Nevertheless these magazines do not convey the realities of working-class life; the frightening reality of mass unemployment only comes into its pages in stories where the hero loses his job – only to find a better one immediately. These publications set out to provide a dream world for both the factory girl and the mother of five. They did so very successfully.

Cheap, mass-produced clothing went some way to eradicating earlier obvious differences in dress between the social classes. Of course, the difference in quality remained, but simple styles and the popularity of the trench coat and the beret enabled the working girl to think she really could look like Greta Garbo. J. B. Priestley, touring England in 1933, writes of 'factory girls looking like actresses'.[33]

The cinema had become a very powerful and influential medium by the 1930s. The talkies had arrived. The number of cinemas in Britain boomed from 3,000 in 1926 to 5,000 in 1939. Forty per cent of Liverpool's population went once a week to see their screen idols and 25 per cent were so hooked that they went twice a week or even more often.[34] Whether the local picture house was a luxurious, carpeted and plush-seated palace with a Wurlitzer organ or just a draughty flea-pit with a concrete floor, it was the gateway to another world. For just a few pence the population could forget The

Slump and escape to the romantic, spectacular and carefre
wonderland created by the Hollywood studios.

It is therefore highly relevant to see what image o
women Warner Bros., and MGM and Twentieth Century
Fox projected throughout cinemas in Britain. Were they an
more real than those of the magazines? They were certainl
more imaginative and did not confine themselves to th
single image of The Housewife. At least three dominant type
flickered across the screen. Firstly, there was the sass
Career Woman. Jean Arthur was the aggressive reporte
who duped country-hick-millionaire, Gary Cooper, int
giving her exclusive stories in *Mr. Deeds Goes to Tow.*
(1936); Joan Crawford was the cub reporter in *Dance Fool*
Dance (1931) and Bette Davis was *Front Page Woman* (1935
The major source of satisfaction for these lady journalists wa
in hooking the hero rather than in getting the scoop, thoug
they usually did that too. In showing women in thes
glamorous professions Hollywood was distorting realit
there were (in real life) less than 1,000 women employed o
newspapers in the whole of the USA. Maybe as the Depres
sion squeezed working women hard, these films were mean
to create a false optimism. The other two screen images fror
the period were more important – the Peroxide Blonde an
the Screen Goddess. Female stars of the early 1930s, follow
ing Anita Loos's advice, were blonde and beautiful and, unt
censorship stepped in, they were also very sexy. Mae Wes
almost a parody of female sexuality, drawled, 'I used to b
Snow White but I drifted.' Jean Harlow was the beautifu
blonde temptress. Neither was a stereotyped, passive femal
and both come across as individual human beings. Marjori
Rosen,[35] the historian of women in films, says of these tw
blonde bombshells, 'Mae West, firing off vocal salvos wit
imperious self assurance and Jean Harlow, merchandisin
her physical allure for the masses, transformed the idea o
passive female sexuality into an agressive statement of fact
It's a far cry from *Peg's Paper* and *Woman*! But the Hay
Office and Randolph Hearst stopped Mae. Harlow die
young. The late 1930s saw the emergence of the great Scree
Goddesses – Garbo and Dietrich. Garbo appeared like
remote, untouchable creature of mythology. She was

agnet to men. A common theme characterized many of her
ms. Her frigid exterior appears impregnable but inevitably
e succumbs to the charms of the hero. She becomes totally
voted to him, only to sink helplessly into ruin when she
ses him. Love humanized and demystified Garbo; she had
separate existence outside her love affair. As she urged
r hero – 'Take me, take me and make me as you desire
e.'[36] She was a blank waiting to be stamped with the
press of the male. Was that why women bought Garbo
rets and plucked their eyebrows? Marlene Dietrich, the
her great Screen Goddess, was in many ways like her, but
like Garbo, she was deadly. She was the destructive ser-
nt of *The Blue Angel* (1930), ruining the old professor, but
quently she came to grief and how reassured male audi-
ces were by her final submission! Such were the Hollywood
ages – all remote from reality. Rosen calls them, 'celluloid
hrodisiacs – talking, walking and comforting a patriarchal
ciety – recently emasculated by the dollar devaluation'.

The dominant images of the 1930s – the Housewife of the
agazines and the cinema stars – were hardly true reflec-
ons of reality. Admittedly, the Housewife is fairly close to
e reality of comfortably-off middle-class women's lives, but
e is as remote as an alien from a far-off galaxy from the
res of the great majority of working-class women. The
ump lowered standards of living that were already
ysmally poor. The only time a woman in South Wales or
e North East would have dressed up was on her wedding
y. Inquiries by social investigators into areas of high
employment reveal a depressing picture of women too
sheartened to even wash themselves. Not for them the
t-out patterns of organdie tea-aprons from the magazines!
s for the cinema, how many women looked like Garbo? How
any were Queen of Sweden, prima donna ballet dancers or
lshevik agents? How many had legs like Dietrich? The
int need not be laboured.

In 1939 the Second World War broke out; so too did the
seted housewife from her suburban home. It was the same
ory as in 1914. Women were needed for the war effort and
w to be a dilettante housewife was considered unpatriotic.
ce again women were brought into munitions factories,

aircraft production and the armed services; at home they to
influential positions in management and the civil servi
Posters proclaimed the new image – the turbanned, trenc
coated female worker. 'Serve in the Waaf with the men w
fly' and 'Cover your hair for safety: your Russian sist
does', said placards and posters. Hollywood presented squar
jawed and square-shouldered independent women for
now largely female audiences; Joan Crawford, Bette Dav
and Katherine Hepburn strode purposefully across t
screen, sometimes as career women and always as t
protagonists. Again it took a war for women to break out
the home and to be 'granted human as opposed to fema
status'.[37]

This book is not concerned with the post-Second Wor
War period – but it must be said the situation was in ma
ways similar to that of the period following the First W;
Once again women were expected to disappear from t
labour force and again become happy housewives. Even mo
emphasis was to be placed on her role and image as moth
particularly after John Bowlby discovered/invent
'maternal deprivation'.

PRACTICAL SCHEDULE

The practical work suggested in this chapter is unlike th
suggested in any of the subsequent chapters in that it can
conducted at armchair level through a programme of readi
and viewing. Old novels and women's magazines form t
basis of the reading programme.

Women's fiction

By this title I mean fiction that is largely about wome
whether it has been written by women or men. Some of t
books in this section, particularly the examples of popul
writing, which I cite at the end of the list, were specifical
aimed at female readers. Before offering a list of fiction
works to read, I should like to point out two useful guides
the literature.

Françoise Basch, *Relative Creatures*, London, Allen Lan
1974; Elaine Showalter, *A Literature of their Own*, Londo

Virago, 1978. The following list is by no means comprehensive: it is a selection. All the books on it are easily available – in second-hand shops, in libraries or in paperback.

Jane Austen, *Pride and Prejudice* (1813), *Mansfield Park* (1814), etc.

Charlotte Brontë, *Jane Eyre* (1847), *Shirley* (1849), *Villette* (1853).

Emily Brontë, *Wuthering Heights* (1847).

Ann Brontë, *Agnes Grey* (1847), *The Tenant of Wildfell Hall* (1848).

William Thackeray, *Vanity Fair* (1847).

Elizabeth Gaskell, *Mary Barton* (1848), *Ruth* (1853), *North and South* (1855).

Elizabeth Barrett Browning, *Aurora Leigh* (1857).

George Eliot, *Adam Bede* (1859), *The Mill on the Floss* (1860), *Middlemarch* (1871).

Mrs Henry Wood, *East Lynne* (1862).

Charlotte Yonge, *The Daisy Chain* (1856).

Thomas Hardy, *Far from the Madding Crowd,* (1874), *The Mayor of Casterbridge* (1886), *Tess of the D'Urbervilles* (1891), *Jude the Obscure* (1895).

George Moore, *A Mummer's Wife* (1884), *Esther Waters* (1894).

George Meredith, *Diana of the Crossways* (1885).

George Gissing, *Thyrza* (1887), *The Odd Women* (1893).

Olive Schreiner, *Story of an African Farm* (1883), *The Heavenly Twins* (1893).

Somerset Maugham, *Liza of Lambeth* (1887), *Of Human Bondage* (1915).

George Egerton, *Key Notes* (1894), *Discords* (1894).

Arnold Bennett, *The Old Wives Tale* (1908), *Hilda Lessways* (1911).

H. G. Wells, *Ann Veronica* (1909).

Henry Handel Richardson, *The Getting of Wisdom* (1910).

May Sinclair, *The Creators* (1910), *Mary Oliver* (1914), *Tree of Heaven* (1917).

Virginia Woolf, *The Voyage Out* (1915), *Orlando* (1928), *A Room of One's Own* (1929).

Mary Webb, *Precious Bane* (1924), *Gone to Earth*, (1917).

Katherine Mansfield, *The Garden Party* (1922).

Radclyffe Hall, *The Unlit Lamp* (1924), *The Well of Loneli-
ness* (1928).
E. M. Delafield, *The Diary of a Provincial Lady* (1931).

The above list is mainly composed of 'good quality'
fiction, but I think it is also important for anyone inquiring
into past images of women to also look at the representation
of women in popular fiction. Past popular fiction is often
easily available in second-hand shops. I cannot present a full
list but a few names worth pursuing are Mrs Opie and T. P.
Prest (both early nineteenth century), Marie Correlli (early
twentieth century), Ruby M. Ayres, Agatha Christie and
Edgar Wallace. Reading these should hardly prove an
arduous task.

Women's magazines

Women's magazines are another interesting source of contemporary images of women. Unfortunately, old ones are not
that easy to locate. Local, or even central, libraries often
regarded them as beneath their dignity to stock – though
they may hold back-copies of monthlies, rather than weeklies. Only major libraries, e.g. the British Library, are likely
to have large collections. It is therefore worth asking friends,
neighbours or people interviewed in a local history project if
they have old copies of women's magazines stacked away
under the stairs or in their attics. I was recently given a pile
of old magazines by a neighbour: they included copies of
Home Cookery 1909, *Home Chat* 1914, *The Home Companion*
1929, *Woman* 1941–6 and copies of *Woman's Weekly* for 1948.

A very good guide to the women's magazine press in
Britain and America exists in Cynthia White, *Women's
Magazines 1693–1968: A Sociological Study,* London,
Michael Joseph, 1970.

Women's magazines have been going strong since the
mid-nineteenth century. Amongst early publications worth
consulting are,
The English Woman's Domestic Journal (1852–79) (BL).
The Mother's Companion (1887–96) (BL).
The Mothers' Friend (1848–95) (BL).
The Lady's Companion (1921–40).
Peg's Paper (1919–40) (BL).

Woman (1937–   ) (Colindale).
Woman's Own (1932–   ) (Colindale).
Woman's Friend (1924–50) (Colindale).
Woman's Weekly (1911–   ) (Colindale).
Home Chat (1895–1956) (Colindale).
People's Friend (of particular interest for Scotland) (1869–   ) (Colindale).

Films

The cinema was from early in this century a powerful agency of mass culture. By looking at old films – in the cinema or on television – we can see how male-created images of what women ought to be, have been changed over the last fifty years; film is an interesting source which demonstrates how images are manipulated to suit the changing needs of industrial society. The main cinematic images, discussed above may be recapped as:

I	1900–1920	a	Girl Child.
		b	The Vamp.
II	1920–1930	a	The Virgin Flapper.
		b	The Chorus Girl.
		c	Working Girls.
III	1930–1940	a	Career Woman.
		b	Blonde Bombshells.
		c	Mysterious Woman.
IV	1940–1950	a	Strong Woman.
		b	Female Victims.
		c	Evil Woman.
		d	Pin up.

By far the best guide to the changing image of women in films is Majorie Rosen, *Popcorn Venus,* New York, Avon, 1973.

It would take up far too much space here to give a long list of films. I suggest that the most useful approach would be to look out for the films of particular actresses, as well as to watch any old films, starring women, which happen to be shown on TV. It would be useful to check on these images and to note any variation on them. The following is a list of some of the actresses who represent the particular stereotypes tabulated above. Often one actress will play more than one stereotype and the list below cannot be taken as totally clear-cut – but it is a starting point.

I   a   Mary Pickford, Lilian Gish.
    b   Theda Bara (for 1920s imitator, see Pola Negri).
II a   Colleen Moore (star of King Vidor films), Eleanor Boardman, Constance Talmadge.
    b   Mae Murray, Gloria Swanson (!), Joan Crawford (!).
    c   Alice White, Louise Fazenda, Natalie Moorhead, Constance Bennett, Lassie Lou Aherne, Clara Bow.
III a   Joan Crawford, Loretta Young, Jean Arthur, Bette Davis.
    b   Mae West, Jean Harlow.
    c   Greta Garbo, Marlene Dietrich.
IV a   Katherine Hepburn, Rosalind Russell, Joan Crawford, Claudette Colbert, Ingrid Bergmann.
    b   Loretta Young, Jane Wyman, Olivia de Havilland.
    c   Bette Davis, Barbara Stanwyck, Lana Turner, Joan Crawford.
    d   Betty Grable, Rita Hayworth, Jane Russell.

Finally, locating lesbians in films of the pre-war era is not easy. Dietrich wore drag in film-stage numbers and flirted with women members of the audience. (*Blonde Venus* 1932 and *Morocco* 1930). Katherine Hepburn dressed as a boy in *Sylvia Scarlett* (1935) and Garbo, in portraying the lesbian Swedish queen in *Queen Christina* (1933), wore male attire and at the beginning of the film was having an affair with her chambermaid. From the same period there are, however, several German films in which lesbianism plays a more central part, e.g. *Die Büchse von Pandora* (*Pandora's Box* 1928) and *Mädchen in Uniform* (*Girls in Uniform* 1931).[38]

Assessing the influence of images: a local project.
This is a somewhat ambitious scheme and I am not certain quite how well it can work. But I think it would be very interesting to actually do as part of a wider local history research project. The aim of this particular section is to try and get some indication of the impact of certain images and stereotypes – as projected by the media – on women's lives.

The emphasis is on the media here: projects centring on other aspects covered in this book e.g. education, waged work or family life will certainly show the influence of stereotyped views of women's role. The main source for this section will be older women themselves and the chief method of investigation will be the oral interview. More information about oral history and how to conduct an interview is given in Chapter 4. The following is a set of suggested questions – which can, of course, be added to – and which may yield some results.

Questions
What did you feel your main role in life should be? To be a wife? A mother? Career woman? Was it possible to be a wife and a woman with a career when you were young? What influenced you to take a particular role? Your family? Friends? School? Things you read? (If appropriate: did you go out to work in the war? What did you do? Did you think at the time that your war-time job conflicted with all you had learned about a woman's role? Did you want to stay on after the war?)

Magazines: do you read women's magazines now? Which ones? Which did you used to read? Why? What did you like most in them? Describe what you liked best. Have any particular stories or articles stuck in your mind? Which?

Novels: do you read novels now? By whom? Did you used to read novels? Who were your favourite writers? What sort of stories did you like? Can you remember any you particularly liked? Did you used to put yourself in the heroine's place? Want to swop places with her? Did you just think it was all fantasy with nothing to do with real life? Looking back, what do you think of those stories now?

Cinema: did you go the cinema? How often? Once, twice a week? More often? Which cinemas? Why did you go? What did you get out of going? Who were your favourite film stars – male and female? Can you remember any of the films they were in? Can you remember the story? Did you want to be like any of the women film stars? Who? Why? Did you try and dress like them, talk like them, etc.? Did you think that your

life could be like the lives of women in the films? Did you
think it had nothing to do with you?

One might come up with some fascinating answers to
these questions. In order to find out what was on in local
cinemas and to find out what images women in your community were exposed to, you only have to look in back
numbers of the local newspaper. It might also be interesting
to get hold of photographs of old film stars and juxtapose them
with local photographs of young women. One might see some
nice points of similarity and contrast.

NOTES

1 J. Berger, *Ways of Seeing,* Harmondsworth, Penguin, 1972,
   p. 46.
2 M. Vicinus (ed.), *Suffer and Be Still: Women in the Victorian Age,*
   London, Methuen, 1980.
3 C. Hall, 'Gender divisions and class formation in the
   Birmingham middle class, 1780–1850', in R. Samuel (ed.),
   People's History and Socialist Theory, London, Routledge &
   Kegan Paul, 1981, pp. 164–75. See also C. Hall, 'The early
   formation of the Victorian domestic Ideology', in S. Burman (ed.),
   Fit Work for Women, London, Croom Helm, 1979.
4 Sarah Stickney Ellis, *The Daughters of England,* London, 1845,
   p. 11.
5 Elizabeth Gould Davis, *The First Sex,* New York, Putnam,
   1971.
6 Sarah Stickney Ellis, *The Women of England: Their Social
   Duties and Domestic Habits,* London, 1839.
7 Ibid., pp. 219–20.
8 See the essay 'Of Queen's Gardens' in *Sesame and Lilies,* London,
   1865, later issued with an additional preface London, 1871.
9 Ibid., pp 90–1. Boys are referred to as 'Kings' and girls as
   'Queens' throughout these lectures!
10 This was the position until the Married Women's Property Act of
   1882.
11 G. Henry Lewes, *Edinburgh Review,* XCI, 155, January 1850.
12 Rees, *Cyclopaedia,* London, 1788, I, pt 2, p. 194.
13 Ruskin, op. cit., pp. 108–9.
14 Coventry Patmore, 'Angel in the Home', F. Page (ed.), *Poems,*
   London, 1949, p. 69. First published 1854–6.
15 Cited in H. M. Roberts, 'Marriage, redundancy or sin: the
   painter's view of women in the first twenty five years of
   Victoria's reign' in M. Vicinus (ed.), op. cit., pp. 45–77.

16 L. Duffin, 'The conspicuous consumptive: woman as invalid', in
    S. Delamont and L. Duffin, (eds), *The Nineteenth Century
    Woman,* London, Croom Helm. 1978.
17 S. S. Ellis, *Daughters,* op. cit., p. 94.
18 'The town mouse and the country mouse', *Temple Bar,* vol. 69,
    1883, p. 72.
19 In M. Hartmann and L. Banner (eds), *Clio's Consciousness
    Raised,* New York, Harper, 1974, pp. 179–92.
20 Charlotte Brontë, *Shirley* (1845). I have used the Penguin
    edition, 1974, p. 235.
21 Cited W. Holtby, *Women and a Changing Civilization,* London,
    John Lane, 1934.
22 Op. cit.
23 For a discussion of this, see R. Evans, *The Feminists,* London,
    Croom Helm, 1979.
24 Cited in Alison Adburgham, *A Punch History of Manners and
    Modes 1841–1940,* London, 1961, p. 150.
25 Ibid.,
26 Ibid.,
27 Thomas Hardy, *Jude the Obscure,* London, 1895. Subsequent
    editions carry a postscript to the preface, in which Hardy quoted
    the remarks made to him by a German critic – as set out in my
    text. I have used the Macmillan edition of 1960.
28 Loveday Brooke was the creation of Catherine Louisa Pirkis.
    One of her stories, 'The Redmill Sisterhood' has recently been
    reprinted. Dora Myrl is the product of M. McD. Bodkin's
    imagination. The extract is from 'How He Cut His Stick'. Both
    stories are in Hugh Greene, *Further Rivals of Sherlock Holmes,*
    Harmondsworth, Penguin, 1976.
29 See J. Darracott and B. Loftus, *First World War Posters,* London,
    Imperial War Museum, 1972.
30 Agatha Christie, *The Secret Adversary,* London, Bodley Head,
    1922, and *The Seven Dials Mystery,* London, Collins, 1929.
31 G. Orwell, 'Boys' weeklies' in *Inside the Whale and Other Essays,*
    Harmondsworth, Penguin, 1957, p. 199.
32 M. Grieve, *Millions made my Story,* London, Gollancz, 1964.
33 J. B. Priestley, *English Journey,* London, 1934.
34 J. Stevenson, *Social Conditions in Britain between the Wars,*
    Harmondsworth, Penguin, 1977, p. 43.
35 M. Rosen, *Popcorn Venus: Women, Movies and the American
    Dream,* New York, Avon, 1973.
36 Ibid. The quotation is from *As You Desire Me* (1932).
37 S. Firestone, *The Dialectic of Sex,* London, Paladin, 1972, p. 33.
38 R. Dyer (ed.), *Gays and Film,* London, British Film Institute,
    1977.

Chapter three

The education of girls

Education is an experience common to almost all women in Britain. It is a compulsory experience and has been since 1880. Its influence has been enormous in propounding a set of values designed to keep women in their place and to teach them the 'natural order' of things. It is therefore an extremely important area of women's history to investigate. It is also a topic on which one can expect to find a wide range of local material and research can consequently be very fruitful.

The great bulk of work undertaken so far on the education of girls has been concerned with the education – or lack of it – of middle-class girls and with the struggle of women of the same class to win a university education for themselves.[1] This middle-class struggle was an important one. These women, through their efforts, set up schools for girls with a curriculum based upon a male model and battered down the barriers to women's entry into the universities. In so doing they challenged the useless and decorative role allotted to many middle-class women in the nineteenth century – a role which stood in stark contrast to the central part played by women of the same class in production in pre-industrial Britain. Nevertheless, it is important to reject the almost exclusive concentration upon the education of a minority of women. It is important now to investigate the education provided for the majority of women in Britain, i.e. the women of the working class. On the other hand, it would be remiss totally to omit the achievements of the middle-class pioneers. These are relevant to the education of working-class girls, particularly in the long run, in that they influenced ideas about the education of girls in Britain and about the training of women teachers. One should also note that some women graduates went on to teach in secondary schools, attended by working-class girls, and may have influenced the aspirations of some of their pupils.[2]

Fortunately, the neglect of the study of the education of
rking-class, and indeed lower middle-class, girls is now
ing rectified. A small number of historians have very
cently begun to produce useful studies of the education of
ese girls.[3] Their contribution is extremely helpful but what
urgently required is many local studies. However, before
rning to the guide to the local sources, I think it will be
eful to present a short survey of the education available to
rls in Britain from 1800 to 1945. It notes the main develop-
ents in the state, private and university sectors.

Before the 1870 Education Act there was little formal
ucational provision for working-class children in England
d Wales, although in some areas opportunities for informal
ucation existed through family, neighbours, friends,
tisan autodidacts and, for older students, through work-
ates and political colleagues.[4] (The Scottish case was rather
fferent but equally inadequate for large numbers of poor
ildren.[5]) There was even less provision for girls than for
ys. If children attended school at all, and they might do so
r a period ranging from a few days to a few years, they
uld have gone to a school run by charity or religious society
specially The British and Foreign School Society or the
ational Society for the Promotion of Education of the Poor),
Dame school, a ragged school, a Sunday school, a part-time
ctory school or, in some cases, a workhouse school. They are
l very interesting to read about and quite a lot has been
ritten on them.[6] Charity and religious society schools are
rticularly of interest because of the way in which they so
ertly socialized the poor into accepting the existing hier-
chy. The lower orders were indoctrinated with the virtues
honesty, thrift and industry. Religion or the doctrine of
olitical economy' reinforced the demarcation between rich
d poor and emphasized the mutual dependence of each
oup upon the other.[7] Workhouses taught their charges
ous lessons too and although many workhouses exploited
ild labour by farming it out, as in the example of Oliver
wist, they also taught practical skills. James Kay
uttleworth and the Poor Law Commissioners of 1839
nished repetitive tasks in workhouse schools – such as
rting bristles and henna and fixing hooks and eyes onto

cards. Boys were trained as blacksmiths, mariners, carpe
ters and shoemakers, but girls learned housework, laund
work and cookery.[8] There were attempts to provide educati
for factory children. Some of these factory schools open
only in the evenings. An evening 'Industrial School' in Leed
opened in 1802 to deal with 'the problem of factory girl
taught reading, writing, sewing and knitting and train
girls for domestic service.[9] The Factory Acts provided th
children between eight and thirteen years should atten
school half-time – mornings or afternoons. The Newcast
Report (1861), commenting on Bradford and Rochdal
deplored the short period of education given to these childr
and showed how girls' timetables could be dominated
sewing.

> The time, therefore, during which a short-timer is under
> effective instruction is very short indeed; short as it is,
> however, in the case of girls, a large portion is abstracted
> for teaching sewing. Mixed schools devote usually about
> an hour and a half, girls' schools about an hour and three
> quarters, to this purpose daily; and, as in a majority of
> cases, by a stupid arrangement, the needlework lesson is
> given only in the afternoon, a mill girl may, during her
> afternoon turn, lasting a week or a month, as the case
> may be, have not more than an hour a day for intellectual
> instruction. Indeed, in not a few private, and some public
> schools, needlework takes up the whole afternoon, and
> the girls may be left for a whole month without even
> having a reading lesson.[10]

Attendance at other schools might be swelled by indu
trial action at a factory. At St Mary's Girls' School in Prest
86 more girls were present on the day of the school inspector
visit than on normal days. The inspector recorded
November 1853 that '86 of the girls in this school are atten
ing in consequence of the millowners having closed the
mills: and the zealous clergyman of the district has wise
induced c. 100 girls in the neighbourhood to attend scho
during the "lock-out" '.[11] I have no information as to wheth
this was indeed a 'lock-out' or if the mill was closed through
cotton shortage.

Dame schools, or schools run by a single woman teacher,
.ctioned both in villages and in the urban centres in the
.eteenth century. They have had a very bad press and are
.ally dismissed as baby-minding hovels, run by old hags.[12]
.eed, there were some dreadful ones. A dame school in a
.ncashire town, visited by an inspector in 1840 was des-
.ed as follows:

.n one of these dame schools I found 31 children, from 2 to
. years of age. The room was a cellar, about 10 feet
.quare and about 7 feet high. The only window was less
.han 18 inches square, and was not made to open.
.lthough it was a warm day, towards the close of
.ugust, there was a fire burning; and the door, through
.vhich alone any air could be admitted, was shut. Of
.ourse, therefore, the room was close and hot; but there
.vas no remedy. The damp, subterraneous walls
.equired, as the old woman assured us, a fire throughout
.he year. If she opened the door the children would rush
.ut to light and liberty, while the cold blast rushing in
.vould torment her aged bones with rheumatism. Still
.urther to restrain their vagrant propensities, and to
.ave them from the danger of tumbling into the fire, she
.ad crammed the children as closely as possible into a
.ark corner at the foot of her bed. Here they sat in the
.estiferous obscurity, totally destitute of books, and
.vithout light enough to enable them to read, had books
.een placed in their hands. Six children, indeed, out of
.he 30, had brought some twopenny books, but these
.lso, having been made to circulate through 60 little
.ands, were now so well soiled and tattered as to be
.ather the memorials of past achievements than the
.neans of leading the children to fresh exertion. The
.nly remaining instruments of instruction possessed by
.he dame, who lamented her hard lot, to be obliged, at
.o advanced an age, to tenant a damp cellar, and to raise
.he means of paying her rent by such scholastic toils,
.vere a glass-full of sugar plums near the tattered leaves
.n the table in the centre of the room, and a cane by
.ts side. Every point in instruction being thus secured

by the good old rule of mingling the useful with the
sweet.[13]

The task of assessing such evidence is difficult since
descriptions of dame schools were mainly written by ca
paigners for a state system to replace them. Recent work a
work in progress is questioning the low assessment of da
schools. By no means all reports on them were bad: ma
were popular institutions and later rivalled infant school
attracting pupils. Joan Burstyn made an interesting po
when she wrote, 'There is a disturbing analogy to be dra
between the industrialization of teaching and the industri
ization of other occupations where small scale worksh
initiated and maintained by women were replaced by sm
scale operations organized by men.'[14] Women were not ag
to have such control over educational content and teach
methods.

There is one other 'accepted truth' about the educatio
working-class children in the period before 1870 which ne
closer examination. It is often said that the content
education for working-class children was hardly differ
tiated by sex at this period and that the only concession to
differences was that girls were taught sewing.[15] This is a vi
which can be questioned. Firstly, it is important to point
that although needlework was only one subject, an inor
nate amount of time was spent on it. The Report for the G
National School at Lambeth in 1827 shows that girls sp
four afternoons a week sewing.[16] There is a revealing co
ment on how the girls viewed this situation in the school's
book for 1867: 'Commenced work this afternoon with a la
attendance in consequence of having told the girls we w
going to have a lesson instead of needlework.'[17]

In schools where any vocational training was gi
before 1870, it is nonsense to talk of lack of sexual dif
entiation. Workhouse and charitable schools trained girl
domestic skills and boys in a wide range of other ski
Minutes and Reports of the Committee of Council show
same differentiation between practical work for the sex
Scottish schools of the 1850s and 1860s were already inc
porating domestic economy into the curriculum for girls (

low).[18] School readers of the pre-1870 period reflect the
ture roles of girls and boys. 'Female Readers' are full of
ecdotes on good and bad maids. The following poem from
e such Reader, *Lessons on Industrial Education for the Use
'Female Schools by a Lady* (1849), presents the ideal of the
tentive and invisible female servant.

The Good Waitress.

The servant who at table waits,
Should have a ready eye;
For 'tis not all, to hand the plates
And silently stand by.

The table neatly to set out,
As it before was planned;
To move with noiseless step about,
To serve with gentle hand.

To cast a look from side to side,
And read in every face
If any want is unsupplied,
Or unfill'd any space.

To have whatever's call'd for near;
To speak no useless word;
To hear, yet never seem to hear,
What passes at the board;

These, of a clever parlour maid,
The special duties are;
And she who hopes to be well-paid,
Must make them all her care.[19]

short, many primary schools today would claim that their
rricula scarcely differentiate between boys and girls and
ey would claim that they offer a non-sexist education,
hilst all the time hammering home stereotyped gender
les and entertaining quite different expectations in the
haviour and achievement of boys and girls. It would,
deed, seem that the content of schools' curricula for the
orking class post-1870 was *more* sex specific than before
at date but the evidence shows the absurdity of thinking
xism in the curriculum did not exist before 1870.

This is the sort of area where local studies could throw a
lot of light. It would be interesting to see how much variation
there was in pre-1870 local practice. There was certainly
great differentiation between the sexes in the field of private
education. The better-off members of the middle class educa
ted their daughters by employing governesses or by sending
their daughters to private academies.[20] The emphasis was on
accomplishments and social graces rather than on intellec
tual stimulus. The latter, it was thought, certainly by the
1870s, would lead to brain fever and barrenness.[21]

Much of the education offered in girls' private school
was of a very low standard. The Taunton Report of 1868 on
private education, stated:

> It cannot be denied that the picture brought before us of
> the state of Middle Class Female Education is on the
> whole unfavourable.
>
>   The general deficiency in girls' education is stated
> with the utmost confidence and with entire agreement,
> with whatever difference in words, by many witnesses of
> authority. Want of thoroughness and foundation; want
> of system; slovenliness and showy superficiality;
> inattention to rudiments, undue time given to
> accomplishments and those not taught intelligently or in
> any systematic manner.[22]

Mr Hammond, a commissioner for the Midlands an
Northumbria, who was later to play an active part in im
proving the number and standard of girls' secondary schools
blamed parents rather than schools for the state of affair
found by the Taunton commissioners. He said that the prim
consideration of parents in selecting a school for their
daughters was 'that instrumental music is supposed to be th
leading subject of instruction for women.'[23] Such an educa
tion, he thought, accounted in part for the 'vapid character
and frivolous pursuits of idle women, who have nothing i
particular to do'.[24] (It was over 75 years since Mar
Wollstonecraft had written *The Vindication of the Rights o
Women,* in which she advocated a broad curriculum for boy
and girls, both rich and poor.) It was precisely this educatio
to be a household ornament which was to make Florenc

ghtingale cry out against 'The Death of the Mind' and ich spurred pioneers, like Ms Buss and Ms Beale, to trans- m secondary education for middle-class girls. Cheltenham dies' College, as a boarding school, and North London llegiate School, as a day establishment, represent the t in the new style of girls' education. They aimed at ering girls an education every bit as good as that offered to rs.[25] Many feminist reformers, given the need to prove the ntal equality of women, would have no truck with special rses or examinations for women. Emily Davies was such uncompromising pioneer in the higher education of men. At Girton College, opened 1870, she insisted that the nale students should study exactly the same course as n, and within the same time limits, despite the fact that ir schooling had usually ill prepared them for this. It was, vever, many years before Cambridge fully admitted men to its degrees. Not, in fact, until 1948. (London iversity had opened its degrees to women in 1898, but not medical degrees. Oxford followed in 1920.) In short, from late nineteenth century a trickle of able and courageous men were to receive the benefits of higher education. Much er the same opportunity would be opened to very able rking-class girls. The pioneers had had to overcome ormous prejudices and in many cases the price they had to for academic success was celibacy. When Vera Brittain s working for Oxford Entrance in 1913, her mother's nds exclaimed, 'How can you send your daughter to lege, Mrs. Brittain. . . . Don't you want her ever to get rried?'[26] In that particular case, they were wrong, but ny women graduates who pursued academic careers were ced to make a choice between career and marriage.

The Elementary Education Act of 1870 (Forster's Act) de schooling theoretically available to all children in gland and Wales up to the age of at least ten. Minimum ted leaving ages were later raised – in 1893 to eleven and 1899 to twelve. The local School Boards, set up by the Act of '0, were empowered to frame by-laws making attendance school compulsory: some cities did this, e.g. Leeds. In 1880 endance was made compulsory everywhere, but it was still free: fees of a few pence a week had to be paid for each

pupil and these were not for the most part abolished ur
1891: in some places fees were still being paid up till 19
The Education Act (Scotland) of 1872 was more far-reach
and aimed at establishing a system of elementary educat
up to the age of thirteen and to make this compulsory.

Forster's Act was intended to plug the many gaps in
voluntary system, which the Newcastle Commission h
shown up. It was agreed by many groups that education wa
'good thing'. Radicals and trade unionists hoped to ra
working-class consciousness by it, feminists to 'rescue' gi
by it and the middle and upper classes to stabilize society
it. Anna Davin has pointed out that historians, analysing
motives behind Forster's Education Act and examining
system of Board Schools it established, have done so in soc
political and economic terms. It is, she argues, primarily
social function that was to be most important in deciding
offer education to girls.

> The political explanations relate most directly to the
> growing labour movement, in which women played no
> part at this time, and to the 1867 Franchise Act, which
> created a million or so new voters, none of them women;
> while the economic context concerns the development of
> a new skilled and literate workforce (including a whole
> range of minor technicians significant in the expansion
> of empire and commerce as well as industry –
> telegraphists, sappers and signalmen as well as the more
> obvious draughtsmen, engineers and clerical workers)
> from which women (to begin with at least) were again
> absent. If such political and economic grounds had been
> the only reasons for introducing general elementary
> education, one might well ask why girls were included at
> all.[27]

Why, indeed, were girls educated at all? The answ
becomes clear when one looks into what and how they w
taught in Board Schools. They were taught to be good wi
to working men and to be good mothers to the next generat
of the workforce. They were taught the bourgeois notion
family – male breadwinner, dependent wife (as a dependa
a brake on her husband's radicalism) and depend

children. The compulsory education of children between the ages of five and ten hampered them from contributing to the family income and made them dependent too on the male breadwinner. I find these ideas set out by Anna Davin entirely plausible. The local research I have carried out makes me reach the same conclusion but I think it is important that a good deal of local research is done in many areas to test out how, and therefore why, working-class girls were educated. Any differences between areas would be particularly interesting.

The Act of 1870 and the Education Act (Scotland) of 1872 established School Boards, which were to be elected, and these in turn set up the familiar Board Schools – solid, often colossal, stone edifices set in bleak asphalt playgrounds enclosed by lavatory sheds. 'Lighthouses, my boy' that is what Conan Doyle in 1893 made Holmes tell Watson. 'Beacons of the future. Capsules with hundreds of bright little seeds in each, out of which will spring the wiser, better England of the future.'[28] Within these lighthouses little girls were being steadily indoctrinated with the domestic ideology.

This is seen clearly in two ways – firstly, by the great emphasis placed upon the teaching of domestic subjects, especially from the 1880s onwards, and secondly, from school text books. I am writing here particularly of England and Wales, since the Scottish systems operated separately and there is yet much work to be done on the education of girls in Scotland. There are many fascinating records available through which domestic science education in schools may be seen but its context needs a little explanation. The teaching of domestic subjects expanded rapidly throughout the 1880s and 1890s. The Code of 1875 made grants available to schools for scholars in the higher standards who passed examinations in two subjects called specific subjects. In 1878 the Code made domestic economy a *compulsory* specific subject for girls. Grants were awarded first for cookery and then for laundry work. In Bristol in the late 1890s the girls were so inundated with practical domestic skills that the Cookery and Housewifery Committee of the Board expressed concern at the overlapping between the teaching of domestic economy and housewifery.[29] The number of girls in England and Wales qualifying for the cookery grant rose from 37,597 in 457 schools in 1882–3 to 134,930 in 2792 schools in 1895–6.[30] Fears of national physical degeneracy among working-class cannon fodder gave a further boost to the teaching of domestic subjects. The outbreak of the Boer War highlighted this. In Manchester 8,000 out of 11,000 volunteers were rejected as unfit. An Inter-departmental Committee, set up by the government to look into national standards of physical health, reported back in 1904. The report laid particular emphasis on the ignorance of working-class wives in the matters of nutrition and hygiene. It led the Board of Education to appoint women inspectors in Domestic Subjects to ensure that girls were given a thorough training for life. These inspectors, when they went on their rounds, were far from satisfied with many schools. They found schools in which the cookery teacher concentrated on getting the girls to prepare easily saleable commodities like toffee and buns (to be sold from the school or cookery centre) and one inspector expressed horror at a school in the North of England where eighteen girls, in the lesson on roasting, prepared and cooked a single chop. They were very scornful of the advice given by another northern teacher who said, 'If you have cholera or scarlet fever in the house put some onions under the bed, and they will sweep away all diseases.'[31]

The second way of learning about how girls were taught their place in the family is to consult old school text books. Examples of these are given below in the section on sources.

Because school had become compulsory, the Boards appointed attendance officers, who instigated a series of graded measures – from warnings to imprisonment – against parents who did not send their children to school.[32] The children could be sent to truant schools. The attendance of girls is well worth looking into. There will probably be many different reasons in different parts of Britain as well as reasons common to all regions. It would also be interesting to know how the reasons for absence of boys and girls varied, if indeed they did.

Secondary education was given little consideration until the early twentieth century. The Scots had paid it more attention and indeed their secondary system proceeded along different lines.[33] In England and Wales secondary education had always been regarded as being the privilege of the middle and upper classes. The Education Act of 1902, implementing the recommendations of the Bryce commission, set up Local Education Authorities to replace School Boards and part of the brief of the LEAs was to provide secondary education. Elementary schools, of course, continued and provided most working-class children with all the schooling they were to receive: the leaving age was twelve. The 1902 Act, however, set up municipal and county secondary schools but the education in them was not free. In 1907 a system of free places – 'the ladder of opportunity' – was introduced so that very able pupils in elementary schools could enter secondary schools. These secondary schools offered an education for children up to the age of sixteen. They offered a wider curriculum than the elementary schools but still included domestic economy for girls. In 1906, the Board of Education, the new government department overseeing national education, even suggested that science teaching for girls 'might be wholly replaced by an approved Scheme of Instruction in Practical Housewifery for girls over 15 years of age'.[34]

It is worth noting that the education offered in girls' 'public day schools' (i.e. private secondary schools) was far more academic and less sex differentiated than that offered in State schools. Domestic subjects were looked down upon but, on the other hand, science and mathematics were not given the provision which they had in boys' schools in the same sector. Consequently, when many middle-class girls went to university, they had already opted for arts subjects.

Official government policy was to continue to differentiate between children on grounds of sex and class. It is often possible to transpose the familiar expressions of 'high ability' and 'low ability' with middle-class and working-class. In 1923 the Hadow Committee addressed itself to the question of 'The Differentiation of the Curriculum for Boys and Girls Respectively in Secondary Schools'.[35] The report outlines existing practice and provides local examples. It shows that in Leicestershire, 'girls are allowed to take Botany instead of

Physics and Needlework instead of Trigonometry'.[36] The report made some interesting statements:

> We do not think it desirable to attempt to divorce a girl's
> education from her home duties and home opportunities.
> On the other hand, there is a real danger of her energies
> being exhausted by home duties and her interests
> absorbed by social engagements to the detriment of her
> mental development.[37]

More than once it states that girls and boys should be given a good general education and said that that education should 'avoid any policy based upon the idea that certain occupations, and certain occupations only, can be successfully undertaken by men or by women'.[38] Yet despite the above remarks, the report did differentiate between the social functions of boys and girls. While both had to be educated to earn a living and to be useful citizens, girls had also 'to be makers of homes'.[39] It notes that girls had to earn their own livings up to the age of about twenty-five and, indeed, later, it points out, if they should be widowed.[40] Despite some of the more liberal statements of the Hadow Report, the basic assumption of it is that boys should be educated for the world of work and girls by and large for the private world of the home.

Later official statements on ideology maintain this dichotomy between the functions of the two sexes. The Norwood Report of 1943 thought in terms of education for boys as that for future supporters of families and that for girls as for future wives and mothers.[41] This report categorized all children as falling within three main categories, according to their levels of ability. This is important because it formed the basis of the tripartite division of secondary education, introduced by the 1944 Education Act. Grammar schools would cater for the elite, who will 'enter the professions or who take up higher administrative or business posts'. The second category, the future technicians, would be provided with a technical education. Given how few women enter 'the learned professions' – an expression which usually means medicine, law and the church – or who gain top administrative posts or, similarly, given how few women become technicians, it seems clear that the Norwood Committee did not have girls and women in mind at all. Anne Marie Wolpe, a sociologist, commented upon this report.

> In other words, although pupils in general were considered in a hierarchical structure in regard to their future position in stratification terms, female pupils were not even considered as people who have a position in any hierarchy except on the basis of what they might attain through their husbands' position in society.[42]

In the third category, however, the place of girls was specifically established. The Secondary Modern School would provide the most suitable type of education for girls. The report singled out girls for special mention in the section headed domestic subjects. The grounds for including domestic subjects were given as 'first that knowledge of such subjects is a necessary equipment for all girls as potential makers of homes'.[43]

This survey of the education of girls does not extend beyond 1945 but I think it worth pointing out that much later reports continued to accept and promote one role for women and another for men. The Crowther Report, published in 1959, stated:

> The incentive for girls to equip themselves for marriage and home-making is genetic. . . . With the less able girls schools can and should make adjustments to the fact that marriage looms much larger and nearer in the pupils' eyes than it has ever done before . . . her interest in dress, personal appearance and problems of human relations should be given a central place in her education.[44]

As late as 1963, the Newsom Report, looking at 'pupils of average and less than average ability' stated:

> We try to educate girls into becoming imitation men and as a result we are wasting and frustrating their qualities of woman-hood at a great expense to the community . . . in addition to their needs as individuals our girls should be educated in terms of their main social function – which is to make for themselves, their children and their

husbands a secure and suitable home and to be mothers.[45]

In short, since the late nineteenth century girls have entered the education system in large numbers. What most of them have got out of it is a confirmation of their role in the domestic sphere. In as far as girls' education has equipped them to enter waged work, it has been as unskilled and ill-paid labour.

QUESTIONS

In investigating the local history of girls' education there are some useful questions to put to the sources. I do not wish to tie anyone with a list of hard and fast questions but the following may provide a useful starting point.

What schools were there? How many? Who provided them? How many children in the community were catered for? Did more boys than girls receive an education? What were the buildings like? What facilities did they have?

Over how long a period did children go to school? Did this change? At what age did they start? Did they pay fees? How regularly did children attend school? Who was absent most frequently . . . boys or girls? Did the children do any paid or unpaid work as well as attend school? If so, what? Were there any particular seasons of the year when absences were especially high? Where were truants sent? How were they treated?

What did the curriculum consist of? How was each school day spent? Was the curriculum/timetable sex differentiated? What books were used in the school? Can you find copies of them? If so try analysing the contents.

Who were the teachers? How and where were they trained? How many children did they teach? What teaching methods did they use? How often did teachers change?

Finally, what changes can you detect, over any given period, in the education of girls in any particular school or group of schools?

These are all questions which can to some degree or other be answered by the sources below.

SECONDARY SOURCES

Some general books on education and on girls' education

C. Adams, *Ordinary Lives A Hundred Years Ago,* London, Virago, 1982.

J. Burstyn, *Victorian Education and the Ideal of Womanhood,* London, Croom Helm, 1980.

M. E. David, *The State, the Family and Education,* London, Routledge & Kegan Paul, 1980.

R. Deem, *Women and Schooling,* London, Routledge & Kegan Paul, 1978.

S. Delamont and L. Duffin, *The Nineteenth Century Woman,* London, Croom Helm, 1978.

C. Dyhouse, *Girls Growing up in Late Victorian and Edwardian England,* London, Routledge & Kegan Paul, 1981.

J. S. Hurt, *Elementary Schooling and the Working Class,* London, Routledge & Kegan Paul, 1979.

J. Kamm, *Hope Deferred: Girls' Education in English History,* London, Methuen, 1965.

P. McCann, *Popular Education and Socialization in the Nineteenth Century,* London, Methuen, 1977.

P. Marks, 'Feminity in the classroom: an account of changing attitudes', in J. Mitchell and A. Oakley (eds), *The Rights and Wrongs of Women*, Harmondsworth, Penguin, 1976.

S. Sharpe, *Just Like a Girl: How Girls Learn to be Women,* Harmondsworth, Penguin, 1976.

P. and H. Silver, *The Education of the Poor,* London, Routledge & Kegan Paul, 1974.

M. Sturt, *The Education of the People,* London, Routledge & Kegan Paul, 1967.

B. Turner, *Equality for Some: The Story of Girls' Education,* London, Ward Lock, 1974.

F. Widdowson, *Going Up Into the Next Class: Women and Elementary Education,* London, WRRC, 1980.

A. M. Wolpe, 'The official ideology of education for girls' in M. Flude and J. Ahier (eds), *Educability, Schools and Ideology*, London, Croom Helm, 1974.

Scotland
A. Bain, *Education in Stirlingshire from the Reformation to 1872*, University of London, 1975.
J. Craigie, *A Bibliography of Scottish Education before 1872*, University of London, 1970.
J. Craigie, *A Bibliography of Scottish Education 1872–1972*, University of London.
F. M. Dean, *Scottish Spinning Schools,* University of London, 1930.
I. R. Finlay, *Education in Scotland,* Newton Abbot, David & Charles, 1973.
S. L. Hunter, *The Scottish Educational System,* Oxford, Pergamon, 1971.
J. Roxburgh, *The School Board of Glasgow, 1873–1919*, University of London.

Articles
J. Burstyn, 'Women's education in England during the nineteenth century: a review of the literature, 1970–76', in *History of Education,* vol. 6, no. 1, 1977.
A. Davin, 'Imperialism and motherhood', in *History Workshop Journal,* Spring 1978.
A. Davin, 'Mind that you do as you are told: reading books for Board School girls, 1870–1902', *Feminist Review,* 3, 1979.
C. Dyhouse, 'Social Darwinistic ideas and the development of women's education in England 1880–1920', in *History of Education,* vol. 5, no. 1, 1976.
C. Dyhouse, 'Good wives and little mothers: social anxieties and the schoolgirls' curriculum', in *Oxford Review of Education,* vol. 3, no. 1, 1977.

Journals
It is worth noting that there are several academic journals on the history of education. The most useful of these to the local historian is *The History of Education Society Bulletin* (University of Leicester). This lists articles published in journals of local history societies and these references can, if they seem worth it, be followed up. Local history journals sometimes publish memoirs as well as studies of local

educational provision. *Oral History,* the journal of the Oral History Society is also worth consulting.

Local books

For the English counties it is worth consulting the hefty volumes of the *Victoria History of the Counties of England.* From c. 1950 onwards the compilers set themselves the task of describing the evolution of every primary school in every parish whose history they wrote. The main facts included are the date of establishment, names of donors, details of enlargement of the site, in the case of voluntary schools, the date of transfer to a School Board or Local Education Authority, the accommodation at the school and attendance figures in at least three widely spaced years.

General local history books may be worth looking at and may well include photographs of the old schools. Some schools actually have their history recorded in books devoted entirely to that subject. Jean McCann's, *Thomas Howell and the School at Llandaff* (Cowbridge, Brown, 1972) is a good example of a well-documented history of one Cardiff girls' school.

Autobiographies

The following list is only a selection.

E. Elias, *On Sundays We Wore White,* London, Robin Clark, 1980 (East London).

W. Foley, *A Child in the Forest,* London, Macdonald Futura, 1977 (Forest of Dean).

M. V. Hughes, *A London Child of the 1870's,* Oxford University Press, 1978 (North London).

E. Mannin, *Confessions and Impressions,* Harmondsworth, Penguin, 1936 (South London).

F. Thompson, *Lark Rise to Candleford,* Harmondsworth, Penguin, 1973 (Oxfordshire).

Recorded oral testimonies

M. Chamberlain, *Fen Women: A Portrait of Women in an English Village,* London, Virago, 1975 (E. Anglia).

J. McCrindle and S. Rowbotham, *Dutiful Daughters: Women Talk about Their Lives,* Harmondsworth, Penguin, 1979 (many Scots interviews).

P. Thompson, *The Edwardians,* London, Weidenfeld &
Nicolson, 1975.
T. Thompson, *Edwardian Childhoods,* London, Routledge &
Kegan Paul, 1981.

In order to demonstrate the value and interest of
biographical material, I include some extracts from three of
the London writers: Molly Hughes, Ethel Mannin and Eileen
Elias.

Molly Hughes was a middle-class girl living in
Highbury, North London, in the 1880s. She recorded
her experiences as a pupil at The North London Collegiate
School in Miss Buss's day. On her very first day there she got
lost:

> Nowhere could I find a room labelled 'Upper Fourth',
> although there were several other species of Fourth.
> Presently I caught sight of a little white haired old lady,
> cap on head, and dressed in black rather the worse for
> wear. Some caretaker or cleaner or something I thought,
> but she may possibly have noticed the names of the class
> rooms; I can but try. So I hailed her in a manner I thought
> appropriate. 'I say, am I going right for the Upper
> Fourth, do you happen to know?' Glaring at me she
> exclaimed, 'Do you know who I am?' 'I haven't the
> faintest idea; I've only just come.' 'I am Miss Buss!' and
> standing back a pace she drew herself up to mark the
> effect on me. It was not at all what she expected, for
> I cheered up and said, 'Oh, then *you* are sure to know
> the way to the Upper Fourth and I do so want to get
> there.'[46]

Molly Hughes shows us much of the detail of the everyday life
of the school. There were rules about everything. It was
forbidden, she recalled, 'to get wet on the way to school, to
walk more than three in a row, to drop a pencil box, leave a
book at home, hang a boot bag by only one loop, run down
stairs, speak in class.' Such misdemeanours were recorded in
the 'Appearing Book' – an exercise book in which the girls
entered and signed for their crimes. The book must have
made interesting reading.

As the culprit was left to enter her own crime, some amusing things were entered in the book that may well puzzle future students of nineteenth-century education. 'I marched with the wrong foot' was the way one girl expressed her failure, to keep in step. 'I was four in a row', 'I spoke in French', 'I called out in Latin'. A technical distinction appears here; to *speak* was to talk to another girl, while to *call out* was to answer before you were asked. 'I left my heart at home', referred to a diagram for physiology.[47]

Ethel Mannin, who went on to become a novelist, described her experiences at a Clapham Board School in the first decade of the twentieth century. She writes of the rigid timetabling, the useless information pushed at the pupils by teachers, the plight of verminous girls isolated on a bench together and labelled 'dirty girls', the condescension shown to poor children who were entitled to free meals and the viciousness of wanton corporate punishment. Any knowledge of sex and reproduction which she acquired came from her peers outside school hours. School sex education consisted of delicate references to the pollination of flowers.

I am reminded of the lovely – and illuminating story of a little girl who had been so enlightened; she had been a bridesmaid at a wedding, and coming out of church asked her mother: 'Will he give her his pollen now, or wait till they get home?'[48]

Eileen Elias, in *On Sundays We Wore White,* vividly records her impressions as a pupil in an elementary school in New Cross, South East London, in the 1920s.[49] She hated 'Mental', Problems and Drill but it is the agony of the sewing lessons that comes across most powerfully in her account. She failed to understand why women at home used sewing machines, but in school sewing was done by hand. In her school they made the patterns as well as the garments. They concentrated on baby clothes.

I struggled miserably week after week with pencil and squared paper, trying to make my own pattern for a baby's matinee coat. Why matinee, I wondered? Surely

you didn't take a young baby to the theatre, and that was
the only place I knew where they had things called
matinees. Our patterns had to be copied onto the paper
from a diagram marked in chalk on the blackboard. It
was entirely incomprehensible to me; I couldn't count
the requisite number of squares and I couldn't draw the
tidy curves and straight lines that the others did so
easily, so that my drawing looked more like some crazy
piece of patchwork than a respectable pattern from
which to cut a coat. Anyway, I thought, why can't they
buy their patterns from Jonesandhiggins like my mother
does? Just one more example of the mysterious ways of
the grown-ups, who seemed bent upon making the
simplest process more difficult.

My pattern never came out the same size as anybody
else's, though I was assured that if I'd done my
calculations right, it would. The teacher seemed more
worried than I did about this; after all, I argued,
babies came in all shapes and sizes, and if it didn't fit one
baby, it would be sure to fit another. But again the
grown-ups wouldn't listen to reason. I had to go over and
over the exercise, till I produced something the right
size.

I would do my best to use this pattern for the cutting
out of a matinee coat in white flannel, and at the end of
it all would feel quite sure that no self-respecting
baby would ever be seen out in a thing like that. We
did feather-stitching round the edges – blue for a boy
and pink for a girl. All the others did neat rows of
feather-stitching, but mine went in crazy curves round
sleeves and neck, with the stitches never the same size.
Tears would fill my eyes as I pushed the needle with the
blue or pink thread in and out of the grubby bit of flannel;
the thread had started such a lovely colour, and the
flannel had been so white; now everything was a dirty
grey. I privately decided that should I have any babies of
my own, they would never wear matinee jackets
designed and sewn by me. I would go straight to
Jonesandhiggins and buy their outfits from the
babywear department.[50]

PRIMARY SOURCES

The first thing to do in embarking upon the study of girls' education in any locality is to find out what schools there were in the district. There are several sources for doing this. For the period before 1870 *The Report of the Census on Education. 1851*,[51] contains the findings of an inquiry into education in England and Wales, conducted as part of the 1851 census. The printed report on this census lists, under the heading of the town, the private schools (i.e. fee-paying), the public schools (i.e. those with some form of local support such as grants, rates, endowments, voluntary subscriptions or with government grants), and Sunday schools. It gives the total number of girls and boys belonging to the schools or actually on the books; the number present on Census day, 31 March 1851 (total by sexes), local population, and the proportion of school children by population. It is important to note that this education inquiry was voluntary and so not every school made a return but, nevertheless, a high proportion of returns was made.

As to the Board and later State schools, the easiest way of establishing just which schools existed is to visit the local record office. They will have indices to their sources on education, which will list the School Boards in a county and will list all the schools under the control of each Board. I think it is the best starting point. Record offices often also have old plans and maps so that it is possible to locate where particular schools were in areas which may have been demolished and rebuilt. They may also have plans of actual school buildings. Write or ring the record office before going so they can sort out material for you before you arrive.

There are also various lists enumerating the School Boards at various times (i.e. *Reports of the Committee of Council for Education* and *Returns relating to Elementary Education*) but the consultation of the local record office files is by far the simplest and most straightforward approach.[52]

Once the number of schools in an area has been established along with the number of pupils they catered for known, it is then possible, if desired, to relate this information to the actual number of children living in an area. This is, of course, particularly applicable to the time before the introduction of compulsory education. It may be quite a demanding exercise, depending upon the size of community investigated, but it is perfectly feasible. The *Census Schedules (Enumerators' Schedules)* from the decennial Census, which are now available up to 1881 and which are particularly useful from 1851, will give the names and ages of children living in any district (see also Chapter 4). There is, of course, no need to do this for 1851. There are further sources for locating private schools.

Town Directories were produced on a large scale, from the 1820s onwards and they usually list Voluntary Schools, Board Schools, Church Schools, Private Academies and Endowed Schools. They also give the names of the teachers.

Private schools often advertised in *local newspapers:* these can be consulted in large reference libraries or, for papers dealing with small towns, often in local libraries. There is another way to determine what private schools there were in any area, i.e. consulting *The Girls' School Year Book*. It is the official book of reference for the Association of Head Mistresses and it provides information on school buildings, staff qualifications, curriculum and fees. The following extract, taken from the 1925–6 volume, shows the sort of information to be gained from consulting it.

Helensburgh

ST. BRIDE'S SCHOOL.

HELENSBURGH, DUMBARTONSHIRE, N.B.

Boarding and Day School for Girls. Founded in 1895.
MOTTO.—"In domo dei ambulavimus cum consensu."

This is one of the three Schools of the Girls' School Company, Limited. For information as to the directorate, general aims, etc., see p. 129.
Staff.
Head Mistress.—Miss Renton, L.L.A., Edinburgh
University Certificate in Arts for Women.

Assistant Mistresses.

Miss Lindsay, M.A. Hons.†
  ,, Churchman, Camb.
     Hist. Trip.
  ,, Jack, Dipl.,
     Sorbonne.*
  ,, Snell, M.A.†
  ,, Joyce, B.A. Hons.
  ,, King, L.L.A. Hons.
  ,, Poole, B.A.
  ,, Robson, B.Sc. Hons.

Miss Just, B.A. Oxon.,
     French.
  ,, Paterson, Dipl. Edin.
     Sch. of Cookery,
     1st Cl. (*Tech.*
     Subjs.).
  ,, Harrison (*Prep.*
     Sch.).§
  ,, Hamilton (*Prep.*
     Sch.).

Class Singing.—Miss Owen, L.R.A.M and A.R.C.M.
Drawing.—Miss Birrell, Art T. Dipl., Glasgow Sch. of
Art.
Gymnastics, Games.—Miss Emblyn Wilson.‖
Dancing.—Miss Webster, Miss Hopkins.
Music:—Piano—Mr. E. Barratt; Miss Owen, L.R.A.M.;
Miss Crawford, L.R.A.M.; Miss Whitehouse, L.R.A.M.;
Miss Ireland, L.R.A.M.
Violin.—Miss L. F. Renton, Leipzig Conserv. and Junior
Assistant.
Solo Singing.—Miss Crawford, L.R.A.M.

Helensburgh is a particularly healthy and
attractive town on the Firth of Clyde. It is a centre for
excursions both by boat and rail, and the situation is
such that plenty of outdoor exercise is available for the
girls both in summer and in winter.

School Buildings. The School is situated in the
high part of Helensburgh overlooking the Firth of Clyde
and it stands in large grounds. The Buildings include
numerous Class-rooms (facing South); Lecture Hall,
large Science Laboratory, Studio, Library, Dining Hall,
Gymnasium equipped with Swedish apparatus, several
Music Rooms, Cloakroom and other accommodation.
There is a small Playing-Field within the School
grounds, and within ten minutes walk, a large Field with
well-equipped Pavilion.

* C.H.L. Hons.　　† Camb. T. Cert.　　§ N.F.U. Hr. Cert.　　‖ Bedford Phys. Tr. Cert.

The School is organised for Boarders in the House system; there are five Houses, each within a few minutes' walk of the School, all under the direction of the Head Mistress assisted by competent House Mistresses.

The number of pupils in the School is about 220 of whom over 100 are Boarders.

Curriculum. The ordinary curriculum includes Scripture, English, History, Geography, French, Latin or German, Science or Greek, Mathematics, Drawing and Painting, Class Singing, Needlework, Gymnastics and Drill.

To suit the varying capacities and requirements of the elder pupils special courses are arranged in which prominence is given to Classics, Mathematics, Science, Modern Languages, Art or Music as may be desired. English forms an obligatory part of every course.

Domestic Science Department. This department is for the domestic training of girls over seventeen. Sessional courses of instruction may be taken in this branch by Sixth Form pupils as options for Mathematics, Latin, etc. One of the Houses is organised for Domestic Science Pupils.

Organisation. The four divisions of the School are: Preparatory School (Kindergarten, Transition, and Form I.), Junior, Middle, and Upper Schools. *Music* forms a special department and is carefully organised. Pupils enter for the Schools and Local Centre Examinations of the Joint Board of the Royal Academy and the Royal College of Music.

Examinations. Girls are regularly prepared for the Leaving Certificate Examinations of the Scotch Education Department, and for the Entrance Examination to the Scottish and English Universities.

The **Session** is divided into Three Terms beginning early in September and in December, and at the end of March. The holidays consist of about ten weeks in summer, and about three weeks at Christmas and at Easter.

Fees. Day School pupils from £5 5s. per term in the Kindergarten to £13 13s. per term in the Upper School.

Inclusive fees for Board and Education vary from 114
guineas per year for girls under ten to 129 guineas for
girls over fifteen. Fees per term for Books and
Stationery, 5s. to 10s. 6d.; for Laboratory, 5s. to 21s.; for
Playground, 2s 6d. to 3s. 6d.

Extra Subjects, per term: Piano, £2 2s to £5 5s.;
Violin, £3 13s. 6d. to £4 4s.; Solo Singing, £3 3s.;
Dancing, £2 2s.; Elocution and Diction, £1 1s.; Special
and Medical Gymnastics, £2 12s. 6d. for twelve
treatments.[53]

Parliamentary Papers

The growing role of the State in education throughout the
nineteenth century is reflected in a massive output of official
reports. They contain an absolutely fascinating wealth of
material. These reports are important because they influenced government policy. They are also particularly
useful for the study of women's history in Great Britain and
Ireland because of the vast amounts of local material which
they contain. Yet one must note in this chapter, as in others,
that this source has a particular bias. The bias is rooted in the
facts that parliamentary reports are official documents produced by upper-or middle-class adult males who can have had
little experience of the working-class, often uneducated, girls
and women.

Sometimes these reports present difficulties for researchers – partly through an elaborate numbering system
and partly because, in some cases, reports can be scattered
over many volumes. But the major education reports are
fairly straightforward, often filling several consecutive
volumes. There are also very good indices and guides to the
reports. I think one should consult the Index to Parliamentary Papers in the library in which one is working to
check what volumes they hold. There is also a very good guide
specifically dealing with reports on education. It is Michael
Argles, *British Government Publications in Education in
the Nineteenth Century*.[54] The problem of the scattered nature
of parliamentary papers may also be avoided by consulting
the more recent editions published by the Irish University
Press.

The actual availability of government reports or parliamentary papers varies from area to area. I have found The Official Publications Room of the British Library an easy place to consult reports because it is a full collection and the volumes are on the open shelves. Education reports are also easily consulted in the library of the Department of Education at Waterloo. Many university and reference libraries will have a wide but not complete range of reports and it is likely that they will have volumes which are of particular local interest. Living in Wales, I find it easy, even in quite small libraries, to get hold of reports dealing specifically with Wales but more difficult to get, for example, Scottish or Irish material.

Reports are quite a useful source for finding out about education before the Board Schools. They sometimes make grim and poignant reading and are invariably interesting. Modern-day official reports lack the impact of these nineteenth-century documents, probably largely because these early records report interviews with staff and children verbatim. A full list of these reports would take far too much space here and Argles's pamphlet has already provided us with the list. I would simply say that among early nineteenth-century reports the following are worth looking at:

Reports of the Education of the Lower orders of the Metropolis, PP 1816 IV, 1818 IV.

Education in Ireland, PP 1825 XII.

Parochial Education in Scotland, PP 1826 XVIII.

Education in Ireland, PP 1829 IV.

Report on state of Education, PP 1834 IX.

Report on Education in England and Wales, PP 1835 VII.

Report on Education of the Poorer Classes in England and Wales, PP 1837 VII.

Report on State of Education in Scotland, PP 1837 VII.

Training and Education of Pauper Children, 1841 (Poor Law Commission).

Report on Education in Wales, PP 1847 XXVII,I,II,III.

This last report caused a furore in Wales not only because of the damning comments made on the state of education in Wales, but because of the slur it cast on the morality of the Welsh working class in general and on Welsh women in particular. This extract shows, not surprisingly, the low academic attainment of girls in a Denbighshire workhouse school.

LLANRHUDD.– This Parish contains 840 inhabitants. It contains no school except the following, the benefit of which is confined to the inmates of the Union workhouse.

Ruthin Union Workhouse School.– A school for boys and girls, taught respectively by a master and mistress in separate rooms of the workhouse. Number of girls, 23; of boys, 21. Subject professed to be taught – the Scriptures and Church Catechism, reading, writing, and arithmetic.

I examined this school February 8. I found all the children present. Out of the whole number 47, 11 were above ten years of age, and 12 had been members of the school for more than two years, yet there was not one who could read a verse of the Bible with ease, or write well upon paper, or work correctly a sum in £.s.d., although arithmetic was the principal attainment of the scholars. Not more than 3 of the girls were able to spell a monosyllabic word. When examined on religious subjects, 10 could repeat portions of the Church Catechism, but without any conception of their meaning; and, in like manner, they had been made to get up by rote a great number of Scripture definitions without the least knowledge of Scripture. Some told me that Samuel was the son of Jesus Christ, Mary Magdalene the mother of our Saviour, and the Virgin Mary his wife: the Virgin Mary was God. The rest appeared not only ignorant but ill-mannered, standing staring me in the face with the appearance of idiots, and giving no kind of answer to any question in Welsh or English. Their knowledge of English was very limited, and is not likely to increase, for no kind of interpretation is adopted; not a word is allowed to be spoken in Welsh, either by the master or scholars. It is difficult to conceive how any progress can be made when their language – the only medium through which the mind receives instruction – is taken from them, and none given in its stead.[55]

The Newcastle Report of 1861 again surveyed popular education in England (*Royal Commission on the State of Popular Education in England,* PP 1861 XXI). It is a very interesting report but a very complacent one, often assuming that the poor had already been 'rescued'. The commissioners concluded that, 'the religious and moral influence of the public schools appears to be very great, to be greater than ever their intellectual influence.'[56] It surveyed a wide range of schools and is particularly interesting on factory schools. It also contains some insights into girls' education – such as the following comment made by Mr Hale, the commissioner for Hull, Yarmouth and Ipswich. Hale made an interesting contribution, which not only accounted for the poor attendance of girls at school but also looked ahead to the job prospects of the girls.

> Sometimes like their brothers they are kept away for the sake of what they can earn by occasional employment (as stringing beads for 1s.6d. a week at Ipswich): but more frequently they are required to help in domestic matters, in seasons of sickness, or when mother is out at work or is secluded by a new birth from the family. In Ipswich there is little employment for women and girls but what can be done in their own homes. A stay factory, a shoe factory, a flax mill and a silk winding room are the only remarkable exceptions: but these are not comparable in size with the cotton mills in Hull or the silk mills in Yarmouth. To the latter may be added the various fish 'offices' of that town, which, however, creates a demand for female labour only during the season and after each catch of herrings. These sources of employment excepted, my district calls for the labour of the female hand only in those miscellaneous forms which are common to all parts of the kingdom alike.[57]

The Taunton Commission of 1864, reporting in 1867–8, has already been mentioned in the introductory survey. It dealt with the private sector and concentrated very largely on boys' schools. It is worth mentioning here inasmuch as ten of its twenty volumes are local studies.[58]

Following the Education Act of 1870 and the setting up

of Board Schools, there were several reports on these elementary schools: these were published in 1871, 1893 and 1899. One of the concerns of the investigators, who reported in 1899, was children working for wages. The report of that year looked at occasional work done by children at busy times of the year – haytime, harvest, turnip pulling and potato picking. It also examined regular, part-time waged work done by boys and girls. I include the following table on girls' work to demonstrate the usefulness of this source.[59]

GIRLS

County.	Age.	Standard.	Occupation.	Hours per Week.	Rate of Pay per Week.
Berks.	6	O	Fetching milk	3	1d.
Cumberland	6	O	Nursing	Often at home	—
Derby	6	I	Domestic	3	3d.
,,	6	I	,,	10	1d.
,,	6	I	Errands	7	5d.
,,	6	I	Nursing	4	½d.
Devon	6	O	Keeping house	6	Employed by parents
,,	6	I	Carries milk (morning and evening)	35	Employed by parents
,,	6	I	Selling cakes	6	6d.
Gloucester	6	I	Minding babies	3	2½d.
Hants	6	I	Piece work in hop gardens	—	Assists parent
Kent	6	I	Taking breakfast	'Cannot say'	4d.
Lancaster	5	O	Sells firewood	6	Profit for father
,,	6	O	Nursing	Not stated	2d.
,,	6	O	Sells firewood	9	Profit for father
,,	6	O	Takes dinners	2½	1d.
,,	6	I	Takes dinners	Tues., Wed., Thurs. and Friday.	1d.
Leicester	6	I	Seaming hose	8	2d. for bank account
,,	6	O	Seaming hose	15	1d.
,,	6	O	Taking dinners	4	2d.

County.	Age.	Standard.	Occupation.	Hours per Week.	Rate of Pay per Week.
London	6	I	Errands	9	6d.
,,	6	O	Minding a neighbour's baby	Every evening 7 to 8	1d.
,,	5	O	Minding a neighbour's baby	Saturday several hours	1d.
,,	6	O	Minding a neighbour's baby	Saturday several hours	1d.
,,	6	O	Goes out cleaning	Saturday several hours	2d.
,,	6	I	Minding a baby	7	Tea and ½d.
,,	6	I	Minding a baby	3	1d.
,,	6	O	Window cleaning, &c.	4	1d. dinner and tea
,,	6	I	Minds a baby	4	1d.
Northumberland	6	I	Nurse girl	11	2d. and food
,,	6	I	Milk girl	7	½d. – works for father
,,	6	I	Nurse girl	29	2d. and food
Notts	6	II	Housework	6	6d.
,,	6	I	Lacework	6 to 8	Helps mother
,,	6	I	Lacework	1	Helps mother
Rutland	6	I	Nursing	18¼	3d.
Somerset	6	I	Errand girl	15	6d.
Stafford	6	I	Taking meals	Not stated	1d.
,,	6	I	Carrying water	Not stated	2d.
,,	6	I	Carrying meals	5	3d.
Warwick	6	O	Helps mother to varnish parts of lamps	Not stated	Helps parents at home
,,	6	O	Helps card hooks and eyes	Not stated	Helps parents at home
,,	6	O	Helps card hooks and eyes	Not stated	Helps parents at home
,,	6	O	Helps card hooks and eyes	Not stated	Helps parents at home
,,	6	I	Goes on errand	3	4d.
Wilts	6	I	Minding baby	6	1d.
,,	6	I	Nursing baby	10	1d.
,,	6	I	Nursing baby	6	1d.
,,	6	I	Nursing baby	6	½d.

County.	Age.	Standard.	Occupation.	Hours per Week.	Rate of Pay per Week.
,,	6	I	Nursing baby	1	1d.
,,	6	I	Nursing baby	2	1d.
,,	6	I	Running errands	3	1d.
,,	6	I	Running errands	3	1d.
Worcester	6	I	Running errands	5	½d.
,,	5	O	Pea picking	15	1s.3d.
York	5	O	Minds the house: mother goes to work	—	—
,,	6	I	Matchbox making	6	2½d. per gross
,,	5	O	Nursing	—	—
,,	6	I	Minds a baby and runs errands	6	2d.
,,	6	I	Nursing	7	1s.
,,	6	I	Taking out groceries for parents	15	2d.
Anglesey	6	O	Selling firewood	12	In father's employ

Finally, *The Minutes of the Committee of Council on Education,* which are available at the Department of Education Library, contain inspectors' reports on British Schools. These were issued annually from 1839 to 1899, but the title was changed in 1857 to the *Report,* instead of *Minutes.* It is an excellent local source. The inspectors' reports range from the very perfunctory to the quite full. This is how the inspector commented on Glasgow's Rottenrow Ragged School in 1858–9. On the day of the inspection 112 boys and 76 girls were present.

The seminary has received two additional improvements since the last inspection. 1. Additional building has been erected at a cost of £1,800 giving the accommodation of an excellent classroom and two apartments for dormitories; the latter kept in the best order, well lighted and ventilated. 2. Skilled Industry has now been introduced for the instruction of the boys in four distinct apartments now fitted up for the purpose in the old premises. The branches of skilled industry for boys are tailoring, shoemaking and carpentry, no one being taught more than one trade. The number trained to each as follows: tailoring, 14, shoemaking 8, carpentry 3 and 2 of better promise than the rest have been taken into the superintendent's office as clerks. The rest of the boys, 85 in number, are taught to make paper bags. Beside 4 in rotation officiate for one month at a time in doing certain portions of the household work, cleaning, washing of floors etc. The girls are taught sewing and needlework and trained to household work. One half day is occupied by all in booklessons, the other half in industrial work. One half of the pupils being employed in each way at one time. Reading, writing and cyphering are taught with fair efficiency, but the latter of course to a limited extent.[60]

School Board records

The Education Act of 1870 set up School Boards. These were elected bodies and it would be interesting to find out how many women were elected to them.[61] Accounts and results of these often hotly disputed elections may be found in local newspapers. The School Boards (and after 1902 the Local Education Authorities) kept records of their deliberations and activities. Precisely what local records are available can be found out by consulting the Education Catalogue in the local record office.

Amongst them will be *School Board Minutes*. Accounts of Board meetings can be somewhat dry reading but the minutes contain a wealth of detail – teachers' and cleaners' names and salaries, purchases made for the schools, attendance figures and proceedings against truants and their parents. There are many human flashes amongst the Minutes. I looked at School Board records for the area in which I went to school, i.e. Barry, South Glamorgan, and they record, 'that Mrs. Gardner of 5 Evans St. had been to Holton Road Girls' School on the 14th instant in a drunken state, and had made use of foul language to the teachers in the presence

of some children'.[62] It was resolved that she be threatened
with magistrate's proceedings. Such parental dramatic
entries into schools in the 1890s as Mrs Gardner's would
seem fairly common judging by other records I have examined in Birmingham, Bristol and the South West. The activities of attendance officers – or Boardies as they are still
known in South Wales – make interesting reading.[63] From
their reports one can see the degree of difference between the
attendance of boys and girls and one can follow the stages of
the proceedings against parents who were not sending their
children to school. (It is always interesting to establish why
the girls were kept away.) The Barry Boardy in January 1898
stated that he had visited 2,780 absentees – the total population of the town at that date was 30,000. He had served 160
notices and initiated 20 prosecutions. He despaired, 'There
are so many truants in the Holton Rd. and Barry Schools that
we do not know what to do with them. Prosecutions nor the
Truant School do them any good.'[64] (Such prosecutions and
the reasons given by the parents for not sending their
children to school can be read in local magistrate's court
records and in newspaper accounts of the proceedings.) I
think that it is worth inquiring what truant schools there
were in any area and looking into their records.

School Board Minutes also list the purchase of furniture
and items of equipment for schools. By looking at these it may
be possible to compare facilities in boys' and girls' schools. A
sexist attitude appeared in the Barry Board Minutes, where
it was noted that the new desks bought for the girls' department in one Barry school were to be transferred to the boys'
department and the girls were to be given the boys' old desks
which were unsuitable for drawing.[65]

Sub-committees were established by School Boards. *The
Minutes of The Cookery Schools Sub-Committees or Cookery
and Laundry or Cookery and Housewifery Sub-Committees*
are a fascinating source, from which the rise of the domestic
ideology in girls' schools can be traced locally. In Cardiff in
1896, for example, the Minutes show that laundrywork was
added to cookery in the girls' curriculum. Cardiff took this
step because London, Bradford, Manchester, Nottingham
and Leeds had introduced laundrywork into their schools,

though Leeds had abandoned it as 'not appreciated by scholars or parents'.[66] The Cardiff sub-committee toyed with the idea of introducing cookery for boys and polled the opinion of parents in the docks area on whether to do so. Of the 68 parents asked on this issue, who had boys in Eleanor St. School, 41 of them said that they would like their boys to learn cookery, but apparently nothing came of this.[67] The records of these sub-committees often contain detailed course syllabuses for cookery, housewifery and laundrywork. The following syllabuses were put into practice in Bristol in 1899.[68]

HOUSEWIFERY.

Lesson 1.		Importance of cleanliness in the home. Order and method in the daily work. Daily routine. (Monday.)	
		Demonstration.	Laying a table. Preparing dinner.
		Practice.	Morning class. – Laying table. Tidying bedroom Afternoon Class. – Clearing table. Washing up. Tidying sitting room and kitchen.
,,	2.	Combustion.	How to lay and light a fire. Best kind of grate.
		Demonstration.	Cleaning kitchen flues and grate.
		Practice.	In above and housework.
,,	3.	Kitchen work.	Cleaning silver, tins, knives and brass. Cost of materials. Disposal of refuse.
		Demonstration.	Cleaning knives and bright things. (Cuts and their treatment). Polishing paste, etc.
		Practice.	Cleaning kitchen.

Lesson 4. Special weekly work in the house.
           Bedrooms.   Ventilation of room and
                              bed. How to make a bed.
                              Bedclothes.
           Demonstration. Making bed and daily
                              bedroom work.
           Practice.   In above, etc.
  ,,   5. Turning out a bedroom. Preparing the room.
           Brushing bed. Walls. Sweeping floor or
           cleaning oilcloth. Washing paint.
           Demonstration. In above.
           Practice.   In above and other work.
  ,,   6. Turning out bedroom 2. Washing china.
           Cleaning marble. Cleaning grate and
           windows.
           Demonstration. In above.
           Practice.   In above with revision.
  ,,   7. Dust, its composition. Why it must be
           removed. Directions for dusting.
           Demonstration. Dusting.
           Practice.   Housework.
  ,,   8. Turning out sitting room. Preparation
           of work. How to sweep and clean carpet.
           Demonstration. Sweeping and dusting a
                              sitting room.
           Practice.   Sweeping and dusting a
                              sitting room, etc.
  ,,   9. Polishing furniture. Care of Polished
           furniture. Recipe for furniture polish.
           Demonstration. Making Polish and
                              polishing furniture.
           Practice.   Cleaning sitting room and
                              polishing furniture.
  ,,   10. Artificial light. Candles, lamps, gas. Best
           kind of lamp. Cleaning and trimming a
           lamp. How to extinguish fire caused by
           lamp.
           Demonstration. Cleaning lamp. Dressing a
           burn.
           Practice.   In above, etc.

Lesson 11. Care of bathroom. Cleaning bath, etc. Stairs
and lobbies (sweeping and dusting).
Demonstration. Cleaning bath etc.
Practice. Stairs and passage.

,, 12. Care of hairtidies. Washing hairbrushes,
clothes brushes and household brushes.
Demonstration. Washing and drying a
hairbrush.
Practice. In above and housework.

,, 13. Recapitulation. Special attention to
preparing dinner with regard to the
housework. Care of larder.
Practice. Preparing dinner and
ordinary housework.

,, 14. Proportionate cost of meals. Economy
of home-made bread.
Demonstration. Bread making.
Practice. Bread making.
Housework.

,, 15. Care of clothing. Mending, patching and
darning. Remove stains. Guarding against
moth and damp.
Demonstration. Removing stains.
Practice. Housework.

,, 16. Preparing for washing day. Airing
clothes.
Demonstration. Sorting and steeping
clothes.
Practice. In above. Cleaning
wash-house.

,, 17. Personal cleanliness. Skin. Baths.
Demonstration. Choice of bedroom
crockery and cleaning
water bottle.
Practice. In above and bedroom work.

,, 18. Fresh air. Composition of air. Respiration.
Ventilation.
Demonstration. Simple methods of
ventilation.
Practice. Housework.

Lesson 19.   On choosing a house or lodgings. Choice of furniture and cost.
Demonstration.   Examination of furniture in centre. Discussion of prices.
Practice.   Housework.

,,   20.   Drainage of a house. Flushing and cleaning pipes. Disposal of refuse.
Demonstration.   Cleaning sink and pipes.
Practice.   In above.

,,   21.   Thrift. Its importance. Portioning out income. Savings.
Demonstration.   Washing sponges and chamois leather.
Practice.   Washing sponges and chamois leather, and housework.

,,   22.   Marketing. Choice of food. Prices.
Demonstration.   Storing dry foods and household requisites.
Practice.   Cleaning cupboards.

Note – The theory lesson will last half an hour, and the practice lesson for an hour and a half.

LAUNDRY WORK.
Syllabus for First Year's Work.

Lesson 1.   Preparation for washing day: use and care of utensils: properties and use of water, soap, ammonia, and vinegar: Rules for drying clothes.
Demonstration: Washing flannels, woollens, stockings, etc.

,,   2.   Practice in above.

,,   3.   Management of fire: Heating and cleaning irons: Arrangement of Ironing table: Disinfecting and purifying clothes.
Properties and use of salt, sanitas, blue, and soda.
Demonstration: Disinfecting, washing, and ironing body linen and handkerchiefs.

Lesson 4.   Practice in above.

,,   5.   Stiffening agents: Properties and use of starch, borax and tallow.
Demonstration: Making clear starch: Washing, starching, and ironing print and muslin.

,,   6.   Practice in above.

,,   7.   Methods of removing stains: Properties and use of salts of lemon, etc.
Demonstration: Removing tea stains, fruit stains, etc. Washing and ironing table linen: Washing and mangling kitchen towels, etc.

,,   8.   Practice in above.

,,   9.   Cold water starching: Use of turpentine.
Demonstration: Making cold water starch: Washing, starching, and ironing collars and cuffs.

,,   10.   Practice in above.

,,   11.   General revision of lesson 1 – 5.
Demonstration: Washing, etc. flannel, stocking, body linen, handkerchiefs, and print.

,,   12.   Practice in above.

,,   13.   General revision of lesson 5 – 10.
Demonstration: Washing etc. muslin, table linen, collars and cuffs.

,,   14.   Practice in above.

Syllabus for Second Year's Course.

Lesson 1.   General revision of lesson 1 – 5 in first year's course.
Demonstration: Washing etc. flannel, stocking, body linen, handkerchiefs, and print.

,,   2.   Practice in above.

,,   3.   General revision of lessons 5 – 10 in first year's course.
Demonstration: Washing etc., muslin, table linen, collars and cuffs.

,,   4.   Practice in above.

Lesson 5.   Preparation and use of gum water.
                Demonstration: Making gum water:
                Washing and ironing lace and silk,
                Goffering lace.

,,   6.   Practice in above.

,,   7.   Polishing agents.
                Demonstration: Washing, starching,
                ironing, and polishing, collars, cuffs, and
                fronts.

,,   8.   Practice in above.

,,   9.   Demonstration: Washing, starching,
                ironing, and polishing a shirt.

,,   10.   Practice in above.

,,   11.   Demonstration: Washing, starching, and
                ironing a Blouse and a frilled pinafore or
                child's dress.

,,   12.   Practice in above.

,,   13.   General revision.

,,   14.   Practice in above.

,,   15.   Use of paraffin.
                Demonstration: Paraffin washing applied
                to workman's overalls, very soiled kitchen
                cloths, etc.

,,   16.   Practice in above.

                Resolved – that 3 lessons per day to be
given at the Centre, viz: one in the morning
and two in the afternoon, and that in order
that this may be carried out the afternoon
session last till 5 o'clock.

                That no girls below Standard VI take
Laundry work except by the special
permission of the Committee.

COOKERY

First Course.

Lesson.	Principal and Primary Method.	Dishes illustrating Prin. and Prim. Method.	Extra dishes (if time allows).
1.	Management of Stove Cleaning. Porridge making	Cleaning flues and grate. Laying and Lighting fire. Making Oatmeal Porridge.	Baking Powder.

Lesson.	Principal and Primary Method.	Dishes illustrating Prin. and Prim. Method.	Extra dishes (if time allows).
2.	Bread (Action of Yeast)	Bread made with Yeast.	
	Scones (Action of B.P.)	Scones made with B.P.	
	Tea making.	A cup of Tea.	
	Coffee making.	A cup of Coffee.	
3.	Invalid cookery	Beef tea and toast	Lemon-
	Steaming	Toast water. Invalid custard.	ade
	Toasting.	Gruel. Egg lightly beaten. Milk jelly.	
4.	Using scraps (remains of joint)	Rendered fat. Bone stock.	
	Stock and Gravy making	Gravy. Cottage Pie.	
	Boiling Potatoes.	Boiled potatoes.	
	Cocoa making.	A cup of cocoa.	
5.	Soup making.	Lentil soup.	Cornflour
	Milk Puddings.	Rice Pudding.	mould.
6.	Boiling Meat and Root Vegetables.	Boiled Mutton and vegetables.	Sauce.
	Using up crusts.	Bread pudding.	
7.	Stewing.	Irish Stew.	Rice
		Stewed fruit (in oven)	mould.
8.	Frying, Grilling	Liver and Bacon. Chop	
	Boiling Puddings.	Suet puddings.	
9.	Roasting or Baking Meat.	Stuffed heart. Gravy	
	Green Vegetables.	Boiled greens	
10.	Frying Fish.	Fried Fish.	
	Pastry making.	Fruit pie or fruit turnovers.	
11.	Examination.		

Second Course

Lesson.	Principal and Primary Method.	Dishes illustrating Prin. and Prim. Method.	Extra dishes (if time allows).
1.	Bread and cake making.	Bread. Plain seed or Currant cake. Buns.	
2.	Invalid Cookery.	Beef tea (various).	
	Poaching.	Savoury custard. Poached egg.	
	Steaming.	'Coddled' egg. Linseed tea. Steamed fish.	

Lesson.	Principal and Primary Method.	Dishes illustrating Prin. and Prim. Method.	Extra dishes (if time allows).
3.	Stock and soup making. Rough puff pastry.	Stock. Potatoe soup. Beef steak pie.	
4.	Cheese Cookery. Baking potatoes.	Welsh rarebit. Cheese and potatoe pudding.	Boiled haricot Beans.
6.	Boiling meat. Sauce Making. Milk puddings.	Boiled salt meat or sheep's head. Sauce. Sago puddings.	Salad.
7.	Steaming puddings. Suet pastry. Short crust.	Beef steak puddings. Syrup tarts. Jam or fruit turnovers.	
8.	Fish Cookery. Cold fish cookery.	Baked fish. Fried fish cakes.	Tea or coffee or Barley water.
9.	Preparing tripe. Stewing. Frying.	Stewed tripe and onions. Tripe fried in batter.	Rice pudding.
10.	Cold meat cookery. Boiled puddings.	Hashed meat with toast. Roly poly puddings.	Cocoa.
11.	Examination.		

Third Course.

Lesson 1. Combustion. Construction and management of kitchen ranges and gas stoves. Economy of fuel.
Demonstration: Cleaning flues, and gas stoves. Lighting fire. Cooking dinner: Fried liver and bacon or fried fish. Potatoes boiled in their skins. Pancakes. Laying dinner-table.

,, 2. *Class Practice* in above.

,, 3. Marketing. Choice of food. Season foods. storage.
Demonstration: Grilled steak. Baked potatoes. Steamed bread or Ginger pudding. Making marmalade.

,, 4. *Class Practice* in above.

,, 5. Dinners suitable for washing days, etc.
Demonstration: Hot pot. Rice pudding.

,, 6. *Class Practice* in above.

Lesson 7.   Proportionate cost of meals. Economy of
home made bread.
Demonstration: Brown bread. White
bread. Tea cakes. Laying tea table.

  ,,   8.   *Class practice* in above.

  ,,   9.   Revision and elaboration of
Lesson 3. – Marketing, etc.
Demonstration: Suitable dinner chosen from
menu drawn up by the Scholars.

  ,,   10.   *Class practice* in above.

  ,,   11.   Revision and elaboration of Lesson
5. – Suitable dinners, etc.
Demonstration: Dinner chosen from menu
drawn up by Scholars.

  ,,   12.   *Class practice* in above.

Sub-committee records also contain information on the sale of food cooked by girls in cookery centres. Not every school had a cookery classroom and girls from various schools would be taught in special cookery centres. (Later whole flats would be set up in towns for school girls to practice all the housewifely arts). The cookery centres kept accounts of their financial outlay on cooking materials and hoped to recoup them by the sale of food from the centre – often a blackboard being put outside to advise the public of the day's speciality. In 1904 the Cardiff School Board drew attention to the teacher at the Court Road Kitchen who was sending the girls out to hawk the food from door to door.[69]

The need to recoup the cost of materials had led teachers in some areas to concentrate on only highly saleable items like toffee and buns: at one Durham school the teacher was taking in orders for fancy cakes.

Another type of committee existed in Birmingham from 1913 onwards and similarly such committees may have existed elsewhere. It was The Central Care Domestic Service Committee, which concentrated on persuading girls to enter domestic service, by acting as an employment agency; it placed girls in a situation, made regular visits to check on the girls' progress and kept a watchful eye over each girl by allocating her to a lady who was to act as a support to her.[70]

No girl was sent out to a job without the employer being thoroughly vetted. The scheme was not, however, particularly successful. The girls had little taste for service and were attracted to war work. In October 1913 it was reported that there had been thirteen positions offered by prospective mistresses and only one filled. In fact, 'there had been no applications properly speaking from the girls during the period. In the case of the one girl placed, the girl applied in the first instance for other work, but was persuaded by Mrs. Ashmore to enter service.'[71]

Records of Individual Schools

The records of individual schools may also be consulted in local record offices or in some cases in the school itself, or with voluntary schools in the vicarage. School *log books*, which had to be kept by all schools in receipt of a state grant from 1862 onwards, make good reading. They contain the details of the day to day running of the school – schemes of work, attendances, purchases, appointments of teachers, inspectors' reports and accounts of moments of high drama in the life of the school. The temporary headmistress of Garrison Lane Board School, Birmingham endured a hard week in September 1877, according to the log book.[72] On Wednesday two abusive women had arrived at the school claiming that a cape belonging to one of their children had been stolen from the Infants' School. On Thursday another mother had assaulted Phoebe Lily, a teacher, for keeping her child in after school. Phoebe Lily was taken along to the police station to summons her assailant and by the end of the week a detective was present in the school to investigate the affair of the missing cape. Phoebe Lily was not, it turned out, a good teacher. When, a little later, the new headmistress was appointed to the school, she reprimanded Phoebe for knitting in class and not paying attention to the needs of the children in her class.

Some log books contain school timetables and most give detailed schemes of work for each class or standard. This often means long lists of 'Object Lessons'. At Blaise Castle National School, Henbury, near Bristol, Class II were given object lessons on subjects ranging from The Primrose and

Root Vegetables to A Coal Mine and A Steam ship. Meanwhile the Infants were being informed on The Daisy, An Onion, The Union Jack, A Glass of Milk and The Princes in the Tower.[73]

The visits of school inspectors, school prize days and the days of government examinations are all recorded in log books. Inspectors' reports were often far from complimentary but they had to be copied out in full into the log. One sees the preparations going on before Prize Day and the log books usually list the winners and their prizes. It is interesting to note the books selected by the teachers as prizes: *Uncle Tom's Cabin*, *The Bible* and *Our Four Footed Friends* were favourites in the 1870s. Not all pupils were good enough to sit government examinations and the log book gives blunt and insensitive reasons for excluding individual pupils – 'Obvious Dullness', 'Imbecile', 'Bad Eyes' and 'No Memory' were all given as grounds for exclusion in Aston Lane Board School in Birmingham.[74]

I looked at the log book for my mother's old school, Hannah Street School, Barry.[75] There the reason for children's absence was most often given as 'bad boots' or 'no boots'. The log records the special feeding of pupils whose fathers were out of work in 1920 because of a coal strike. The girls' fathers were mainly employed on Barry Docks loading coal for export. The prevalent domestic ideology came out strongly, not only from the provisions for cookery, etc., but from such accounts as that of a special outing for the girls to a newly built council estate, where the clerk of the works pointed out all the labour-saving devices and the special features of the drains to the senior girls.

Some schools kept special *Punishment Ledgers*. A reading of the Aston Lane School, Birmingham, Punishment Ledger shows the changing mode of chastisement.[76] In 1901 hand smacking and locking girls in a private room was abandoned in favour of caning on the hands. The crimes there included – 'a rebellious attitude after scolding', 'impudence', 'being late six times in one week', 'telling stories' and 'rudeness to a teacher'. A poignant feature of that book is that pupils themselves wrote the entries in the ledger. It was set out as follows.

Name	Offence	Date of Offence	Punishment Awarded	Date of Punishment
Ida Stubbard	For commencing in first class at beginning of year old bad habit of staying away to mind baby.	6.9.1917.	1 stripe with cane	same
Edna Hill	Insolent Expression under Correction.	26.9.1917.	1 stripe with cane	same
Annie Stevens	Ran Home from cookery.	8.11.1917.	2 stripes with cane	9.11.1917.

It is also sometimes worth consulting *school registers*. They contain a certain amount of biographical material.

Certain schools kept very full records on individual pupils. Carlton House Industrial School for Girls in Bristol kept *Reports on Pupils* from 1875 to 1900.[77] It was a specialized residential school which took in girls who were in need of care and whose parents never sent them to school. The reports are often horrific and very sad. The following extract is the account of one of the school's successes, Cecelia Wilkes.

Wilkes.

Cecelia. Admitted April 14th 1877. Aged 10 years. This child is illegitimate and has been deserted by mother and father 6 years. She has hitherto been dependent upon an elderly grandmother, who is a charwoman, Sylvia Bowden by name, living at 50. Philip St., Bedminster. Cecelia had occasionally attended St. Luke's Ragged School at Bedminster, but she knows little more than her letters. She has only once been inside a place of Worship and that was a Roman Catholic Chapel. She bears a fair character and appears to be a bright and promising girl. Cecelia Wilkes sent to Torquay Hospital for Changes. October 25th. 1880. Returned from Torquay May 25th 1881. Greatly Improved. Left for service (on licensing June 27th 1881) in Bristol. March 22nd 1882. returned to school. Aug. 22nd 1882. Discharged by Secretary of State in order to emigrate to America. 1882 Mr. Whitewell visited C. W. in New Brunswick. Address 18. Garden

Street, St. John's, New Brunswick. 1884 Same Address.
1885 Married to an Engineer, Mr. Adams. In 1887
visited Bristol, called at the school.

Other activities of this school are recorded in *The
Matron's Journal*. It contains a wealth of detail of the daily
life of girls in this institution and of their relationships with
their families outside. It contains details of how the matron
tried to place them all in suitable positions in domestic
service outside the home. Sometimes she was successful, but
many of the girls were troublesome. Jemima Smith was one
such difficult charge. On her, the journal reads:

19 November 1873. Jemima Smith left her situation
today. This is the 5th situation in 4 months. She wants
too much money and her friends are no good to the girl.
21 November 1873. Engaged Jemima Smith in another
situation.
13 December 1873. Engaged Jemima Smith in another
situation. I fear said girl will go back to her friends.[78]

School books: exercise and text books

Pupils' exercise books, where they survive, may be worth
looking at. Some are kept in local record offices – usually
under the heading of Educational Miscellanea – and others
may be in the private possessions of older women or their
relatives. Exercise books, especially from secondary schools,
reflect a very dull teaching system. Among those I have
looked at I have found detailed accounts of The Voyages of
Saint Paul, The Baltic Sea and Its Boundaries, countless
maps of The Major Rivers of the World (especially the Rhine
and the Rhone) and pages and pages of parsed sentences and
of long mechanical sums.[79]

One of the most interesting exercise books, which I
happened to stumble across in a little museum in the
Western Isles of Scotland, came not from a school but a
training college. It belonged to a student at the West of
Scotland College of Domestic Science in 1921.[80] It contained a
hundred handwritten pages and an index – to such items as
starching, bleaching and ironing. This short extract comes
from the section headed:

To Iron Drawers or Knickers

First tapes, bands, trimmings and hems, embroidery on legs.
Begin by ironing the front of the left leg as far as possible double.
Right leg in the same manner.
Turn and iron back as above
Open out and iron upper front and back separately.
To fold.
Lay the waist at the left band, straight fold towards you.
Tapes straight down.
Fold sloped part towards you forming a straight line.
Fold the waist down one third, legs up one-third.
If liked, turn back the front of the upper leg to show the embroidery.
If very full a pleat may be put down the centre of the leg before cross fold.

Old school text books are usually easier to locate. Second-hand and junk shops usually have old ones used locally. If you know what texts were employed in a school and you can find that out from school log books, then it may be possible to locate very old ones in major libraries, like the British Museum. Anna Davin has analysed text books used in London Board Schools.[81] I have perused text books used in some South Wales industrial towns. Collin's *Progressive Reader* (1877),[82] used in Caerphilly Board School, is full of anecdotes encouraging the poor to keep their place. When the 'jolly cobbler' was given a bag of money by a rich banker, he stopped whistling and singing and lost his peace of mind. Only by returning the money could he sing, whistle and sleep again. *A Reading Book for Use in Female Schools* (1864) was in use in Maesteg in the 1870s.[83] Like most readers, it is an anthology of poetry and prose. In poetry the themes of death, the angel mother and child piety predominate. The prose extracts advocate honesty, cleanliness and industry – especially among female domestic servants. Readers of this little work were told,

It is a sin to steal a pin.
Much more to steal a greater thing.[84]

Efficiency and good management were praised and the following extract on bad management contains a salutary warning:

BAD MANAGEMENT

'There are the beds to be made – and the breakfast things to be washed, and the pudding and the potatoes to be boiled for dinner.' A bad manager receives those directions from her mistress, and to work she goes, with bustle enough, perhaps, as if she would accomplish it all long before dinner time. She makes the beds, and comes down to wash the breakfast things – 'Oh dear, oh dear, was ever any thing so provoking – not a drop of water in the kettle, and the fire just out.' Then the sticks and the bellows go to work, (by the way, I never knew any but a bad manager who found it necessary often to use the bellows) – at length the water boils, and the clock strikes – 'Why, what o'clock is that? – my pudding ought to be in, and it is not made, nor any water set on for it, well, I must use this, and do the tea-things afterwards.' The pudding is made, and put in, half an hour later than it should be – then to work again, to heat water for the tea-things; it boils – but she must now put the potatoes on, or they will not be half done by dinner time. The potatoes are put on, and the water poured out; but now the family are assembled for dinner, and the cloth must be laid; and the potatoes are all raw, and the pudding but half boiled – and the water cold, and the tea-things not washed up – and the mistress displeased, and the house thrown into confusion. It never seems to occur to a bad manager, that there are some things, which if once set agoing, go on by themselves. If she had supplied the fire with coals, it would have drawn up – and set on the kettle, the water would have boiled for the tea-things, while she made the beds; and the fire would have been at liberty for the pudding water to be set on, and all the mischief would have been prevented. (Cottage Comforts).[85]

Throughout this little book, the sayings of Poor Richard contain pointed warnings and gems of insight: 'Sloth like rust consumes faster than labour wears, while the used key is always bright,' or 'Laziness travels so slowly that Poverty soon overtakes him.'[86]

This reader contains very little factual information – except a very boring history, spanning the period from the Old Testament to the Seventeenth century (40 pages) and an account of The Principal Manufactures of England (1 page). But presumably girls did not need to know very much since this book contained the following comment on female education: 'What a woman knows is comparatively of little importance to what a woman is.'[87]

Records of teaching unions
These records concentrate mainly on the activities of women as teachers but they may also throw some light on the education of girls. The main collections to consult are:
The Association of Assistant Mistresses, founded 1884.
The Association of Head Mistresses, founded 1874.
The National Union of Teachers, founded 1870.
The National Union of Women Teachers, founded 1909 (see Chapter 4).

Newspapers and journals
Local newspapers are a helpful source in several ways. As already mentioned, they report School Board elections: some papers also reported Board meetings. In addition they published attendance cases, school prize days, sports days, school expeditions and outings and plans for proposed new buildings.

Among journals, the following may contain some relevant information *School Attendance Officers Gazette* (BL) *The Governess* (and *Head Mistress*), 1882–4 (BL); *Journal of Women's Education Union*, 1873–82 (BL); *The School Mistress* 1881–1935, which then became *Woman Teacher's World* (BL); *The School Master* and *Woman Teacher's Chronicle* 1872 – (now *The Teacher*), the journal of the National Union of Teachers (BL and NUT Library).

Photographs
School photographs are an excellent source. Many old photographs show pupils actually in the classroom engaged in

activities rather than the later photographs of classes of pupils sitting on benches in bleak school playgrounds. In London the GLC has a large collection of fascinating school photographs, which can be consulted by the public. The London photographs illustrate the domestic ideology well and show how it was conveyed to young girls through lessons in cookery, laundry, childcare and even spring cleaning! The GLC collection also shows girls engaged in a variety of bizarre exercises in school playgrounds and dressed in very constricting clothing for drill exercises. In Glamorgan Record Office, for example, I was able to find superb photographs both of girls sewing at their desks, in a classroom with walls decorated by charts of cocoa beans and eskimos, and of girls engaged in drill. The most amazing example came from a Penarth school where girls in long dresses and pinafores stood at their desks between the bench and linked table, swinging dumb bells. That was a very large photograph and we (myself and a local group working on women's history) used it in an exhibition on women's lives in Penarth.

It is also worth looking out for photographs of young women in further or higher education e.g. evening institutes, training colleges, etc.

Oral history
One of the most interesting and rewarding ways – and perhaps the most accurate – of discovering the educational experience of girls under past educational systems is to interview older women on the subject of their school lives. The interview programme in which I have been most actively engaged has concentrated on the working lives of women and the education of these women has formed only an introductory part of my inquiries. Therefore a far fuller section on oral history, its value and the techniques involved is given in Chapter 4.

I would like just briefly to outline some questions which I have put to respondents on their education and to quote just one extract from one such respondent.

Some suggested questions
Did anyone give you any lessons before you went to school?

Who? What in? How old were you when you first went to
school? What did the youngest children do in school? What
sort of school was it? (Church? State? Mixed or single sex?)
How big was the class? Were the children all the same age?
What subjects were you taught? Did the boys study different
subjects from the girls? If so, what? Did you attend a cookery,
laundry centre, etc.? Did you sew in school? How much time
was spent on it? What were the teachers like? Do you think
that they treated boys and girls differently? How? How were
the girls and boys punished?

What social class did the children in your school come
from? How were they dressed? What did their fathers do?
Were there school dinners? Were exams important in your
school? Were there ever any treats or outings? If so, what?
Where?

Were you ever late? Why? What was the punishment?
Did you often miss days at school? Why? What happened to
you then when you came back to school? Did parents ever
come to the school? Why? Were they welcome? What did your
parents think about the education you were getting? What
did you think about the education you were getting? Were
you given any careers advice in your school? If so, what? How
old were you when you left school? Did you go on to any other
school? (If so, repeat the above questions.)

Extract from an Interview with Nora (b. 1919. Attended
school in Fulham)

We were all girls. We used to go to other schools for
cookery. That was called housewifery and cookery. That
was rather interesting. I liked that. I did plenty of
housework at home so I didn't have to learn an awful lot
there.

In sewing, as Christmas came near the teacher
thought it would be nice if we made our mother a
Christmas present. The cost of it would be 6d. which
when I was 10 or 11 wasn't bad. We could pay at a penny
a week. So I chose to make my mother a coffee coloured
organdie tea apron. This is what I wanted to make for my
mother but my poor mother, as I told you previously, was
a step woman and she didn't have time for that. But how

nice that in a child's mind to think that my poor mother
that went out scrubbing steps and working in laundries
all hours of the day, I visualized her dishing up tea in a
tea apron.

Only I never got to make it because when I came
at lunchtime the teacher inspected hands and I had
been home and laid the fire in the kitchen range of
course with mum at work – and I'd washed up the
breakfast things. The teacher said if I couldn't get
my hands cleaner I would be allowed to make the apron.
So of course when I washed my hands they naturally
came up cleaner. So I was not allowed to do the apron.
I had to do hemming stitches on a piece of calico.
This teacher I think would be dead now but this hurt
me very much as a little kid not to be able to make
my mum the apron – not that she could ever have worn
it.[88]

Miscellanea

Local record offices often hold a whole variety of miscellan-
eous educational records. These could range from prefects'
badges, proficiency certificates and awards to teachers to old
school wall charts. Locally, I have found under this heading,
a certificate of proficiency for something or other awarded to a
great uncle of mine. I have also found an interesting needlework sampler book: this was a book containing pages made of
cloth which were elaborately decorated by a variety of
tortuous needlework stitches and which was distributed by a
company which made embroidery threads.

Some record offices may, under this heading, hold old
drawings of the interiors of schools and plans of these schools.
It is worth consulting the works of M. V. J. Seaborne,[89] who
wrote on school architecture and organization to see what
sources he consulted.

Amongst the odd pieces of archive material held by the
GLC Archive I found the following notice. It instructs school
girls on why and how they should furnish comfortably the
home of a working man. The illustration tells all. It seems to
have been pinned up in all the cookery centres of the London
Board.

HOUSEWIFERY.

(1) GUIDING PRINCIPLES TO ENSURE HEALTH
AND HAPPINESS.

(a) In selecting a house see that it is thoroughly
drained, well-lighted, and capable of thorough
ventilation.

(b) Endeavour to obtain a knowledge of the chief
elements of food, their uses, and the best methods
of cooking.

(c) Learn the best methods of keeping your home
thoroughly clean and wholesome.

(d) Study how to PREVENT disease as well as how
to restore to health those who are sick.

(e) Provide recreations and amusements in the
home so that the members of the family may be
made happy and kept from seeking their
pleasures in questionable places.

(f) Be careful and thrifty so that you may be
independent in your old age.

(2) COST OF FURNISHING A WORKING MAN'S
HOME.

SITTING ROOM—

	£	s.	d.		£	s.	d.
Four chairs –	0	16	0	Cover for same –	0	3	0
Two easy chairs	1	5	0	Curtains – –	0	2	6
Strong deal table	1	2	6	Straw-matting –	1	0	0
Fender – –	0	13	9	Chamber ware –	0	3	11
Fire irons –	0	9	6	Blankets, sheets,			
Curtains –	0	5	6	counterpane –	1	15	0
Table Cover –	0	8	6	Fender – –	0	6	0
Screen – –	0	9	0	Towel horse –	0	3	6
Small table –	0	7	6	Bath – –	0	2	3
Lamp (safety) –	0	16	0	Folding bed (com-			
Pictures and orna-				plete) – –	4	12	0
ments – –	1	0	0				
Rug – –	0	12	9	KITCHEN—			
Linoleum (good)	1	10	0	Earthenware and			
				cutlery – –	2	10	0

BED-ROOM—				Washing & clean-			
Bed (complete)	3	10	0	ing utensils	– 4	10	0
Two chairs	– 0	6	0				
Washstand	– 0	10	6		£29	18	2
Deal toilet table	0	7	6				

NOTES

1   See, for example, S. Delamont and L. Duffin, *The Nineteenth
    Century Woman*, London, Croom Helm, 1978; B. Turner,
    Equality for Some: The Story of Girls' Education, London, Ward
    Lock, 1974; M. Bryant, *The Unexpected Revolution: A Study of
    the Education of Women and Girls in the Nineteenth Century*,
    University of London, 1980; S. Fletcher, *Feminists and
    Bureaucrats: A Study in the Development of Girls' Education in
    the Nineteenth Century*, Cambridge University Press, 1980;
    J. Burstyn, *Victorian Education and the Ideal of Womanhood*,
    London, Croom Helm, 1980.

2   One thinks of the fictional example of Winifred Holtby's, *South
    Riding*.

3   Fortunately this is now being rectified. Carol Dyhouse's work is
    really very useful in respect of the education of working-class
    girls and shows how domestic subjects loomed large in girls'
    school lives. See C. Dyhouse, 'Good wives and little mothers:
    social anxieties and the schoolgirls' curriculum', *Oxford Review
    of Education*, vol. 5, no. 1, 1977, and C. Dyhouse, *Girls Growing
    Up in Late Victorian and Edwardian England*, London,
    Routledge & Kegan Paul, 1981. See also A. Davin, 'Mind that
    you do as you are told: reading books for Board School girls,
    1870–1902', in *Feminist Review*, 3, 1979; P. Marks, 'Femininity
    in the class room; an account of changing attitudes', in J.
    Mitchell and A. Oakley, *The Rights and Wrongs of Women*,
    Harmondsworth, Penguin, 1976. Amongst short but useful
    surveys of the education of working-class girls are R. Deem,
    Women and Schooling, London, Routledge & Kegan Paul, 1978;
    and S. Sharpe's, *Just Like A Girl: How Girls Learn to be Women*,
    Harmondsworth, Penguin, 1976. Joan Burstyn surveys the
    literature on girls' education in 'Women's education in England
    during the nineteenth century: a review of the literature' in
    History of Education, vol. 6, no. 1, 1977.

4   R. Johnson, ' "Really Useful Knowledge": radical education and
    working class culture 1790–1848', J. Clarke, C. Critcher and R.
    Johnson (eds), *Working Class Culture*, London, Hutchinson,
    1979.

5 Scottish educational provision differed from that offered to children in England and Wales. Before 1872 (when School Boards were set up in Scotland) a variety of schools existed which did not exist south of the border, e.g. parochial schools, spinning schools for girls, burgh schools, academies and in the Highlands Gaelic Society Schools. In the course of the nineteenth century, Scotland, especially Glasgow and Clydeside, was rapidly industrialized and school provision was found to be inadequate.

As in England and Wales, government grants have been made available to some schools from the 1830s onwards and shortly afterwards Her Majesty's Inspectors of Schools began to make regular visits to schools in Scotland and to report back to the Committee of Council on Education. Their reports are discussed below. From 1864 to 1867 the Argyll Commission enquired into the state of schools, both elementary and secondary, and the report of this commission makes an interesting source of Scottish local history.

The operation of the Scottish educational system was to differ in several respects from the system in England and Wales. There are some useful surveys of the Scottish educational system and it would be helpful to consult these. I have found the following books useful as an introduction: I. R. Finlay, *Education in Scotland*, Newton Abbot, David & Charles, 1973; and S. L. Hunter, *The Scottish Educational System*, Oxford, Pergamon, 1971. For more detailed information see J. Craigie, *A Bibliography of Scottish Education before 1872*, University of London, 1970; and *A Bibliography of Scottish Education 1872–1972*, University of London, 1975.

6 On these earlier schools see for example, P. and H. Silver, *The Education of the Poor*, London, Routledge & Kegan Paul, 1974. S. J. Curtis, *History of Education in Great Britain*, London, University Tutorial Press, repr. 1968, is a dull survey but it does give an outline. One of the best is M. Sturt, *The Education of the People*, London, Routledge & Kegan Paul, 1967.

7 See J. M. Goldstrom, 'The content of education and the socialization of the working class child 1830–1860', in P. McCann (ed.), *Popular Education and Socialization in the Nineteenth Century*, London, Methuen, 1977. Also R. Johnson, 'Educational Policy and Social Control in Early Victorian England,' in *Past and Present* no. 49, 1970.

8 M. Sturt, op. cit., p. 89.

9 Cited by S. Frith, 'Socialization and rational schooling: elementary education in Leeds before 1870', in McCann, op. cit., p. 73.

10 *Report of the Royal Commission on Popular Education* (Newcastle Commission), PP 1861 XXI, Report of J. S. Winder, p. 238.

11 *Minutes of the Committee of Council on Education*, Preston, 1853–4.

12 See, for example, Sturt, op. cit. and Turner, op. cit.

13 *Report of the Committee of Council on Education*, 1840, pp. 161–3.

14 J. Burstyn, loc. cit., p. 13. See also R. Johnson, loc. cit. and, for a local study which seeks to reassess dame schools, J. L. Field, 'Private schools in Portsmouth and Southampton, 1850–1870', *Journal of Educational Administration and History*, vol. X, no. 2, 1978, pp. 8–14.

15 S. Delamont in Delamont and Duffin, op. cit., p. 164–5; P. Marks in Mitchell and Oakley, op. cit., p. 184.

16 P. and H. Silver, op. cit., p. 48.

17 Ibid., p. 103.

18 *Minutes and Report of the Committee of Council on Education*, 1850–1870.

19 Cited P. H. J. H. Gosden, *How They Were Taught*, Oxford, Blackwell, 1969, pp. 20–1.

20 In order to see what proportion of the middle class could afford to have their daughters educated by governesses and in private schools see P. Branca, 'Image and Reality: the myth of the idle Victorian woman', in M. Hartman and L. Banner (eds), *Clio's Consciousness Raised*, New York, Harper, 1974.

21 L. Duffin, 'The conspicuous consumptive: woman as invalid', in Delamont and Duffin, op. cit.

22 Cited from the Taunton Report by the Hadow Committee in the *Report On The Differentiation of the Curriculum for Boys and Girls Respectively in Secondary Schools*, 1923, p. 28.

23 *Royal Commission on Schools not comprised within the two recent Commissions on Popular Education and Public Schools*, PP 1868 VIII, p. 476. For the part played by Hammond and others in raising the number and standard of girls' secondary schools, see S. Fletcher, op. cit.

24 Ibid., pp. 493–4.

25 Delamont in Delamont and Duffin, op. cit., p. 156.

26 V. Brittain, *Testament of Youth*, London, Virago, 1978.

27 Davin, loc. cit., p. 89.

28 Cited in D. Rubinstein, 'Socialization and the London School Board, 1870–1904: aims, methods and public opinion', in McCann, op. cit.

29 Bristol Record Office, Bristol School Board, Minutes of Cookery and Housewifery Committee 1898–1903, ED MB/C1. p. 16.

30 Dyhouse article, loc. cit., p. 21.

31 *Special Report on The Teaching of Cookery to Public and Elementary School Children in England and Wales, by the Chief Woman Inspector of the Board of Education*, 1907, pp. 2–3.

32 See Rubinstein in McCann, op. cit., for the activities of London attendance officers and for proceedings against parents. Also J. S. Hurt, *Elementary Schooling and the Working Classes 1816–1918*, London, Routledge & Kegan Paul, 1979, particularly Chapter 7, which is headed 'Unwillingly to School'. See also J. M. Roxburgh, *The School Board of Glasgow, 1873–1919*, University of London, 1971, especially Chapter 9.

33 See Hunter, op. cit., on Scottish Secondary Education.

34 J. Kamm, *Hope Deferred: Girls' Education in English History*, London, Methuen, 1965, p. 236.

35 The Hadow Report, op. cit.

36 Ibid., p. 56.

37 Ibid., p. 125.

38 Ibid., p. 39.

39 Ibid., p. 126.

40 Ibid., p. 127.

41 *Report of the Committee of the Secondary School Examination Council: Curriculum Examinations in Secondary Schools*, (Norwood Report), 1943; A. M. Wolpe, 'The official ideology of education for girls', in M. Flude and J. Ahier (eds), *Educability, Schools and Ideology*, London, Croom Helm, 1974, p. 142.

42 Wolpe, op. cit., p. 145.

43 Deem, op. cit., p. 17.

44 *Report of the Central Advisory Committee for Education, Fifteen to Eighteen* (Crowther Report), London, HMSO, 1959.

45 *Report of the Central Advisory Committee for Education, (England): Half Our Future* (Newsom Report), London, DES, 1963.

46 M. V. Hughes, *A London Girl of the 1880's*, Oxford University Press, 1977, pp. 19–20.

47 Ibid., p. 22.

48 E. Mannin, *Confessions and Impressions*, Harmondsworth, Penguin, 1936, p. 42.

49 E. Elias, *On Sundays We Wore White*, London, Robin Clark, 1980.

50 Ibid., pp. 158–9.

51 *Education, England and Wales*, PP 1852–3 XC.

52 For a survey of these various lists, see R. B. Pugh, 'Sources for the history of English primary schools', in *British Journal of Educational Studies* vol. 1, no. 1, 1952.

53 *The Girls' Schools Year Book*, London, The Year Book Press, 1925, pp. 142–3.

54 M. Argles, *British Government Publications in Education During the Nineteenth Century*, History of Education Society, Guides to the Sources of Education No. 1, University of Lancaster.

55 *Report on Education in Wales*, PP 1847 III, p. 67.
56 Cited U.R.Q. Henriques, *Before the Welfare State*, London, Longmans, 1979, p. 239, *Report of Commissioners, Appointed to Inquire into the State of Popular Education in England* . . . (Newcastle Report) 1861.
57 Ibid., PP 1861 III, p. 247.
58 *Report of Commissioners Appointed by Her Majesty to Inquire into the Education given in Schools in England not comprised within Her Majesty's two recent Commissions on Popular Education*, Taunton 1867–8 21v.
59 *Report on Elementary Education*, PP 1899 LXXV, pp. 451–3.
60 *Report of the Committee of Council on Education*, 1858–9.
61 See Hurt, op. cit., p. 97, for a short national survey of women's representation on School Boards.
62 Glamorgan County Record Office, Cardiff. Barry School Board Minutes 1895–8.
63 See n. 32.
64 Glamorgan County Record Office, op. cit., Barry School Board Minutes 1895–8.
65 Ibid., 1892–5.
66 Glamorgan County Record Office, Cardiff School Board, Minutes of the Cookery Schools Committee, vol. I.
67 Ibid.
68 Bristol Record Office, Bristol School Board, Minutes of the Sub-Committee on Cookery 1898–1903.
69 *Special Report on the Teaching of Cookery, op. cit.* (1907) pt. I, p. 4.
70 Birmingham Central Library, Central Care Domestic Service Committee Minute Book 1913–15.
71 Ibid., 13 October 1913.
72 Birmingham Central Library, Log Book of Garrison Lane Board School.
73 Bristol Record Office, Log Book of Blaise Castle National School, Henbury.
74 Birmingham Central Library, Log Book of Aston Lane Board School.
75 Glamorgan County Record Office, Log Book of Hannah Street School, Barry.
76 Birmingham Central Library, Aston Lane Board School, Girls' Punishment Book.
77 Bristol Record Office, Carlton House Industrial School, Report on Pupils 1875–1900.
78 Ibid., Matron's Journal.
79 Glamorgan County Record Office, Notebooks of Emma Edmunds 1859–1940, D/DX fq 1–3.

80 Tobermory Museum, Isle of Mull. Notebook of Christina MacKinnon.

81 Davin, loc.cit.

82 Glamorgan County Record Office, *Collin's Progressive Reader* 1877, D/D xq 36/2.

83 Ibid., D/D x 174/2, *A Reading Book for Use in Female Schools*, 1864.

84 Ibid., p. 38.

85 Ibid., pp. 51–2.

86 Ibid., p. 139.

87 Ibid., p. 307.

88 Oral interview, Nora: tape no. 8 side 1.

89 M.V.J. Seabourne, *The English School, its Architecture and Organization 1370–1870*, London, Routledge & Kegan Paul, 1971; and *The English School: its Architecture and Organization 1870–1970*, London, Routledge & Kegan Paul, 1977.

Chapter four

Women's waged work

The following short survey of women's work from the Industrial Revolution to the Second World War can scarcely be complete or adequate. However, it is important to indicate the range of work done by women outside the home, to note changes which took place over time and to be aware of some of the detailed work which has already been published on certain women's jobs. My essentially practical aim is to enable researchers to rediscover the work done by women in their own localities in the past.

It is useful at this point to draw attention to two very useful tools of analysis or methods of approach to a study of women's waged labour. Firstly, the idea and practice of the sexual division of labour is important. In conducting local research into the work done by women, we should check if the same work was done by men. If not, why not? For the most part women did 'women's work', i.e. low-paid work. The sexual division of labour therefore split the working class along lines of sex. It split the unity of that class and often the enmity between the two groups is seen in trade unions. The second tool of analysis which I regard as very useful is to note the way in which women were regarded as a cheap reserve pool of labour, which could be brought in and out of the workforce, to suit the requirements of capital and/or state. This can be checked and confirmed, or not, through local studies.

The Industrial Revolution, as Ivy Pinchbeck rightly pointed out, did not create women workers.[1] Women had worked for centuries on the land – as the wives of farmers, as servants-in-husbandry (i.e. living-in farm workers) and as day labourers. The employment of female day labourers suited the well-to-do landowners, who owned the increasingly large units of agricultural production. These women did hard, heavy work – digging up, cutting and loading crops onto waggons – and they could be employed for about half a man's wage. Working women in agriculture stood in contrast to the wives and daughters of the farmers. The latter, like the wives of urban capitalists, were withdrawn from production and became merely that symbol of success – a decorative wife. John Robey's satiric verse sums up what had happened to the hitherto busy farmer's family.

1743

Man to the Plough,
Wife to the Cow,
Girl to the Yarn,
Boy to the Barn,
And your Rent will be netted.

1843

Man, Tally Ho
Miss, Piano,
Wife Silk and Satin,
Boy, Greek and Latin,
And you'll all be Gazetted.[2]

Agriculture, however, declined as an employer in the nineteenth century and the number of women working on the land fell most sharply. In England and Wales in 1851 144,000 women were employed in agriculture, in Scotland 5,000 and in Ireland 144,000: by 1881 these figures were 40,000, 7,000 and 36,000.[3] It was a dramatic decrease in England, Wales and Ireland. (In Scotland the picture was quite the reverse.) Maybe this was all the result of the farmers' preference for employing adult males, maybe due to a rise in male earnings approaching a family wage or maybe due to the nineteenth-century expansion of the domestic ideology which regarded some but not other forms of women's work, as unsuitable and coarsening.

The swift progress of the Industrial Revolution in the late eighteenth and early nineteenth centuries had profound effects on women's work. The Industrial Revolution – a short-hand phrase denoting the invention of new machinery, the organization of production in factories and the rapid growth of towns – brought about a decisive separation between home and work. Generations of women in pre-industrial society had engaged in production at home – e.g. spinning or lace-making. Industrialization shifted production into factories. Many women became factory workers in, for example, textiles, boot and shoe making and in pottery making.

Cheap labour is a fundamental requirement of the capitalist mode of production and female labour was and is cheap labour. By introducing machinery and low-paid women into factories, manufacturers sought to break down many specialist skills into a series of mechanical operations and to keep wage bills low. This is seen in the textile industries, where women were most conspicuous. Only in the woollen industry were women not strikingly more numerous than men. These figures have some defects but they give a fair idea.[4]

	Cotton		Wool		Flax/Jute		Silk	
	M	F	M	F	M	F	M	F
1850	142	189	72	82	21	48	13	30
1861	183	269	81	92	27	67	16	37
1874	188	292	125	135	52	120	13	32

Figures in thousands

The employment of large numbers of women in factories must have brought about changes in domestic arrangements and in the relationships between men and women. For many women the factory offered companionship and independence. Lettice Bell, a middle-class evangelical, wrote of the boisterous and confident manner of factory girls.

> There is no mistaking her in the streets. The long day's silence is made up for the moment she is free, by loud and boisterous laughter and a flow of language peculiar to her and her alone. No pavement ever seems quite wide enough for her requirements, as she strolls along from side to side, arm in arm with two kindred spirits.[5]

It is important too, however, to remember the long hours, the dangers and the low wages earned by women. Women often earned half the wages of male operatives. Women working in the laundries of Glasgow, Edinburgh or Aberdeen were working 15½ hour days in 1905.[6] In the Glasgow tailoring industry in the 1890s men were paid 3/6d and women 9d for making the same garment.[7] Not only did women work in factories but they also laboured in heavy industry – e.g. in coal and iron – but as the nineteenth century progressed such 'unfeminine' labour was regarded as particularly unsuitable for women and undermining of the family. Progressively legislation therefore pushed women out of coal mining.[8] But the point is that women had been working in heavy industry and in factories for much of the nineteenth century. It was certainly not an innovation of the First World War.

Many other women were tied to the home yet were desperately in need of money to support themselves and their children. Some form of outwork or homework was often their only option. This was, and still is, a particularly exploitative form of employment of women. Women sewed garments at home, assembled matchboxes, curled feathers, made paper flowers, wire brushes, ropes, nets, nails or chains, etc. Much of this work was brought to the public attention by The Sweated Industries Exhibition of 1906 and by such widely publicized action as the Cradley Heath chain-makers' strike in 1910. However, homework continued. Local research has shown that homework flourished between the wars in the Luton hat trade, Nottinghamshire lace making and London rag trade.[9] Further local research may well bring to light other forms of outwork which continued into the 1920s and 1930s. Homework, of course, is still carried out.

In the mid-nineteenth century, the census of 1861 reveals that 2.7 million women over fifteen years of age were in waged employment. The figure represents just over a quarter of the total female population – a proportion that was to remain stable for some time to come. Nor should we assume that they were all single women. It has been said as a generalization that women usually gave up work on marriage – but this generalization is not borne out when examined in relation to specific industries.[10] Married women worked at the pit head in Wigan, on farms in East Anglia, in the silk industry in Essex and in jute making in Dundee.[11] Actually, nineteenth-century contemporaries often assumed that nearly all working women were married women and chided them for neglecting their homes and families! The single women in the workforce – the mill girl was normally portrayed as single and as an immoral flirt – were equally to be condemned as it was assumed that they would marry and therefore they were viewed as potentially irresponsible wives and mothers. Clearly, there is a great need for research here to establish through local studies whether the workforce was predominantly single or predominantly married or a mixture of both. Further questions present themselves. If married women went out to work, for what period of their lives did they go? How old were their children? If very young, who cared for them? Census records are a useful source of information on this, but we should note that much of the work done by married women was invisible, i.e. untaxed and unregistered. Taking in washing, going out cleaning and babyminding at home were all largely invisible occupations.

Returning to the 1861 census figure for working women, one fact demands attention. Of the 2.7 million employed women, no less than 2.0 million were in domestic service. Until the Second World War domestic service remained the largest single category of female employment.

The work itself varied enormously according to the type of household, the character of the employer and the number of servants kept. But generally it was characterized by low status, low wages and long hours of strenuous repetitive tasks, unregulated by any protective legislation. Domestic service was often a lonely, isolating and bewildering experience – especially for girls entering single servant households, removed from familiar surroundings and subjected to an alien middle-class culture. Often it was a major jolt for a country girl to find herself working in a large and noisy city. Service demanded of these girls and women an attitude of deference, an acceptance of a fixed and lowly place in the social order – externalized by a servant's uniform and by the practice of disregarding the servant's first name and bestowing a more suitable one on them. This last practice seemed very common from interviews conducted with ex-domestic servants and is often still resented.

By the end of the nineteenth century we can clearly see

the sexual division of labour in operation. Women were concentrated into a few low-paid industries – where the great majority of employees were female – and in domestic service. Finally, it was as a product too of another aspect of industrialization that women entered office work. The introduction of new machinery into business, especially typewriters and telephones, eased women's entry into offices. The entry of women into offices as typists or telephonists tended to lower the status and wage of employees in that section!

Outworkers and domestic servants were isolated and divided workers. They were to remain for the most part outside any co-operative protection or trade unionism.[12] Nineteenth-century trade unions, like their twentieth-century counterparts, were male-dominated and most had the interest of male trade unionists at heart. Unions were threatened by the way in which female labour was being used to undercut male wages and to 'dilute' male craft skills. Their reaction did not help women workers, but we must be quite clear that it did not *cause* women to be in such a lowly place in the labour market.[13]

Trade unionism was strongest amongst women in factories and there are many examples of women acting in a confident manner to assert their rights as workers.[14] In 1832 1,500 women card-setters at Peep Green, Yorkshire, came out on strike for equal pay. The Lancashire cotton mill women were active in trade unions. In 1859 the North East Lancashire Amalgamated Society was formed for both men and women and in 1884 the Northern Counties Amalgamated Association of Weavers was established for male and female workers, who were receiving the same rate of pay. But the most significant development in nineteenth-century female unionism was the emergence of separate women's unions. In 1874 Emma Paterson formed the Women's Protective and Provident League, later to become the Women's Trade Union League. The League assisted local unions, particularly in the case of strikes. In 1888, for example, the dandy loom weavers of Leeds and the women tailors also of Leeds were assisted by the League. The League acted as the mouthpiece for women workers, campaigned for factory legislation and urged the appointment of women as factory inspectors. Considerable impetus was given to women's trade unionism and the late nineteenth century saw a great deal of industrial action by women. Not only was there the famous Bryant and May's matchgirl strike (1888), but among others the Dewsbury textile workers, who came out in 1875, Aberdeen jute workers in 1884, Dundee jute workers in 1885 and Bristol confectionery workers. It is not possible to list them all here. The important point is that women were ready to take action over unfair dismissals, wage cuts and the lengthening of working hours. Women's unions, under the inspiration of the League, campaigned for better wages and working conditions.

The single-sex union development of the nineteenth century continued up to the First World War. In 1906 Mary MacArthur formed the National Federation of Women Workers, (NFWW) which did more to organize women in the workplace than any other body. It was a general labour union and it took up the cause of the very badly paid and the exploited – those in sweated and home industries. Mary MacArthur's organization of the Cradley Heath chain workers in 1910 is well known. In the next year she was involved with striking jam and pickle workers, rag pickers, bottle washers and distillery workers in London.

Sarah Boston comments, 'Reading accounts and records of these and other strikes of the period one gets the feeling of a sudden welling up of confidence among women workers. They marched in their Sunday-best, picketed, organized and raised funds with gusto.'[15] For many women, membership of a union gave them confidence and a chance to speak in public. It is a reflection on this era of separate female unions that in 1906 the female membership of all unions was nearly 167,000 and in 1914 it had risen to nearly 358,000.

The attitude of male trade unionists towards their women co-workers ranged from the supportive to the down-right hostile. The TUC itself in 1877 declared that men's 'wives should be in their proper sphere at home, instead of being dragged into competition of livelihood with the great strong men of the world.'[16] The attitude of many trade unionists towards women was clearly to be revealed at the end of the First World War.

The immediate effect of the outbreak of the First World War in 1914 was large-scale unemployment of women. This was particularly the case in such industries as jewellery, confectionery, millinery and dressmaking. By 1915, however, women began to move in large numbers into munitions production and by 1916 the problem of female unemployment had disappeared. The explanation for this is linked closely to the introduction of conscription for men in January 1916. A whole range of traditionally considered 'men's jobs' were opened to women. They were employed in engineering, heavy industry and the transport industries. Many of them had previously been employed in now slack industries, e.g. textiles or had been in domestic service. Yet although they took over men's jobs, they rarely were paid men's rates – though many, even so, had never been better off.[17]

Increased industrial employment of women during the war led to a great rise in female trade union membership.[18] The reactions of the male-dominated unions varied and was often ambiguous. The NUR, The Electrical Trades Union and the General Union of Municipal Workers admitted women for the first time.[19] Other unions, usually representing skilled men, were very suspicious. They felt threatened by the cheaper rates paid to women, by dilution (i.e. replacing skilled men by unskilled women and machines) and by the suspicion that employers would keep on cheap female labour after the war. One important development concerning women and trade unionism during the war should be noted. Although the NFWW had recruited large numbers during the war, many women had joined mixed trade unions. Negotiations to amalgamate the NFWW with the National Union of General Workers began in 1917 and were completed shortly after the war ended. The Women's Trade Union League became amalgamated into the Women's Department of the TUC. Henceforth women's role within trade unionism was to be in mixed, i.e. male-dominated, unions.

The end of the war brought about massive unemployment of women. Over 600,000 were registered as unemployed in the spring of 1919.[20] That figure does not give a true picture since not all unemployed women registered. It may well have been 1½ million. The government dismissed women from munitions factories and from the civil service: a few remained in jobs previously held by men – such as railway booking clerks – because they were cheaper to employ. The Restoration of Pre-War Practices Act and trade union male prejudice restored 'men's jobs' to men. Government and unions expected women to revert to traditional sex roles and there was particular hostility to married women workers. The domestic ideology, designating that a woman's place is in the home, re-emerged with vigour. From this period emerged the dominant image of the Housewife – whose role in life was to tend her husband and children and to keep her home (increasingly equipped with consumer goods) spick and span. It did not seem to matter that working-class families could scarcely manage on a single wage or could not afford to buy the consumer goods which advertisements depicted as essential for a comfortable home.[21]

It is difficult and inadvisable to generalize about women's work between the wars and a great deal of local research is required. The one certain fact about the economy of the period is that it was dominated by The Slump, and mass unemployment. At the end of the First World War women had been forced back into hated domestic service. Unemployed women who refused places as domestics – where wages were very low, lost their entitlement to unemployment benefit![22] In fact, it has been estimated that only 4 per cent of unemployed women received benefit.[23] Governments, including Labour governments, and the middle classes urged the return of all the 'idle women' into domestic service. Training centres were set up to train them as cooks and cleaners. In a few not very well paid jobs, however, women had clearly come to stay. This was true in offices – but they had usually to leave on marriage. This strong antipathy to married women at work is seen clearly in the case of teachers – where the marriage bar was wideningly and more stringently applied.[24] In short, the female labour market was composed very largely of young, single women – who were expected to give up outside employment on marriage.[25] However, one of the reasons that it is difficult to generalize about the inter-war period is the fact that the economic depression was not uniform in its impact throughout Great Britain. Its effects on, for example, South Wales, Clydeside or Durham were very different from its effect on South East England. In the south and midlands, light industries such as electrical, motor-car components, cosmetics and certain branches of light engineering were being set up and were employing women on production lines. Industrialists used women as cheap labour and justified it by speaking of women's manual dexterity.

Given the regional variations, there is a pressing need to look closely at the impact of the Depression on women's work. This gap can only be filled by many local studies.

In 1939, with the outbreak of the Second World War, the notion that a woman's place is in the home became untenable again. The reserve army of labour was wanted once more. By 1940 the presence of large numbers of women in war indus-tries and replacing men in other jobs became essential. There does not appear to have been the same willingness among women to dash into war work as there had been in the First War. In fact the response was poor. This was due probably, in part, to a repugnance to dangerous factory work (a repug-nance not shown by women from sweated industries and domestic service in 1914), and probably also, in part, to the persuasion throughout the 1920s and 1930s that a woman's role was as a housewife. By the spring of 1941 it became necessary to register women aged between 16 and 49, who could then be 'compulsorily directed to other full time civilian employment'. By December women without children could be conscripted into the armed forces. Both moves show that women were regarded as mobile workers, who could be trans-ferred from one part of the country to another as and when they were required. Once again women were doing men's jobs – making and flying aeroplanes, making munitions, working in transport, in industry and on the land.[26] Despite the initial reluctance of women to volunteer, a patriotic fervour seems to have developed among women workers, which was probably used against them in making them accept low wages. Male workers and many trade unions again viewed them with suspicion: they were not admitted into the AEU until 1943. Both groups regarded them as a temporary work-force. But how did the women view themselves? How did young single women and older married women regard their work experience? As something to continue in or as a temporary expedient? The end of the Second War was followed by the laying-off of women from men's jobs. They were expected to disappear into the home and to breed. The situation was, however, not to parallel exactly that at the end of the First War. The rise of many part-time jobs for women was to bring them once more into the labour market in large numbers.

QUESTIONS

What paid work (including outwork) did women do in your locality? How did women find jobs – through friends? Advertisements? Did women move to other areas (or into your area) to find work? Was there any/much choice of work? Was it specifically women's work? Did men do the same job? What wages were women paid? What wages were men paid if doing the same or similar job? What were the conditions, hours of work?

Did the women join a union? Which? Is there any evidence of industrial action? Over what? How long did such action last? Was it successful?

What war work did women do in the First and Second World Wars and what were their hours? Conditions? Wages? Child care provision? Did they travel far to get there? What did they do at the end of the war?

How high was unemployment amongst women? Did they register as unemployed? Did they receive dole/benefit?

How did women rate various jobs? E.g. shopwork compared to factory work or to domestic service?

Were there any social clubs or social activities connected with their employment?

SECONDARY SOURCES

In order to save time and trouble, the best starting point for an investigation into women's work in the past is to look at books already published. Sheila Rowbotham's *Hidden From History* (1973) still serves as a useful introduction. The following are more specialized.

Nineteenth-century
Sally Alexander, 'Women's work in nineteenth century London; a study of the years 1820–50', in J. Mitchell and A. Oakley (eds), *The Rights and Wrongs of Women*, Harmondsworth, Penguin, 1976.

Sandra Burman, *Fit Work For Women*, London, Croom Helm, 1979.

Alice Clark, *Working Life of Women in the Seventeenth Century*, London, Routledge & Kegan Paul, 1982.

Ross Davies, *Women and Work*, London, Hutchinson, 1975.

Alexander Fenton, *Scottish Country Life*, Edinburgh, J. Donald, 1976.

Margaret Hewitt, *Wives and Mothers in Victorian Industry*, London, Rockliff, 1958.

P. Hollis, *Women in Public: The Women's Movement 1850–1900*, London, George Allen & Unwin, 1979.

Angela V. John, *By The Sweat of Their Brow: Women Workers at Victorian Coalmines*, London, Croom Helm, 1980.

Jenny Kitteringham, 'Country work girls in nineteenth century England', in R. Samuel (ed.), *Village Life and Labour*, London, Routledge & Kegan Paul, 1975.

Theresa McBride, *The Domestic Revolution: The Modernization of Household Service in England and France 1820–1920*, London, Croom Helm, 1976.

Wanda Neff, *Victorian Working Women: A Historical and Literary Study of Women in British Industries and Professions*, New York, Columbia University Press, 1929.

Ivy Pinchbeck, *Women Workers and the Industrial Revolution*, London, Virago, 1981.

L. Tilly and J. Scott, 'Women's work and family in nineteenth century Europe', *Comparative Studies in Society and History*, January 1975.

Working women writing and speaking for themselves
John Burnet (ed.), *Useful Toil: Autobiographies of Work People from 1820's to 1920's*, Harmondsworth, Penguin, 1974.

Mary Chamberlain, *Fen Women: A Portrait of Women in an English Village*, London, Virago, 1975.

Doris Nield Chew, *Ada Nield Chew: The Life and Writings of a Working Woman*, London, Virago, 1982.
Dolly Davey, *A Sense of Adventure*, London, SE1 People's History, 1980.
Winifred Foley, *A Child in the Forest*, London, Macdonald Futura, 1977.
Edith Hall, *Canary Girls and Stockpots*, Luton, WEA, 1977.
Flora Thompson, *Lark Rise to Candleford*, Harmondsworth, Penguin edition, 1973.
The publications of the Federation of Worker Writers and Community Publishers contain many pamphlets on local autobiographies.

Trade unions
Sarah Boston, *Women Workers and the Trade Union Movement*, London, Davis-Poynter, 1980.
Sheila Lewenhak, *Women and Trade Unions*, London, Ernest Benn, 1977.
A. Marsh and V. Ryan, *Historical Directory of Trade Unions*, London, Gower, 1979.
T. Olcott, 'Dead centre: the women's trade union movement in London', *London Journal*, vol. 2, 1976.

The First World War
Gail Braybon, *Women Workers in the First World War*, London, Croom Helm, 1981.
Arthur Marwick, *Women at War 1914–1918*, London, Fontana, 1977.

Between the wars
Winifred Holtby, *Women in a Changing Civilization*, London, 1934.

The Second World War
Raynes Minns, *Bombers and Mash: The Domestic Front 1939–45*, London, Virago, 1980.
Denise Riley, 'The free mothers: prenatalism and working mothers in industry at the end of the last war in Britain', *History Workshop*, vol. 11, Spring 1981.

RECORD SOURCES

The census

Census information becomes available to the public only after a lapse of one hundred years. The census records of 1881 became available in January 1982: 1891's will be available in January 1992.

The first census of any real use is that of 1841, which lists every household, the name of the head of household and all the others in the house, their relationship to the head and their ages and occupations. The census returns of 1851 are much more useful – both because they recorded people's ages more accurately and because they also state where each person was born. It is therefore possible to trace migration from this source. For example, if one is studying women working as domestic servants in a town or city, it is possible from 1851 onwards to see from which villages or other towns these women came.

The census records are comprised of:

1 *Census schedules or Enumerators' schedules* These are the actual books or copies of them compiled by the Enumerators as they went from house to house. They may be consulted in the Public Record Office, London, but local returns are normally available (on microfilm or in transcript) in local record offices and sometimes in large libraries.

2 There also exist printed *Census Reports*. These are synopses of the schedules and they give population figures for each parish.

From the census schedules we can find out much of the work done by women. The schedules record the woman's name, age and occupation. One has to be a little wary of the age given. Young domestic servants frequently gave their age as fifteen in order to gain a position and were therefore compelled to keep up the fiction. The Registrar General complained about this in 1881.[27] Another point is that despite the apparently comprehensive nature of the census, a great deal of women's work remains invisible. We cannot discover from the census records if a woman took in washing or went out cleaning. Nevertheless it is an excellent source as the following excerpt from a village in the Vale of Glamorgan shows. It comes from the schedule for Llantwit Major (Llanilltud Fawr) in 1851.[28]In conjunction with census information see also Commercial Directories.

Address	Name	Rel'ship.	Cond.	Ages. M.	F.	Occupn.	Born.
12 Dimlands House	Eliz. Carne	Head	Wid.		78	Lady. Landed Prop.	Alpbinggon? Devon.
	Kate Thomas	Serv.	U		23	Lady's Maid	Lantwit
	Margaret Williams	Serv.	U		46	Cook	Margam
	Eliz. Morgan	Serv.	U		27	Dairy Maid	Landow
	William Jenkins	Serv.	U	37		Farm Bailiff	Lantwit
	Edwin Phillips	Serv.	U	28		Groom/ Coachman	Glos.
13 Siginston Village	William Edmonds	Head	M	45		Carpenter	Marcross
	Gwenllian „	Wife	M		40	Carpenter	Llanmihangel
	Catherine Thomas	Mother-in-law	U		78	Ag. Lab. Widow/Pauper	Tythegstone
14	Thomas Thomas	Head	M	33		Farm Lab.	Lantwit
	Mary Thomas	Wife	M		35		Llansamlet
15	John Jenkins	Head	Wid.	68		Farmer of 87a. Empls. 1 lab.	Marcross
	Edward Jenkins	Son	U	34		Son	Marcross
	Margaret Saunders	Sister-in-law	Wid.		80	Annuitant	Ystradyfodwg
	Barbara John	Serv.	U		22	House Serv.	Lysworney
	Thomas David	Serv.	U	19		Farm Lab.	St. Hilary

Estate records
Ironically, it is sometimes easier to find out about the lives of women living and working in the countryside than it is to find out about women working in towns. This is mainly because the records of large estates are often preserved in record offices. For example the estate accounts of Picton Castle, Pembrokeshire, are held in the National Library of Wales.[29] They include a receipt book of servants' wages. From this one sees kitchen maids in the 1780s being paid £2 per half year plus a small allowance to buy tea. Sometimes the accounts of much smaller farms survive and one may see from these the wages paid to women servants in husbandry.

The records of private businesses
The records of privately owned businesses may also prove a fruitful source. Again it is a matter of tracking them down. In

the National Library of Wales, for example, there are the records, albeit scanty, of a small-town Welsh milliner. Some major employers e.g. colliery owners and ironmasters have donated their past records to local repositories but, on the other hand, many have not. It is advisable to begin a search in the record office and if no records are held there of firms which employed women, it may well be worth contacting the firm itself – if it is extant. A letter to the Public Relations Officer makes a tactful beginning: in it state your interest, inquire what archives the firm holds and request permission to see them. The actual records held by individual firms vary a lot but the following examples may give an idea of the type and range of material held by a very large company. They all come from the archives of J. S. Fry and Sons Ltd., at Somerdale near Bristol. The company is now part of the Cadbury Schweppes enterprise. Fry's, as a Quaker company, was a very benevolent and paternalistic employer. 'Everything that can be done to make the workers comfortable seems to have been anticipated', stated *The British Workman* in 1894.[30] Fry's employed large numbers of women – making confectionery, making boxes, packing chocolates and also as clerical workers. Their records are very full. As model employers they provided education for the workers and ran a Girls' Continuation School. It can be considered as day release: the girls attended one day a week for eight hours. The activities of the school are recorded in the *Work's Magazine*, which was first published in 1921. The school opened in 1920 and a year later it was noted, 'Today there are more than 600 pupils on the register, with an average attendance of 96% a very jolly time they have.'[31] The women workers (i.e. 'the girls') there were studying English literature, hygiene, nursing, first aid, dancing, singing, and needlework as well as cookery and laundrywork. Quite exceptional facilities were offered but we should be aware of the potential bias of firms' records: phrases like a 'jolly time' should alert us to this bias. The magazine shows the great range of social activities, including many team games. Perhaps surprisingly, one of these was cricket. In the summer of 1921 the first eleven won 8 matches, lost 9 and drew 1: five of the opposing sides were male. Other printed material amongst the factory archives includes Work Staff Regulations. It contains, for example, overtime rates for men and women. These are set out here.

Overtime	Grade 3 Women	Grade 3 Men
Work after 2 p.m. on Saturday	3/–	5/–
Sunday 8 a.m.–12 noon	5/–	7/6
Sunday after 12 noon	5/–	7/6

Other regulations include sections on walking in the factory in an orderly manner and the regulations for the Girls' Department (sic) forbade the linking of arms.

Among other records held by the firm are Wage and Salary Registers, Superintendents' Wage Books and Lists of Young Persons Employed in the Factory. From this last source it is possible to calculate the age on entry of these young employees. Finally, this particular firm has a superb collection of photographs. They show women at their work and they clearly show working conditions. Many other photographs show workers in their leisure time. Had I not looked at photographs, I would not have realized that the male and female workers had separate dining halls and used separate entrances to the factory.

Records of government or local authority training centres

During the 1920s and 1930s great emphasis was placed on training women as domestic servants. Special training centres were set up to teach young women the skills of service. The records of Barry Domestic Training Centre, run by Glamorgan County Council, are held in the local record office. They include a Register of Inmates, Admissions and Discharges: it gives the girl's name, parentage, home (often an institution), her admission date to the centre and the list of positions taken up by each girl. These young South Walian women and girls were being sent, as the register shows, chiefly to the West Midlands and Bristol. They were sent to service in private houses, but increasingly into large institutions e.g. hospitals. From such registers we can see the 'publicization' of domestic service. It is well worth inquiring at record offices as to whether they hold such records.

Trade Union records

The active role played by women in trade unions has been shown above. Trade union records ought therefore to be worth examining. Some will be held locally by local trade union branches or libraries or record offices. For example, Leeds Central Library holds a collection of the records of the Leeds Branch of The National Union of Women Workers.

The headquarters of major unions may hold past records concerning women workers. For example, information on women school teachers is held by the Association of Assistant Mistresses and the Association of Head Mistresses. Also in London two other collections may prove useful. The Trade Union Congress Library holds e.g. the records of the Women's Trade Union League (1895–1921). The Library of the Labour Party holds, amongst other things, the records of the Women's Labour League, The Standing Joint Committee of Industrial Women's Organizations and the Railway Woman's Guild.

Criminal records

I include a reference to criminal records here because they often give the age and occupation of the charged person. The main types of court records, which can be consulted locally, are those of the Court of Quarter Sessions and magistrates' courts. Assize Court records are normally kept in central repositories, e.g. Public Record Office, National Library of Wales. Unless one is really interested in all the details of the case itself, it is easier to read the printed accounts of trials at the Assizes with which newspapers dramatically supplied their readers.

Some cases involve thefts by women from their employers. Eliza Wheeler, for example, a dairy maid who was born in Herefordshire, was sent for trial to Glamorgan Assizes. She was convicted of stealing a shawl from her mistress and since she had a previous record, she was transported to Van Diemen's Land (Tasmania).[32] In a study of three hundred female transportees from Wales to Australia, which I undertook, I found that most gave their occupations as some form of domestic service, laundry or farm work. Few were in skilled jobs: there were some cooks, dairy maids and dressmakers. Sometimes, when asked by the court what jobs they did, their answers came alive. Anne Williams, a Welsh monoglot from Anglesey replied that she was a 'farm servant, milk and wash'. It was the sort of statement she would have made at a country hiring fair.

Diaries
Diaries qualify as a record source. I suggest that researchers could inquire of women, who are taking part in the interview programme, whether they kept and still have old diaries. If there are any available they could be very useful.

Parliamentary Papers
Nineteenth-century Parliamentary Papers are a rich and excellent source of women's history. The detailed reports of government commissions include a great deal of evidence given by women workers in a wide range of occupations. They are available in major libraries, e.g. the British Library, a university or city library. It is also best to consult the index first if you do not know what you are looking for. Look under such headings as Women, Employment, or specific occupations e.g. Agriculture, Lace Making, Brick Making, etc.

It should be pointed out that the commissioners reflect the prejudices of their period and it is therefore worth reading general histories of the period. One should also note that although many of the respondents were women, the commissioners were men and it was they who framed the actual questions. But it is not only the evidence from women which is important. Often men, both questioners and respondents, make telling points and incidental revelations about their attitudes towards women and to the family. Sometimes silences and reading between the lines will tell even more. Parliamentary papers are a very useful source, which has been available to researchers for many years but only recently have new questions been brought to this source. Questions concerning the sexual division of labour, relationships between male and female workers and on how women's role in the workforce was perceived by women and men can render this 'old source' a fund of new information.

The following list of reports is by no means complete. It is intended to give an idea of the range of material available. The extracts will, I hope, whet the appetite of any one who thinks of these reports as dull reading. They certainly are not. I include here a select list of reports on agriculture, industry and domestic service together with some illustrative extracts.

Agriculture
Report on Agricultural Distress, PP 1821 IX; PP 1822 V.
Report from S. C. on Labourers' Wages, PP 1824 VI.
Report from S. C. . . . on Agriculture, causes and extent of Distress, PP 1836 VIII.
Report from Lords' S. C. on State of Agriculture, PP 1837 V.
Report from Commissioners on the Employment of Women and Children in Agriculture, PP 1843 XII.
Sixth Report of Children's Employment Commission, PP 1867 XVI.
Report of Commissioners on Children's, Young Persons' and Women's Employment in Agriculture: 1st Report and 2nd Report, England, PP 1867–8 XVII and PP 1868–9 XIII; 3rd Report, Wales, PP 1870 XIII; 4th Report, Scotland, PP 1870 XIII.[33]

The first two extracts are both from the 1860s. They deal with two aspects of female farm labour which were highly shocking to bourgeois notions of respectability i.e. the gangs and the bondagers.

The Gangs

By an agricultural gang is meant a number of persons, men, women, girls, lads, and boys, employed by and under the control of one person, who lets them out to different farmers in turn for certain kinds of work. In some of these gangs the males and females work together, in other gangs they work separately. . . .
      As the gangman makes no inquiry as to the character of those he employs, the gang will sometimes

include idle labourers who dislike regular and sustained employment, young women of immoral character, married women of slatternly, immodest, and idle habits, and young children. . . .

In a gang of such a character it necessarily follows that even those who were steady and respectable when they joined it must become corrupted. When the gang is mixed, where I mean males and females work together, the evil becomes greater. The dress of the women is to a certain extent almost of necessity immodest. When the crops are wet they tuck up their dresses between their legs, often leaving the legs much exposed. The long absence and distance from home often render it necessary that the women should attend to the calls of nature, and this they frequently do in the presence of the lads, boys and men. Thus a girl who is when she joins these gangs modest and decent gradually loses her modesty. *Sixth Report of Children's Employment Commission 1867*, XVI, pp. 83–4.)[34]

Women bondagers in Northumbria

As there are very few villages in this part of Northumberland [Glendale Union, extending in a southerly direction from Wark and Carham on the Tweed, over an area of 147,698 acres, with a population of 13,210], the farmers are almost entirely dependent on their cottagers for the labour of their farms. . . . To secure this, the hind [labourer] is bound to find the work of a suitable woman whenever she is needed.

The woman thus hired is called the 'bondager' or 'bound woman'. Her earnings are paid to the hind, who engages to give her wages, lodging, food, and washing.

Women are extensively employed throughout the whole year, and their labour is considered essential for the cultivation of the land. The work of two women is usually required for every 75 acres of the light land, and a larger proportion for that which is heavier. . . . Their labour consists in the various operations of cleaning the land, picking stones, weeds, etc.; turnip hoeing, hay making, and harvest work, rooting and shawing, that is, cleaning turnips; barn work, with the thrashing and winnowing machines, filling dung carts, turning dung heaps, spreading the dung, and sowing artificial manure; turnip cutting in the winter for sheep, etc.; and occasionally driving carts or harrowing; in some instances forking (pitching) and loading hay or corn, though when such is the case two women are put to the work for one man.

The Northumbrian women who do these kinds of labour are physically a splendid race; their strength is such that they can vie with the men in carrying sacks of corn, and there seems to be no work which affects them injuriously, however hard it may appear . . . (*First Report. Commission on Children's, Young Person's and Women's Employment in Agriculture* PP 1867–8 XVII)[35]

Industry

Very many investigations were made into nineteenth-century industries and these reports contain a great deal of information on women workers. Here are some examples down to c. 1850.

Report . . . on Petitions of Cotton Spinners in Lancashire, PP 1778–1852 V.

Report . . . on Petitions of Persons concerned in the Woollen Trade and Manufactures, PP 1802–3 V,VII.

Report . . . Disputes between Masters and Workmen engaged in Cotton Manufacture, PP 1802–3 VIII.

Report . . . on Petitions of Clothmakers, Shearmen, Weavers and Clothiers, PP 1805 III.

Report on the State of Woollen Manufacture, PP 1806 III.

Reports . . . on Petitions of Cotton Manufactures and Journeymen Cotton Weavers, PP 1808 II; PP 1809 III; PP 1810–11 II.

Report on Framework-knitters' Petitions, PP 1812 II.

Report . . . on the State of Children in Manufactories, PP 1816 III.

Reports on Ribbon Weavers' Petitions, PP 1818 IX.

Report . . . Petitions of Hosiers and Frame work knitters, PP 1819 V.

Report . . . on Artisans and Machinery, PP 1824 V.

Report . . . on Combination Laws PP 1825 IV.

Report . . . State of British Wool Trade, PP 1828 VIII.

Report . . . Fluctuation of Employment in Manufacturing Districts, PP 1830 X.

Report . . . on the Silk Trade, PP 1831–2 XIX.

Report on Manufactures,

Commerce and Shipping, PP 1833 VI.

Report . . . on the Bill to regulate the Labour of Children in the Mills and Factories, PP 1831–2 XV.

Reports of the Commissioners, Factories Inquiry Commission:

First, PP 1833 XX; *Second*, PP 1833 XXI; *Supplementary Report*, PP 1834 XIX, XX.

Reports of Inspectors of Factories, PP 1834 XLIII; 1835 XL; 1836 XLV; 1837 XXXI; 1837–8 XXVIII, XLV; 1839 XIX; 1840 XXIII; 1841 X; 1842 (Sess 2) VI; 1843 XXVII; 1844 XXVIII; 1845 XXV; 1846 XX; 1847 XV.

Persons Employed in Mills and Factories . . ., PP 1836 XLV.

Report . . . on Hand Loom Weavers' Petitions, PP 1834 X; 1835 XIII.

Report from Commissioners on . . . the State of Handloom Weavers, PP 1839 XLII; 1840 XXIII; 1841 X.

Report on Payment of Wages, 1 PP 1842 IX.

Reports of Commissioners, Children's Employment Commission:

First Report (Mines), PP 1842 XV; *Appendix*, PP 1842 XVI; *Part II*, PP 1842 XVII.

Second Report of Commissioners on Trade and Manufactures, PP 1843 XV; *Appendix* PP 1843 XIV,XV.

Report . . . Midland Mining Commission, PP 1843 XIII.

Reports of the Commissioner . . . to Inquire . . . Mining Districts, PP 1844 XVI; 1845 XXVII; 1846 XXIV; 1847–8 XXVI; 1849 XXII; 1850 XXIII; 1851 XXIII; 1852 XXI.

Reports of Commissioners . . . Condition of Framework knitters, PP 1845 XV.[36]

A few short extracts from parliamentary returns on industry will show the type and range of material available.

Coalmining: an East Lothian pit woman

Isabel Hogg, 53 years old, coal-bearer. Been married 37 years; it was the practice to marry early, when the coals were all carried on women's back, men needed us; from the great sore labour false births are frequent and very dangerous. I have four daughters married, and all work below till they bear their bairns—one is very badly now from working while pregnant, which brought on a miscarriage from which she is not expected to recover.

Collier-people suffer much more than others—my guid man died nine years since with bad breath; he lingered some years, and was entirely off work eleven years before he died.

You must just tell the Queen Victoria that we are guid loyal subjects; women people here don't mind work, but they object to horse-work; and that she would have the blessings of all the Scotch coal-women if she would get them out of the pits, and send them to other labour.

(*Note* by the Sub-Commissioner: Mrs Hogg is one of the most respectable coal-wives in Penston; her rooms are well furnished, and the house the cleanest I have seen in East Lothian.) (*Reports of Commissioners, Children's Employment Commission (Mines)*, PP 1842 XVI p. 460)[37]

Sheffield cutlery workers

Sophia Cockin, adult.—I rent this room, and employ a few girls in it on cutlery. I began cutting work at 6 years old. They lifted me on a stool to reach my work, as I was not big enough to get up myself. My lass, now dead, began cutting when two weeks turned 6 years old. Bless you! you'll find little ones at it up and down now, some, I daresay, nearly as young as I was. The trade is up and down, so that people are obliged to put their children to it as soon as they can bring on anything. There's many a little nattling job that little ones can do in it.

When I first began, I and my sister worked for mother, and then in a shop like this for my uncle. Even then he would have us up at 5 and 6 in the morning, and keep us at work sometimes till 8, but many a time till 10, 9, and 11 at night. At first, when at work late, I have fallen asleep with the work in my hand, and my mother would hit me over the head to wake me up. When I were a lass I have many a time worked all night on Friday; and after I grew up and married, for years I never went to bed on Friday night, because I was slaving for my children. On other days I have often worked from 4 and 5 a.m. till 12 at night.

I have a cough (she had coughed several times), and a pain in my chest. It is from the dust made by the lathe. I am very tired of the work now, but am obliged to keep on at it. It is easier for the bones now that we use steam power, but it is worse for the chest, as so much more dust is made. Working the lathe with the foot I should sweat even at Christmas on the coldest day with frost and snow on the ground.

The girls don't get caught here in the shafting, though we hear of such things at some places. I have been very careful about machines ever since I was a girl of 9 or 10 years old. We girls in some works of this kind were playing at hiding, and one about 14 years old hid beside a drum in a wheel not then working, and it was started and crushed her to pieces. They had to pick up her bones in a basket as they found them, and that's how they buried her.

Girls are soft, giddy things. That one there, now about 14, is a dragon for getting into danger, and I have great trouble with her. If I was not looking she would be putting her foot on the shaft, very likely, and once she sat down upon it, just to see how it felt when it was set agate.

The master does not have the shop cleaned; we must do it ourselves. But after working so long we are too tired. That heap of bone dust (a bushel or two) in the corner has been gathering for many a week. It is three weeks since we swept the rest of the shop. The dust is swept into the corner. (*Children's Employment Commission, 4th Report 1865. Report on Metal Manufacturers of the Sheffield District* PP 1865 XX p.42)[38]

Domestic service
Domestic service was the largest source of employment
throughout the nineteenth century and for much of the
twentieth century. The very women who were under the
noses of the parliamentarians at home were the last to whom
official attention was paid. Reports of interest on these
women begin at the turn of the century.
*Report by Miss Collett on money Wages of Indoor Domestic
Servants*, PP 1899 XCII.
*Report of Women's Employment Committee of the Ministry of
Reconstruction*, PP 1918 XIV.
*Report of Women's Advisory Committee on the Domestic
Service Problem*, PP 1919 XXIX.
*Ministry of Labour Report . . . Supply of Female Domestic
Servants*, PP 1923.
Report on Post War Organization of Domestic Employment,
PP 1944–5 (Cmd 6650), i.
Report . . . Minimum Rates of Wages . . . Domestic Help, PP
1942–3 (Cmd 6841), iv.
The two following extracts are both taken from the first-
named report above, i.e. Miss Collett's – it is a refreshing
change to read a report made by a woman. The table shows
the regional variation within Great Britain and Ireland of
servants' wages and the commentary gives some interesting
insights into the lot of the many servants who worked alone
in single-servant households.

> In these one-servant households can be found the
> greatest variety of conditions in striking contrast with
> the general uniformity in wages. At the top, the want of
> 'professional' training alone disqualifies the most
> efficient general servants for promotion to the
> households employing many servants and paying higher
> wages; while, at the same time, the thoroughly good
> general servant can secure for herself such warm
> appreciation from the family she serves, that her
> privileges and freedom quite outweigh the attractions of
> better paid service in richer households. At the bottom,
> the young 'slavey' of the lodging house or the coffee shop
> has to work harder and under more unfavourable

Average Wages of Female Domestic Servants
(at selected Age Periods) according to class of work.

Class of Work.	Age Period.	London.	England and Wales (excluding London).	Scotland.	Ireland.
	Years	£	£	£	£
Between maid	19	12.4	10.7	—	—
Scullerymaid	19	13.7	13.0	—	—
Kitchenmaid	20	16.6	15.0	15.0	11.3
Nurse-housemaid	21 and under 25	14.9	16.0	14.0	—
General	21 and under 25	14.9	14.6	15.3	10.3
Housemaid	21 and under 25	17.5	16.2	17.1	13.3
Nurse	25 and under 30	21.0	20.1	19.5	13.8
Parlourmaid	25 and under 30	22.2	20.6	20.1	16.0
Laundrymaid	25 and under 30	27.3	23.6	20.0	—
Cook	25 and under 30	21.8	20.2	20.6	17.2
Lady's maid	30 and under 35	28.1	24.7	24.4	24.0*
Cook-housekeeper	40 and upwards	41.6	35.6	22.0	—
Housekeeper	40 and upwards	34.3	52.2	45.0	—

* Only one case.
(*Miss Collett's Report*, 1899 XCII, p. 13.)

conditions perhaps than any other class of the
community.

The rough-mannered servant girl accustomed to
service with rough-mannered employers has little before
her as she grows older. As soon as she reaches an age
when she wants more than a very small sum in wages,
she is dismissed and replaced by another young girl. Her
previous experience is against her amongst mistresses
looking for older servants, and the customs of well
ordered, or at least conventionally ordered households,
often do not attract the girl herself. This class of girl in
very few years disappears from the ranks of domestic
servants, and in doing so, is generally in a worse position
than the factory girl in the same grade. (*Miss Collett's
Report*, 1899 XCII, p. 15)[39]

Surveys
The usefulness of social surveys as a source is shown more

fully in Chapter 5, but since several major investigations took place which throw light on women's work they should be noted. I list some interesting ones here.

Charles Booth, *Life and Labour of the People of London* (17 vols), London, Macmillan, 1889–1903.

Henry Mayhew, *London Labour and the London Poor*, London, Griffin, Bohn & Co., 1861.

The Women's Industrial Council also sponsored investigations into women's waged work. Among them are,

Clementina Black, *Married Women's Work*, London, Bell, 1915.

C. V. Butler, *Domestic Service*, London, Bell, 1916.

B. L. Hutchins, *Women's Wages in England in the Nineteenth Century*, London, 1908.

Among other bodies to initiate investigations were the Women's Trade Union League and the Fabian Society. One further report I would like to single out is –

H. Llewellyn Smith (ed.), *The New Survey of London Life and Labour*, London, P. S. King, 1934.

Newspapers

Clearly one of the most useful sections of newspapers as a source of information on women's employment is the situations vacant column. Both in the nineteenth and early twentieth centuries advertisements seeking domestic servants predominate. The *Evening Express*, widely read in South Wales, in 1887 announced such vacancies in its 'Wanted' column as:

> Good Plain Cook Wanted; small dairy and baking: must understand soups and entrees: pastry etc.: kitchen maid kept. Wages £30: all found but beer.
>
> The Castle, Saundersfoot

and

> A Respectable Girl, about 18 years of age as Housemaid: tall and of good appearance: one who has not been out before preferred: must be willing and handy with her needle.
>
> Plymouth Road, Penarth.[40]

Articles on women's work are fairly common, especially at times of proposed legislation and in wartime.

Journals

The most useful journals and periodicals dealing with women's work have emanated from the trade union movement or other organizations concerned with the employment of women. These frequently contain information on wages and working conditions in a wide variety of industries and often include reports from local branches concerning their activities. I would single out the following.

1 *The Woman Worker: Official Organ of the National Federation of Woman Workers*, 1907–10, 1916–21. (BL; Fawcett 1907–9). This contains many local reports, educational articles and very cheap recipes. Margaret Bondfield contributed an account of the living–in system for shop girls, who lived in hostels without hot water, cooking facilities or any choice of who their room mate was to be (November 1907). Another interesting article in this journal gives an account of Scottish women who were employed as fish gutters in Yarmouth. They found it very hard to find accommodation and lived in *totally* unfurnished rooms. (December 1908).

2 *The Woman's Industrial News* (1895–1919) (BL; Fawcett 1903–19) This is a particularly good source on homeworkers at the beginning of this century and contains much Scottish information. Among the homeworkers reported on are 'hollow ware' workers in Lye (i.e. painters and grainers of tin trunks), spring mattress makers in London and linen finishers in Belfast. (April 1911). For sewing 384 dots on a handkerchief women in Belfast received 1d. The handkerchieves were sold at 6/8 per dozen. Among other groups described in this journal are pit women, waitresses, servants and barmaids.

3 *Women's Union Journal: Organ of the Women's Provident League* (1876–1890); superseded by *Women's Trade Union Review* (1891–1919), (Fawcett 1876–80, 1891–1900, 1911–19). Again it contains local reports and articles on women in local industries, e.g. seamers and stitchers in Leicester (February 1877), brickmakers in Oldbury (May

1881), a report on the Bristol Union of Working Women and on Nottingham Mutual Benefit Society (January 1882).

Among other journals worth consulting are:

Women Workers, Quarterly Magazine of Birmingham Ladies' Union of Workers (1891–24) (Birmingham Central Library).

Woman Clerk: Organ of the Association of Women Clerks and Secretaries (1925–31) (BL).

Woman Engineer: Organ of the Women's Engineering Society (1919–70) (BL; Fawcett 1919–25).

Woman Teacher: Organ of the National Union of Women Teachers (1919–61) (BL).

Magazines which are not connected with trade unions should also be consulted. The *Englishwoman's Review* contains articles on women's work. *The Illustrated London News* and *The Graphic* contain many woodcuts of idealized scenes of women at work.

Commercial Directories

Commercial Directories, regularly compiled for towns from the mid-nineteenth century list the names of people engaging in business in British towns. These are usually divided up according to specific trades, e.g. blacksmiths, innkeepers, tailors, milliners.

An indispensable guide is Jane E. Norton's *Guide to National and Provincial Directories of England and Wales excluding London, published before 1856*, Roy. Hist. Soc., 1950.

Catherine Hall's work on Birmingham shows what a marvellous source these directories are. From these she was able to trace women as coachmakers, plumbers, iron and steel merchants and in the guntrade. In the period she examined, c. 1780–1850, she was able to see how women were pushed out of many trades and into a much narrower range of work – i.e. in retail trades, dressmaking, millinery and school teaching.[41]

Photographs

Photographs of women at work are well worth seeking out and examining. The visual image brings history to life and often a photograph will convey, much more clearly than written descriptions, the nature of the work, the tools used and the work dress worn. Valuable and fascinating as this is as a source, one must be aware of its limitations. There are certain technical considerations. Early photographs look very posed and indeed they were – on account of the long exposure times required. There could be no clear photographic reproductions of dark industrial interiors until the use of flash photography in the 1890s. There are other things to consider too. One should ask what the purpose or function of a photograph was or is. If it was social reform, commercial purposes, war-time propaganda, etc., then we should view the photograph in the light of that knowledge. These motives, of course, rarely apply to photographs found in family albums – but then photographs of people at work do not usually figure prominently in albums.

There are certain very famous photographers who photographed women at work and whose representations of women engaged in a variety of jobs are well worth looking at. Frank Meadow Sutcliffe (1853–1941) recorded the working lives of fisherwomen along the Yorkshire coast and of women agricultural workers in the same county. They are somewhat idyllic and romantic, yet they do convey the arduous quality of the work done. His work is widely reproduced and the collection of his photographs may be seen at the Sutcliffe Gallery in Whitby. A. J. Munby was not himself a photographer but he was responsible for many photographs of working women, particularly pitwomen in Lancashire. He was constantly ushering pit women into local photographers' studios in the 1860s and 1870s. Munby's collection of photographs show the pit women themselves, their costume and the tools they used.[42] Horace Nicholls on the other hand was himself a very skilled photographer: he is best known for his photographs of such occasions as Derby Day. During the First World War Nicholls produced a memorable series of photographs of women at work – in munitions factories, as tram drivers, chimney sweeps and agricultural workers. These are now in the Imperial War Museum.

There are certain major collections of photographs, which contain many representations of women workers. The

National Museum of Labour History in East London has a very large collection of photographs of women engaged in many jobs, including many different kinds of outwork. To consult this collection it is necessary to join The National Labour History Society and to pay a search fee. Other very large collections include The Imperial War Museum and The Greater London Council's photographic archive. But many local museums may have useful photographic material of more particular local interest. One photograph of women stripping bark (for tanning leather) in the Wyre Forest I found in a small but well arranged museum in Bewdley, Worcestershire.

Finally private individuals keep old photographs. It is most important to advertise for or ask individuals for old photographs. I am aware most family albums celebrate rituals – holidays, weddings, christenings, etc., but they may well include the odd photograph of a female member of the family at work. Shop girls were often photographed outside the shop for instance. I include a photograph here of my mother in her first job – as a cinema usherette at the Theatre Royal, Barry, in the 1920s – and the photograph of the First World War postwoman comes from her granddaughter's family album.

Postcards
The Victorians also had the fortunate habit of making postcards of practically everything, including people at work. Many of these are still around in second-hand shops.

Paintings
A move towards social realism amongst some nineteenth-century painters meant that women's work became a fit subject for paintings – if not always for exhibition. Among British artists who depicted working women, are Richard Redgrave and G. F. Watts.[43] Redgrave chose such themes as *The Poor Teacher* – a painting in which he shows a sad and lovely young governess reading a letter from home as she stood amongst the gaiety of her wealthy charges. In *Going into Service*, exhibited at the Royal Academy in 1843, Redgrave depicts a young girl leaving home in a wagon to

take up a post as a servant. In *The Sempstress* (1844) and
Fashion's Slaves (1847) he took up the cause of exploited
needlewomen: in *Fashion's Slaves* he shows an angry rich
woman severely scolding a weary seamstress who was late in
completing a garment. G. F. Watts too championed oppressed
needlewomen in his very poignant *The Seamstress*, which
was painted about 1850. In it, the emaciated and exhausted
seamstress sits in a poor room, lit by a single candle, with her
hand to her head and an unfinished shirt resting on her lap.
She looks like I always imagine Thomas Hood's seamstress
looked in the popular poem 'The Song of the Shirt'.[44]

A. J. Munby, mentioned above as a commissioner of
photographs, also sketched pit women but British pit-brow
lasses lack an artist such as Constantin Meunier who painted
Belgian women coal workers. Fisherwomen seem to have
caught the eye of some British painters: Stanhope A. Forbes
painted Cornish fish sellers.[45] It is often forgotten that Sylvia
Pankhurst was an artist as well as a campaigner and her
paintings of women workers in England and Scotland should
not be overlooked[46] Not only are they well executed but
they accurately record women's work in the Staffordshire
potteries, Leicestershire boot factories, Glasgow cotton mills,
in the Berwickshire countryside and on the Yorkshire and
Scottish coasts.

The artists who I have mentioned were all quite well
known, but there may well have been many other artists who
recorded working women at work. The People's Palace in
Glasgow, for example, has a superb pictorial record of a
woman at her employment. A proud and independent
Glaswegian shopkeeper of the 1790s stands at her counter.
She is finely dressed and wearing jewellery: her shop is well
stocked and on the counter before her she lines up silver
coins. It really would be marvellous if local researchers
discovered other portraits of successful women.

Trade union banners
These are an unusually lovely source of history. Often beauti-
fully made and bearing images, many are a delight to see.
They are also informative. A useful guide to them exists in
John Gorman's, *Banner Bright*.[47]

Some banners portray women as workers, e.g. The Blackburn District Weavers, Winders and Warpers Association, which is kept in the county Borough of Blackburn Museum, portrays a woman worker at her loom.[48] Women are seen doing specific tasks in banners such as those of the Union of Shop, Distributive and Allied Workers and The National Amalgamated Society of Male and Female Pottery Workers.[49] Women often figure in banners as representing some abstract idea, such as Justice or Socialism. They also feature on other banners as the wife or widow of an injured male worker. Such widow and orphan scenes often decorate the back of male trade union banners. The National Union of Vehicle Workers (Aldgate Branch), portrays on the reverse a sickroom scene, with wife and child kneeling at the man's bedside and with trade union officials standing by. Two vignettes in each top corner carry the story forward. One shows the widow, receiving death benefit from the union, and the other shows her and her small child at the graveside.[50]

Trade union emblems and banner designs were produced on surfaces other than the actual banners. The emblem of the Glasgow Association of Cotton Spinners c. 1820, is painted on a tin tray and is on display at The People's Palace in Glasgow.

It is certainly worth making inquiries at museums and at local trade union offices to locate old banners and other artefacts. They make marvellous items for exhibitions on women's history.

Posters

Posters have already been mentioned in connection with images of women (see above Chapter 2). They are also a source of evidence for women's work. Some have been collected by museums but occasionally they survive *in situ*. I came across a 1950s British Rail recruitment poster for women recently at Paddington Station. It had survived on a notice board because the practice had been to pin each new poster over the one previously displayed. But on the whole such posters are not easy to find.

Wartime posters are probably the best preserved. The Imperial War Museum has a collection, some of which have been printed.[51]

Oral sources

Often the most useful source of all for any local inquiry into women's work is the oral interview. Social historians have in recent years paid increasing attention to oral history and since so little has been recorded in written and printed evidence of the everyday experiences of working women the interview is of paramount importance. It is easy to criticize this particular historical source or research method and yet it may be argued that it has no more obvious faults than any other source.[52] Memory may fade – but it tends to be as vivid after nearly fifty years as after one.[53] Perceptions alter according to the later experience of the interviewee or the changing attitudes of society, but changing perceptions are in themselves historical material. I believe that the advantages of interviewing far outweigh the shortcomings. Actually talking to older people in the community is a useful and rewarding experience, bridging the gap between generations, increasing understanding and tolerance.

Many older women actually enjoy being interviewed; it is often the only recognition they have ever received that their working lives are important. Only by interviewing them can we rescue information which would otherwise be totally lost. Finding older people to interview is not usually difficult. If an individual or group has no immediate contact with older women in the community then letters to the local newspaper or appeals to the local radio station, asking for memories, can yield results. It is also possible to contact old people's groups and clubs. I have also found that once one has found one older woman to interview, she recommends other friends to be interviewed.

The interview

I have no doubt that the interview is best conducted in the respondent's home, where she feels at ease. Ideally only the interviewer and respondent should be present. A tape-recorder (cassette recorder) is essential. You cannot remember the conversation, actual words used, nuances, hesitations, reactions – if you simply take notes. There is no substitute for the actual recording. I prefer the sort of tape-recorder which has a built in microphone — thereby avoiding thrusting an intimidating microphone at the respondent. Interviewees actually forget the existence of the machine quite quickly and it is useful therefore to have long-running cassettes (ideally 60 or 90 minutes) in order not to remind them unnecessarily of its technological presence.

The first point to bear in mind before an interview is to be as well informed as possible. The more local and specific knowledge the interviewer already has, the more rewarding the interview should prove. I favour a very informal interview where the respondent is allowed to talk at length and to digress. Much of the most valuable information I have taped has been as a result of allowing the respondent to chat on, rather than as a result of pointed questioning. However, some questions are very important and useful and it would be a pity to miss them out. The following form a useful nucleus for an inquiry.[54] Quite how many questions are asked, and in what depth they are pursued should be left to the discretion of the interviewer, who should always remember that she/he is there to listen rather than to talk.

Some suggested questions

Did you do a part-time job while you were still at school? What? How did you find it? What wages? What hours did you work?

When did you start full-time work? How did you find it? What were the hours, meal breaks, wages? Did you train? What were you paid in training? Did you get paid holidays? Was it 'good money' in your job? Did men and women do the same job? Were they paid the same wage? How much of your wages did you keep? Give to your mother? Were you in a union? Which? What did the union do for the people? Were you ever on strike? Why?

How did you get on with your work mates? Were they your friends outside? Was there any social club or any organization to do with your job which you joined? Were there any childcare facilities attached to your workplace?

How did your employer treat you? Did you like your job?

Once you have conducted the interview don't run away but stay for a chat. If people are nice enough to talk about themselves they often want to know about you.

The next steps are as follows. Immediately put the respondent's name and the date of the interview onto the actual cassette and onto the box. It is also useful to compile a card index of tape recordings giving the following information:

Name

Date of Birth

Address

Recorded at

Interviewer[55]

Paul Thompson makes many useful suggestions for indexing and storing the information, which I cannot improve upon, and anybody undertaking an oral history project is very well advised to use his book. Among his very useful suggestions is the making of contents cards – these give a *brief* summary of the tape. The transcription of a tape is a long and arduous business. It takes 5–6 times as long to write something out as to listen to it. It may not always be necessary – but if a group decides to publish a pamphlet on local women's lives it would be very useful to transcribe whole interviews. This obviously raises the question of permission and it is essential to obtain the respondent's permission before using this evidence.

Finally if an individual or group becomes very interested in oral history, they could join the Oral History Society which produces a useful journal and pamphlets.[56] *The Women's History Issue* (vol. 5. no. 2. 1977) shows the kind of information some women historians have gathered from oral testimonies. A local group could fairly easily attempt a series of interviews of women in the same age group or of women in the same occupation and reach some generalizations therefrom: a group could record a series of individual interviews with older women and publish their biographies. Finally, I keep speaking of older women and many people refer me to very, very old women. Indeed, one of my most lucid and lively respondents was well into her nineties but it is not necessary to seek out the very old. Women in their fifties and sixties have their tale to tell.

Below are some extracts from various interviews I or friends have conducted. I have chosen just four, but the respondents come from different parts of the country, did different jobs and vary in age.

Respondent 1

Bessie. b. 1917. Kidderminster. Carpet factory worker. Began work the day after she left school at 14. She began in the carpet factory as a bobbin winder at 11/10d p.w. until she was 16. She then became a skilled pattern setter.

Bessie

Bessie started work the day after she left school at 14, in 1933. She described what she did as follows:

Prepare it for the weavers. It is a skilled job and we were paid piece work. We were given a pattern in very thick paper – that was pinned onto a drum, what they called a drum. It was about seven rows to the inch. Therefore in one inch you changed that pattern seven times. We were given the colours. In one colour alone you could have seven shades – seven shades of blue, seven shades of pink. It was very, very interesting.

We worked from seven o'clock in the morning till one o'clock . . . with a break of half an hour. Then from two o'clock till half past five and that was our day finished but we also worked on Saturday morning from seven o'clock till twelve o'clock.

Once you saw your first week's pay packet, automatically you tried to get more. The more you turned out the more money you would get. Of course, the people by the sides of you they tried to beat you and get more money. My job was clean – but the winding was a very very dirty job. Before the war before the nylon came into it, it was all wool. It was just all flights that came from the nylon came from the wool – little bits in the air. There were mice and rats. They got in the yarn and made a bed. I remember my friend removing one set of bobbins. It was just a family of mice and they ran in all directions. The factory was next to a canal. . . .

On my job you worked with a friend, which you called a butty. As long as you got on with that girl and she worked well you stuck with her for years and years and years. But of course if she didn't work well or I didn't work well you'd want to part because your money relied on that. It needed two of you – one on one side of the frame and one on the other. You'd set your pattern and you'd come into the middle and you'd meet.[57]

Respondent 2
Alice. b. 1890 in the Forest of Dean. Domestic servant in South Wales valleys, Cardiff, Weston-super-Mare, Cheltenham and Gloucester. Like many other girls Alice was a loyal member of the Anglican Support Organisation for domestic servants – the Girls' Friendly Society. She frequently cycled from Cheltenham to Gloucester with one hand on the handlebars and with the Girls' Friendly Magazine, 'Friendly Leaves', in her other hand. She only fell off once.

During the First World War Alice was employed in the household of an elderly lady with grand ideas. She (the lady) was the daughter of an ex-Lord Mayor and she lived with her companion in a semi-detached house. All meals were very formal.

Alice

I did used to cook them a late dinner and I did used to lay all the table. Her companion had showed me how I got to lay it. All silver and it had got to be laid out as though it was for the Lord Mayor. The spoons got to be in their place. Fish knives and forks had got to be in their places. The serving out spoons had got to be in their places. . . .

Seven o'clock was late dinner, cooked dinner always and I had got to lay all this dining table in the middle room as if it was in here [respondent's home]. She's come out from her room now – I'd get the dinner and I'd got to have my black dress on and my little white apron and my lace cap and my cuffs. O all ohh la la posh. Well any rate and alongside the dining-room was a drop down table, you know, to put your tray on. They go into dinner now – oh this used to amuse me. They did use to go upstairs to dress for dinner girl – the both of them. They'd come down. You know the big tulle scarves – you've seen them on the pictures–and the big wide stairs to come down and

I'd be standing by my table now all my dishes and the
meat covered over with a big silver cover with a big
handle on and I'd be standing waiting for them two to
come down and have their dinner. They'd be coming
down those stairs girl, trailing dresses, trailing behind
them, these big tulle scarves all around them – and the
old lady did used to wear a little tarara (sic) every day.

I did used to say – there was nothing wrong really –
ah yer silly old buggers.[58]

Respondent 3
Katie. b. 1898. Cardiff. Trained in shorthand and typing.
Office worker in Sheffield and London. She was at a Mayfair
Employment Agency in 1935.

Q – Is that the place where you were referred to only by
numbers?
A – Yes, only by a number – no names at all. This agency
was run by a woman, Miss Sandemann, who was very
strict on proper behaviour in the office. Nobody was
allowed to use your name. You had a number and you
were referred to as a number. My number was 55. So I
was 55. I was then sent out on jobs to do private
secretarial work for Lords and Ladies. Lady R. – was one
of them that I went to. Any place at all in the localities
that wanted secretarial help. I took a German man out
sight seeing in London for a fortnight. I had to take him
down in the tube all over London – all the museums. I
was with him from nine o'clock in the morning until I
took him to his hotel at ten o'clock at night. . . . I would
read to him. If it was a fine day I would sit in Hyde Park. I
would read to him and get him to read back to me. When
he was going up and down in the tubes, in the lifts, I
thought afterwards in later years he was measuring the
distance from the ground to the basement for subversive
activities. I wondered if he was a German intelligence
officer that I was escorting around London. Very likely
he was. That wasn't my business. I was employed. I was
paid.

[On her employer.] She treated me very well. We
had a break in the morning at ten o'clock – coffee or tea or

milk. We had a full luncheon. We had tea at four o'clock. Of course we had to work till six. She took to me because I never refused a job. Some of the other girls got frightened but I never refused a job. I had to go once to the city to share pushers. I didn't know what they were doing. I had to get on the telephone, open the directory, find a good address and get on to people to push shares. That was a job I didn't bargain for.[59]

Respondent 4
Nora. b. 1919. Seven Dials, London. Worked in a dairy, a cigar factory and then as a hand shirt ironer until the Second World War. This extract covers the early 1930s.

My mother decided that I too should take up the family profession of hand shirt ironer, which I did. I went to a little place in Piccadilly Circus. We had a coke stove with old fashioned flat irons. They used to give me a penny a week to make the stove up with the coke and I used to have to go around to Berwick Street to the pub to bring them half a pint of beer in a jug and two pennyworth of pickle onions – which I hated because I was only fifteen and all the boys used to chi ike (sic) me –
but they (the ironers) had all been to school with my mother so I could not refuse.

My aunt paid me 6/– a week. I was her learner and she paid me out of her own money because the business wasn't doing well enough to pay learners. I used to iron the backs of the shirts, the collars, the sleeves and the cuffs and she used to finish them off. She used to get 4d for each shirt that I had apart from what she did herself and she was one of the best ironers in the West End – she was well known. She was so good and quick she could walk out anyday and get a job anywhere in the West End.

You were four weeks just doing the cuffs because you put six pleats in the back of a shirt and three pleats down each sleeve. There were no pins when you folded them – you had to put 10 stripes one side and ten stripes the other – but you learned to do it all exact.

I left then when I learnt and went to a little laundry in Knightsbridge and I worked there and then from there

I went across to Harrods as a shirt presser. I started there at £2.00 when I was eighteen. That was very good – until I was conscripted in the war and learnt to be an engineer.[60]

For the purpose of this book I have conducted interviews in various parts of England, Wales and Scotland but I realize that I was a most effective interviewer in the area which I knew best. I greatly enjoyed interviewing an aunt in her eighties and her niece in her fifties, who for the last thirty years had run a croft just outside Tobermory on the island of Mull. It was a fascinating eye-opener to me but I think a Scottish interviewer would have profited more and not had to bother the respondents by ignorant questions on points of information.

Songs
Songs too can be a revealing source. It would be very exciting and it would be a very valuable service to discover or keep alive working women's songs. Certainly plenty existed. There were street sellers' songs. The women broom makers and sellers of Wyrley, near Cannock, sang such verses as,

Come buy 'em, come buy 'em
My bonny new brooms
A penny I axes
To sweep up your rooms.[61]

Many songs reflect women's work in factories and some arose out of industrial actions. When the chain makers of Cradley Heath went on strike in 1910 this was their rallying song.

CRADLEY SONG: ROUSE, YE WOMEN
Tune: Men of Harlech.
Rouse, ye women, long enduring,
Beat no iron, blow no bellows
Till ye win the fight, ensuing
Pay that is your due.

Chorus

Through years uncomplaining,
Hope and strength are waning, –
    Your industry
    A beggar's fee,
And meagre fare was gaining.
Now a Trade Board is created,
See your pain and dearth abated,
And the Sweater's wiles checkmated
Parliament's decree!

Rouse, ye women, rouse, around you
Towns and Cities cry, 'God speed you,'
Rouse, shake off the fears that bound you
    Women, rouse. Be true.

    Chorus

At length the light is breaking,
The Sweater's throne is shaking,
    Oh, do your part,
    With all your heart,
A sweeter world in making!
Stand together, strong and splendid,
In your Union till you've ended
Tyranny, and with toil blended
Beauty, Joy and Art.[62]

There are collections of women's songs in print. *My Song is My Own* is very useful for British women's history and it contains many work songs.[63] One of the songs from this collection is 'The Jute Mill Song', which comes from Dundee.

                Jute Mill Song.
O dear me, the mill's going fast,
The poor wee shifters canna get their rest;
Shifting bobbins coarse and fine,
They fairly mak' you work for your ten-and-nine

O dear me, I wish the day was done,
Running up and down the pass is no fun,
Shifting, piecing, spinning, warp, weft and twine,
To feed and clothe my bairnie aff'n ten-and-nine.

O dear me, the world's ill divided,
Them that work the hardest are the least provided;
But I must bide contented, dark days or fine,
There's no much pleasure living aff'n ten-and-nine.[64]

Museums

In recent years the image of museums in Britain has changed greatly. Although many museums still concentrate largely upon *objets d'art* and stuffed animals in glass cases, there has been a distinctive move towards a type of museum which records and displays the life of ordinary people in Britain. In these museums working and home life are often reconstructed and many give demonstrations of craft, industrial and domestic production.

There are quite a number of museums which may prove useful in the search for women's history. Agricultural life is fairly well covered. In Wales, at the Welsh Folk Museum, St Fagan's, cottages from all parts of the Welsh countryside have been reconstructed and there is a permanent display of many facets of rural life. At Reading, the Grove Rural Life Museum, reflects aspects of English rural life in the nineteenth century. East Anglia has the Abbot's Hall Museum of Rural Life at Stowmarket. The Irish Agricultural Museum at Wexford is being developed to display Ireland's agricultural past. In Scotland there are numerous museums reflecting country life such as those at Fife, Glamis and Inveraray. The Auchindrain Museum of Country Life, near Inveraray, is unusual and special in that it preserves an actual West Highland farming village. Walking along wet, grassy tracks from one tiny damp cottage to another one really gets the impression of being transported back a century.

A growing number of museums are attempting to preserve aspects of the lives of the urban proletariat. The Gladstone Museum of the Potteries at Stoke on Trent reconstructs working conditions in that industry – though the emphasis there is more on the work process than on the workers. The museum at Beamish, Co. Durham, preserves aspects of industrial life as well as rural life. In Glasgow the working life of men and women is recaptured in The People's

Palace – a museum which is alert to women's role in the workforce.

A quick way to check on what museums exist is to consult *The Good Museums Guide*[65] though it is not absolutely comprehensive. Separate guides exist for Scotland and Ireland.[66]

Museums are well worth visiting for several reasons. Firstly, the best museums do recapture something of the past. Not only did I feel the dampness at Auchindrain and comprehend the struggle for survival, but I never would have realized how far across a chain maker's kitchen the sparks fly had I not watched chains being made at The Black Country Museum at Dudley. Secondly, many museums have good libraries and photographic collections. Thirdly, they often publish very useful material. The National Museum of Labour History, Limehouse, E. London, produces illustrated broadsheets on themes, including the Bryant and May match girls' strike of 1888, the East End Rag Trade and the life of Mary MacArthur.[67] It has also produced notes for teachers on women's work and on the suffrage movement. To take another example, the Black Country Museum, mentioned above, has produced reprints of magazine articles from the 1890s on the theme 'The White Slaves of England': amongst this group are the Cradley Heath women chain makers and the Bromsgrove nail makers.[68]

Labour history societies
There are now a number of societies which concentrate on labour history. These, or one of them, may be worth approaching for assistance and their journals may prove useful. The national labour history societies are:

The Society for the Study of Labour History (England)
Scottish Labour History Society
Society for the Study of Welsh Labour History (Llafur)
Irish Labour History Society.

They produce the following journals respectively, *Bulletin of the Society for the Study of Labour History*, *Scottish Labour History Society Journal*, *Llafur* and *Saothar*. *The Bulletin of the Society for the Study of Labour History* also provides up-to-date addresses for both national and regional societies dealing with labour history. The English regional groups are:

North East Group for the Study of Labour History

North West Group for the Study of Labour History

Yorkshire, Humberside and North Midlands Group for the Study of Labour History

West Midlands Group for the Study of Labour History

The Holberry Society for the Study of Sheffield Labour History.

The amount of attention given to women's history varies from society to society. The North West Labour History Society in conjunction with Manchester Women's Group, has devoted a whole issue of its journal to Women and the Labour Movement.[69] Llafur has printed an analysis of the omission of women from Welsh History and is making women's history the subject of its annual weekend school.[70] The Irish Labour History Society, which covers Eire and Northern Ireland, is also taking an increased interest in women's history. Mary Daly's article in *Saothar* on women in the Irish workforce is a very welcome piece of work.[71]

Films

Original films dealing with aspects of women's working lives in the past still survive. They are not all in any one place. A very useful reference work is, Elizabeth Oliver, *Researcher's Guide to British Film and Television Collections*, London, British Universities Film Council Ltd, 1981. This provides lists of the central film repositories in mainland Britain and Northern Ireland together with an indication of their contents. Among the large film collections, the Imperial War Museum has films relating to women on the domestic front, factory and munition work, nursing and the women's service. The National Film Archive has collected old films and newsreels. The EMI-Pathe Library allows public access to its newsreel collection, which covers the period 1896–1972.

Recently several films have been made on women's work. They include *The Song of the Shirt* (a rather long and somewhat esoteric film on the exploitation of seamstresses in nineteenth-century London) and *Rosie the Riveter* (dealing with women's work in America during the Second World

War). Both can be hired from The Other Cinema. The last-mentioned film is, of course, American but it is superbly well made and will hopefully inspire British film makers to similar ventures. Finally, Sarah Boston made an excellent film on the subject of the *Chain Makers of Cradley Heath*. This was made by the BBC.

NOTES

1 I. Pinchbeck, *Women Workers and the Industrial Revolution 1750–1850*, London, Virago, 1981.
2 Op. cit., p. 36.
3 G. Best, *Mid-Victorian Britain*, London, Fontana, 1979, pp. 127–9.
4 Ibid., p. 126.
5 Cited A. Davin, 'Women and history' in M. Wandor (ed.), *The Body Politic*, London, Stage 1, 1972.
6 M. Irwin, *Women Workers in Laundries*, Report 1905, consulted in the Mitchell Library, Glasgow.
7 M. Irwin, (Assistant Commissioner to the Royal Commission on Labour), 'Women's Industries in Scotland', *The Proceedings of the Philosophical Society of Glasgow*, 1896, consulted in the Mitchell Library, Glasgow.
8 A. V. John, *By the Sweat of their Brow: Women Workers at Victorian Coalmines*, London, Croom Helm, 1980.
9 Homeworking, – Past, Present, Future: Notes for Workshop 1981. Unpublished Paper distributed at South East London's Women's History Workshop, June 1981.
10 See S. Alexander, A. Davin and E. Hostettler, 'Labouring Women: A Reply to Eric Hobsbawm', *History Workshop Journal*, Autumn 1979, pp. 174–82.
11 For Scottish evidence, see M. Irwin, 'Women's Industries in Scotland', loc. cit.
12 For the history of women in trade unions, see S. Lewenhak, *Women and Trade Unions: An Outline History of Women in the British Trade Union Movement*, London, Benn, 1977; and S. Boston, *Women Workers and the Trade Union Movement*, London, Davis Poynter, 1980.
13 See S. Alexander's introduction to M. Herzog, *From Hand to Mouth: Women and Piecework*, Harmondsworth, Penguin, 1980.
14 See Lewenhak, op. cit., and Boston, op. cit.
15 Boston, op. cit., p. 70.
16 Cited L. Mackie and P. Pattullo, *Women at Work*, London, Tavistock, 1977, p. 163.

17 Lewenhak, op. cit., p. 149.
18 Boston, op. cit., p. 126.
19 G. Braybon, *Women Workers in the First World War*, London, Croom Helm, 1981, p. 68.
20 Boston, op. cit., p. 137.
21 See above, Chapter 2.
22 Boston, op. cit., pp. 150–3.
23 *Ministry of Labour Report on the Supply of Female Servants*, 1923, cited in Lewenhak, op. cit., pp. 183–4.
24 The GLC Archive contains several files of information on the operation of the marriage bar throughout Britain: the then LCC was surveying the scene elsewhere before introducing the marriage bar in London. EO/STA/2.
25 In 1921 50 per cent of women workers were under 25 and 70 per cent were under 35. These figures are taken from S. Anthony, *Woman's Place in Industry and Home*, London, 1935. Cited Braybon, op. cit., p. 217.
26 For a detailed account see R. Minns, *Bombers and Mash*, London, Virago, 1980.
27 *General Report on the Census*, PP 1883 XXX, p. 33, cited in G. Best, op. cit., p. 124.
28 From a transcript made by D. E. Gibbs, *Llantwit Major: Its People in 1851*, Llantwit Major Local History Society.
29 National Library of Wales, Aberystwyth, Picton Castle Accounts 568.
30 From an unsigned article entitled 'The Cup that Comforts: A Walk around Messrs. Fry's at Bristol', *The British Workman*, XL, 1894.
31 J. S. Fry Archive, Somerdale, *Works Magazine I*, 1921–2.
32 D. Beddoe, *Welsh Convict Women*, Barry, Stewart Williams, 1979. Glamorgan Quarter Sessions Minute Book 1842.
33 This list is largely based on the sources used by I. Pinchbeck, op. cit., p. 322.
34 For a longer extract from this report, see E. R. Pike, *Human Documents of the Victorian Golden Age*, London, Allen & Unwin, 1967, pp. 217–20.
35 Similarly, see ibid., pp. 224–7.
36 This list is based on Pinchbeck, op. cit., pp. 323–4.
37 Cited E. R. Pike, *Human Documents of the Industrial Revolution*, London, Allen & Unwin, 1970, p. 1257.
38 Cited E. R. Pike, *Human Documents of the Victorian Golden Age*, pp. 193–4.
39 *Report by Miss Collett on the Money Wages of Indoor Domestic Servants* PP 1899 XCII.
40 *Evening Express*, 11 August 1887, Cardiff Central Reference Library.

41 C. Hall, 'Gender divisions and class formation in the Birmingham middle class, 1780–1850', R. Samuel (ed.), *People's History and Socialist Theory*, London, Routledge & Kegan Paul, 1981, p. 164.

42 See D. Hudson, *Munby: Man of Two Worlds*, London, Abacus, 1974; M. Hiley, *Victorian Working Women*, London, Gordon Fraser, 1979.

43 See H. M. Roberts, 'Marriage, redundancy or sin: the painter's view of women in the first twenty-five years of Victoria's reign', in M. Vicinus (ed.), *Suffer and Be Still*, Indiana University Press, 1972.

44 T. Hood, 'The Song of the Shirt', *Punch*, vol. V, 1843, p. 260.

45 See, for example, *A Fish Sale on A Cornish Beach* in Plymouth City Art Gallery.

46 See R. Pankhurst, *Sylvia Pankhurst: Artist and Crusader*, New York and London, Paddington, 1979.

47 J. Gorman, *Banner Bright*, London, Allen Lane, 1973.

48 Ibid., p. 153.

49 Ibid., p. 152, p. 158.

50 Ibid., pp. 94–5.

51 J. Darracott and B. Loftus, *First World War Posters*, London Imperial War Museum, 1972 and *Second World War Posters*, London, Imperial War Museum, 1972.

52 P. Thompson, *The Voice of the Past: Oral History*, Oxford University Press, 1978. This is an invaluable guide to the techniques and uses of oral history.

53 Ibid., p. 102.

54 For a fuller list of questions, see ibid., p. 249.

55 Ibid., Chapter 7.

56 See e.g. S. Purkis, *Oral History in Schools*.

57 Oral Interview. Bessie. Tape no. 16. side 1.

58 Oral Interview. Alice. Tape no. 5. side 1.

59 Oral Interview. Katie. tape no. 11. side 1.

60 Oral Interview. Nora. Tape no. 7. side 1.

61 From 'Songs and cries of Wyrley broom sellers' in J. Raven, *Blackcountry Songs and Rhymes*, vol. 1, Wolverhampton, Broadside Records.

62 Cited R. Woolley, *Gi' It Sum 'Ommer*, Midlands Tales 3, 1979.

63 K. Henderson, F. Armstrong and S. Kerr, *My Song is My Own*, London, Pluto, 1979.

64 Ibid., p. 154. Dundee Jute Song was written by Mary Brooksbank, a lifelong socialist and a jute worker herself.

65 K. Hudson, *The Good Museums Guide*, London, Macmillan, 1980.

66 *Museums and Galleries in Scotland*, published by the Council for Museums and Galleries in Scotland and the Scottish Tourist Board, 1981.

67 T. McCarthy, 'Women: Notes for Teachers and School Students'.

68 R. Sherard, 'The chainmakers of Cradley Heath', Pearson's Magazine, 1896, and 'The nailmakers of Bromsgrove', in ibid., are both reprinted and available in The Black Country Museum leaflets nos. 5 and 6.

69 North West Labour History Society Bulletin 7, 1980–1. Also now published as a separate pamphlet.

70 D. Beddoe, 'Towards a Welsh women's history', *Llafur*, vol. 3, no. 2, Spring 1981.

71 M. Daly, 'Women in the Irish workforce from pre-industrial to modern times', *Saothar*, 7, 1981.

Chapter five

Women and family life

Most women in Britain in the period under review have married and raised children. They have become 'housewives' – whether or not they had a job outside the home. The home and the family have been the setting for much of their lives. It is therefore a very important area of study in women's history.

The range of duties implied in the term housewife has changed greatly over the centuries. It has been shown above how in pre-industrial Britain the housewife was the organizer of a self-sufficient economic unit and how industrialization removed many middle-class women from production and closeted them within the home, which had become a refuge from the outside world.[1] This process, coupled with the rise of the domestic ideology, fixed the place of middle-class women firmly in the home.[2] Yet although the dominant stereotype of the idle, sickly Victorian lady seems all-pervasive, it is important to remember that it applies to only a small minority of upper middle-class women. Patricia Branca's[3] analysis of the incomes of the great majority of middle-class families has demonstrated that most middle-class women simply could not afford to delegate housework and childcare to a regiment of domestic servants, nannies and governesses. By examining a Victorian household manual – Mrs Warren's *How I Managed My House on £200 a Year*, Branca shows a woman totally occupied with housework, washing, cooking, coping with money problems and arguing with her one and only maid-of-all-work. For working-class women, industrialization and the rise of the domestic ideology had quite different implications. On the one hand, they were brought into factories as cheap labour and, on the other hand, they were reprimanded for not being at home to care for their children.[4] There are enormous contradictions in this. The important point is that many married women were in many periods also employed outside the home. We have seen how women in great numbers were brought in and out of the workforce to suit the changing needs of the economy. But there were also married women, who despite economic fluctuations, steadily remained at home to care for husband, house and children. For them the home was always the main focus of their lives.

This is not a theoretical study of the family[5] but rather a practical guide on how to find out about aspects of women's lives within the family. The aspects on which I concentrate are – housing, domestic work, childbearing.

QUESTIONS

There are many questions to pose to a variety of sources but in order not to repeat myself, some of the main questions are set out under the heading of *Oral History*.

SECONDARY SOURCES

General
Michael Anderson, *Approaches to the History of the Western Family*, London, Macmillan, 1980 (this summarizes all the main findings on this subject).

Nineteenth century
Carol Adams, *Ordinary Lives*, London, Virago, 1980.
G. Best, *Mid Victorian Britain 1851–75*, London, Weidenfeld & Nicolson, 1971.
J. A. and O. Banks, *Prosperity and Parenthood*, London, Routledge & Kegan Paul, 1971.
Barbara Ehrenreich and Deirdre English, *For her Own Good: 150 years of Experts' Advice to Women*, London, Pluto, 1979 (useful for the twentieth century).
Peter Laslett and Richard Wall, *Household and Family in Past Time*, Cambridge University Press, 1972.
Laura Oren, 'The welfare of women in laboring families, England 1860–1950', in M. Hartman and L. Banner (eds), *Clio's Consciousness Raised*, New York, Harper, 1974.

See also Barbara Kanner's bibliography in M. Vicinus (ed.), *Suffer and Be Still*, London, Methuen, 1980 and in *A Widening Sphere*, London, Methuen, 1980.

Women Writing on their Own Lives
John Burnett, *Useful Toil*, Harmondsworth, Penguin, 1977.
M. Llewelyn Davies (ed.), *Life As We Have Known it by Cooperative Working Women*, London, Virago, 1977.
M. V. Hughes, *A London Child of the 1870's*, Oxford University Press, 1977.
M. V. Hughes, *A London Child of the 1880's*, Oxford University Press, 1977.
M. V. Hughes, *A London Child of the 1890's*, Oxford University Press, 1977.

Twentieth century
M. L. Eyles, *The Woman in the Little House*, London, Grant Richards, 1922.
Ellen Malos, *The Politics of Housework*, London, Allison & Busby, 1980.
John Stevenson, *Social Conditions in Britain between the Wars*, Harmondsworth, Penguin, 1977.
Paul Thompson, *The Edwardians*, London, Weidenfeld & Nicolson, 1975.
See also the Virago reprints mentioned under *Surveys*.

Women Speaking and Writing for Themselves.
See also secondary sources for Chapters 3 and 4.
Eileen Elias, *On Sundays We Wore White*, London, Robin Clark, 1978.
Jean McCrindle and Sheila Rowbotham (eds), *Dutiful Daughters: Women Talk about their Lives*, Harmondsworth, Penguin, 1979.
Joan Kent, *Binder Twine and Rabbit Stew: Stories from a Country Childhood*, London, Coronet, 1978.
Molly Weir, *Shoes Were for Sunday*, London, Pan, 1973.
Phyllis Wilmott, *Growing up in a London Village: Family Life between the Wars*, London, Peter Owen, 1979.

Surveys

From the late nineteenth century onwards a series of surveys
into poverty and its effect on home life were instigated.
Charles Booth investigated poverty in London in the 1890s
and Seebohm Rowntree in York later in the same decade.
Between 1909 and 1913 Maud Pember Reeves and a group of
Fabian women addressed themselves to the question of how a
working-class woman manages to keep her family on *Round
About a Pound a Week*. It was the title of their report which
was published in 1913.[6] This detailed survey of working-class
women's family lives is a valuable source and it is quoted
below. Other inquiries into poverty followed the First World
War. Detailed investigations took place in London, in York
(again by Rowntree over thirty years after his original
inquiry) and on Merseyside and Tyneside. There were
inquiries centring on unemployment such as the Pilgrim
Trust's *Men Without Work*[7] (Deptford, Leicester, Rhondda,
Crooke in Co. Durham, Liverpool and Blackburn) and the
Carnegie Foundation's *Disinherited Youth*,[8] which looked at
South Wales. This last report concentrated on unemployment among coal miners but it commented too on unemployment's effect on the womenfolk. The following passage
illustrates the insights given by this particular source.

> The outstanding fact about many of these homes was
> that the men in them appeared to have higher standards
> of personal cleanliness than those reflected by their
> living conditions. It seemed, very largely, their
> womenfolk who had lost all pride in personal appearance
> and the appearance of the home. Men folks were obliged
> to go out of doors, even if only to the Employment
> Exchange; this was a reason for washing and dressing
> up. The women had not this incentive. Their outings
> extended little beyond the small shops at the corner of
> the street, and to these they could 'slip-down' without
> washing. To them there seemed little point in washing
> the children, as they just got dirty anyway. All this is
> highly regrettable and, quite apart from unemployment
> and bad housing conditions, many of the women, even if
> given the opportunity and money for improved

standards, would find it an exceedingly difficult task to break away from their acquired habits. But we must face the fact that to live constantly on a depressed standard of living, where life is a hand-to-mouth existence, is, except for the bravest souls, to experience the bitterness of defeat.

There were other inquiries too – too many to list here. A useful resume of their findings is given by John Stevenson[9] and Laura Oren examines their findings with specific reference to women.[10]

There is one more inquiry, which I should like to single out and rank alongside that of Mrs Pember Reeves's investigation of 1913. It is Margery Spring Rice's, *Working Class Wives: Their Health and Conditions* (1939).[11] (Both surveys have recently been reprinted.) The Spring Rice survey was conducted by volunteers, such as health visitors, into the health and living conditions of 1,250 women in many different parts of Britain. The following extracts from *Round About a Pound a Week* (1913) and *Working Class Wives* (1939) will indicate their value as a source. *Round About a Pound a Week* was concerned with a number of working-class homes in Lambeth, where the family lived on between 18 and 30 shillings a week.

> They are not the poorest people of the district. Far from it! They are, putting aside the tradesmen whose shops line the big thoroughfares such as Kennington Road or Kennington Park Road, some of the more enviable and settled inhabitants of this part of the world. The poorest people – the river-side casual, the workhouse in-and-out, the bar-room loafer – are anxiously ignored by these respectable persons whose work is permanent, as permanency goes in Lambeth, and whose wages range from 18s. to 30s. a week.[12]

The survey looked in detail at housing, rents, sleeping accommodation, household budgets, diets and 'mothers' days'.
On sleeping accommodation: this is how some Lambeth families slept. The references to the banana-crate cot stems

from the fact that the surveyors insisted on the new baby having its own cot.

1. Man, wife, and three children; one room, 12 feet by 10 feet; one bed, one banana-crate cot. Man a night-worker. Wages varying from 16s. to 20s. Bed, in which woman and two children slept all night, and man most of the day, with its head half across the window; cot right under the window.
2. Man, wife, and four children; one room, 12 feet by 14 feet; one bed, one cot, one banana-crate cot. Wage from 19s. to 22s. The bed and small cot stood alongside the window; the other cot stood across it.[13]

On household budgets: these are presented in full, as in the example of Mr P.

Mr. P., printer's labourer. Average wage 24s. Allows 20s. to 22s. Six children.
November 23, 1910, allowed 20s.

	s.	d.
Rent	8	0
Burial insurance (2d. each child, 3d. wife, 5d. husband; unusually heavy)	1	8
Boot club	1	0
Soap, soda, blue	0	4½
Wood	0	3
Gas	0	8
Coal	1	0
	12	11½

Left for food   ...   7s. 0½d.

November 30, allowed 20s.

Rent	8	0
Burial insurance	1	8
Boot club	1	0
Soap, soda, blue, starch	0	5
Gas	0	8
Coal	1	0
	12	9

Left for food   ...   7s. 3d.[14]

Detailed menus are also included, such as that of a very good
manager – Mrs X – who was given 22s. 6d. by her husband.
They had four children and rented one room for 4s. 6d.

> Sunday. – Breakfast: One loaf, 1 oz. butter, ½ oz. tea, a
> farthing's-worth of tinned milk, a half-pennyworth of
> sugar. Kippers extra for Mr. X. Dinner: Hashed beef,
> batter pudding, greens, and potatoes. Tea: Same as
> breakfast, but Mr. X. has shrimps instead of kippers.
> Monday. – Breakfast: Same as Sunday. Mr. X has a little
> cold meat. Dinner: Sunday's dinner cold, with pickles, or
> warmed up with greens and potatoes. Tea: One loaf,
> marmalade, and tea. Mr. X. has two eggs.
> Tuesday. – Breakfast: One loaf, 1 oz. butter, two
> pennyworth of cocoa. Bloaters for Mr. X. Dinner: Bread
> and dripping, with cheese and tomatoes. Tea: One loaf,
> marmalade and tea. Fish and fried potatoes for Mr. X.
> Wednesday. – Breakfast: One loaf, 1 oz. butter, tea.
> Corned beef for Mr. X. Dinner: Boiled bacon, beans and
> potatoes. Tea: One loaf, 1 oz. butter, and tea. Cold bacon
> for Mr. X.
> Thursday. – Breakfast: One loaf, jam, and tea. Dinner:
> Mutton chops, greens, and potatoes. Tea: One loaf, 1oz.
> butter, and tea.
> Friday. – Breakfast: One loaf, 1 oz. butter, and tea.
> Dinner: Sausages and potatoes. Tea: One loaf, jam and
> tea.
> Saturday. – Breakfast: One loaf, 1 oz. butter, two
> pennyworth of cocoa. Dinner: Pudding of 'pieces', greens
> and potatoes.
> Tea: One loaf, 1 oz. butter, and tea. Fish and fried
> potatoes for Mr. X.
> These children look fairly well and seem vigorous. The
> baby is being nursed. The other three live chiefly on
> bread, with potatoes and greens and a tiny portion of
> meat at dinner.[15]

Finally 'mothers' days' are one of the most interesting
features of the survey. They really show the stamina of these
women and the demands made on them. This is Mrs T's day.
She was married to a builder's handyman, on 25s. a week.

She, her husband and six children lived in two upstairs rooms. All their water had to be carried in pails from the ground floor. The investigators commented, 'She is gentle and big and slow, never lifts her voice or gets angry: seems always tired and dragged. She is very clean and orderly.'

6.0 – Nurses baby.

6.30 – Gets up, calls five children, put kettle on, washes 'necks' and 'backs' of all the children, dresses the little ones, does hair of three girls.

7.30 – Gets husband's breakfast, cooks bloater, and makes tea.

8.0 – Gives him breakfast alone, nurses baby while he has it, and cuts slices of bread and dripping for children.

8.30 – He goes, gives children breakfast, sends them off to school at 8.50. and has her own.

9.0 – Clears away and washes up breakfast things.

9.30 – Carries down slops, and carries up water from the yard; makes beds.

10.0 – Washes and dresses baby, nurses him, and puts him to bed.

11.0 – Sweeps out bedroom, scrubs stairs and passage.

12.0 – Goes out and buys food for the day. Children home at 12.15.

12.30 – Cooks dinner; lays it.

1.0 – Gives children dinner and nurses baby.

1.45 – Washes hands and faces, and sees children off to school.

2.0 – Washes up dinner things, scrubs out kitchen, cleans grate, empties dirty water, and fetches more clean from yard.

3.0 – Nurses baby.

3.30 – Cleans herself and begins to mend clothes.

4.15 – Children all back.

4.30 – Gives them tea.

5.0 – Clears away and washes up, nurses the baby, and mends clothes till 6.30.

6.30 – Cooks husband's tea.

7.0 – Gives husband tea alone.

7.30 – Puts younger children to bed.

8.0   – Tidies up, washes husband's tea things, sweeps kitchen and mends clothes, nurses baby, puts elder children to bed.

8.45 – Gets husband's supper; mends clothes.

10.0   – Nurses baby, and makes him comfortable for the night.

10.30 – Goes to bed.[16]

Margery Spring Rice's survey covered many similar aspects but concentrated in more detail on women's health. (Even in 1939 a woman had no right to free medical attention.) I would just like to quote one extract – the diet of 37-year-old Mrs C. of Rotherham. She lived in municipal housing, had eight children and husband was unemployed. The family lived on £2.5s. 0d, of which 7s. 10d. went as rent. She gave her diet as:

Breakfast: Tea, don't usually eat any breakfast.
Dinner: Bread and lard or margerine; dinner, occasionally which includes stew meat and potatoes. By the time you have served 9 of them you have had yours.
Tea: Consists of tea, bread and butter, tinned tomatoes and black pudding.
Supper: 3d. of chips and 1d. fish for five or six of us about 3 times a week.[17]

There is a large section on health. Many women suffered from anaemia and many from headaches. Of those advised to wear spectacles, many could not afford them or bought them in Woolworth's. One woman said her eyes were hurt by the light when she went out of 'her dark smelly kitchen'.[18] This is a very useful survey because it looks at women in town and country in England, Scotland and Wales. Sometimes it has a rather patronising note. A young woman in Accrington is derided for complaining that she had no electricity and no refrigerator for keeping milk and food. She is snidely called 'a superior young woman . . . who goes to League of Nations meetings, lectures and concerts'.[19] Then there was the Llanelly woman, who did not care at all about housework. Of her, the visitor wrote, 'she is a most improvident young woman; – the rare type which *makes* a slum'.[20]

Household manuals/advice books

These abound in plenty and can often be picked up cheaply in second-hand bookshops. Patricia Branca used Mrs Warren's book to good effect, but the major drawback with these is that they were largely aimed at the middle class and they reflect a high standard of living. They are nevertheless great fun to read, especially the illustrated ones.

Mrs Ellis wrote a whole series of volumes advising the middle-class women of England on how to run their homes.[21] She stressed the fact that women should be content to be inferior to men.[22] She advised the middle-class women of England 'Look at your duties first, examine them well, submit yourself without reserve to their claims and having made them habitual reap your reward in that happiness of which no human being can deprive you and which no earthly event can destroy.'[23] She portrayed the role of women as that of wife, mother, and housekeeper. Young girls before marriage should practise housewifely virtues on their brothers.[24]

Very many household manuals and cookery books have been published this century. Amy Atkinson's and Grace Holroyd's, *Practical Cookery* had reached its sixth edition by 1911.[25] It was updated with a section on cookery by gas. It contains a variety of recipes from a grandiose asparagus soup, made with fifty heads of asparagus, to such humble dishes as sausage and tomato pie. It also contains very interesting advertisements – for example for gas cookers and for various quick methods of cookery such as 'Soyer's Paper Bag Cookery'. I think it is very useful to compare the recipes in these books – even the ones which appear to be cheap – with what working people actually ate. This can be done either by reading social surveys or by interviewing older women. Atkinson and Holroyd's sixth edition was published just about the time of the Fabian women's survey of Lambeth: they appear to have been writing about two different planets.

Marjorie Swift's, *Feed the Brute* (1925) portrays an anxious housewife who strives to cook good nourishing meals and serve them up daintily, but yet grieves in secret because her husband, weary and tired after a long day's work, never seems to notice her efforts.[26] Ms Swift thought the housewife should not hanker after any verbal expression of appreciation from 'the brute' – but be pleased that he ate it! I found this a particularly insidious little book. It made its philosophy quite explicit:

> The well fed man is a happy man – and a very easily 'managed' one too. And since we women know that to maintain harmony *every* man however clever, however efficient, however charming, must be 'managed', let us feed him well first and manage him afterwards.[27]

Many cookery books of the 1920s and 1930s, through which I have browsed, give no indication of hard times. They portray pretty, well dressed – sometimes bejewelled – housewives, presiding over tables full of fancy cakes. They also strangely reinforce the role of the housewife as sole cook and cleaner in the home.

Miss A. M. Kaye's, *A Student's Handbook of Housewifery* was published in 1940. It is primarily a guide to cleaning the home. Its illustrations show mops, pails, carpet sweepers, vacuum cleaners and brushes. The well-equipped home should have twenty different brushes! The linen cupboard should hold a list of things which spans seven pages of the book: for the table alone (and she said she was writing of 'the average house') the linen cupboard should hold tablecloths (white damask), breakfast cloths, kitchen cloths, table napkins (two sizes), breakfast napkins, tea napkins, sideboard cloths, carving cloths, trolley covers, tray cloths, afternoon tea cloths and table mats.[28] But most staggering and most out of touch with the reality of most women's lives was her prescribed list of *daily* cleaning. It is based on the philosophy – 'It is easier to keep things clean than to clean dirty things'. She stated,

The Daily Work of a House consists of
  (i) The removal of all surface dust.
  (ii) The keeping clean and bright of all polished surfaces, i.e. polished wood floors, furniture, windows, mirrors, etc.

1 George Elgar Hicks, *Woman's Mission: Companion to Manhood* (courtesy of The Tate Gallery, London)

2 The New Woman, 1895, as seen by *Punch* (reproduced by permission of *Punch*)

3 Learning to blacklead a grate and to lay a fire, Dulwich
  Hamlet School, 1907 (courtesy of the Greater London
  Council Photographic Collection)

4 Typing class, Blackheath Road Institute, 1914 (courtesy of the Greater London Council Photographic Collection)

5 Charlotte Chesterton, postwoman in Kidderminster
  during the First World War

6 My mother (second from left) in her first job as a cinema usherette, at the Theatre Royal, Barry

7 A Glasgow shopkeeper of the 1790s (courtesy of the People's Palace Museum, Glasgow)

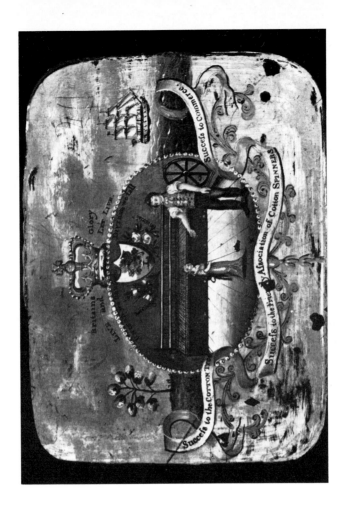

8 Tin tray bearing the emblem of the Glasgow Association of Cotton Spinners (courtesy of the People's Palace Museum, Glasgow)

9 Advertisement for Wilson gas cookers, 1911

10 Advertisement for Soyer's Paper Bag Cookery, 1911

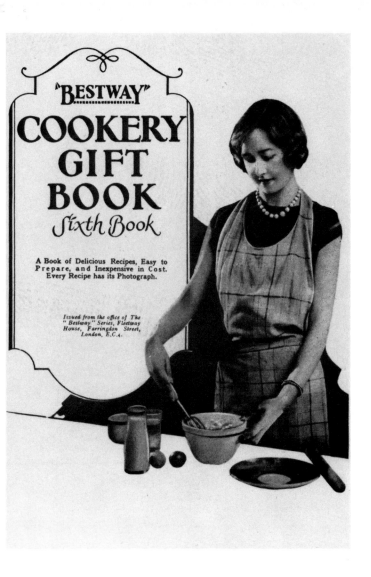

"BESTWAY"
COOKERY
GIFT
BOOK
Sixth Book

A Book of Delicious Recipes, Easy to Prepare, and Inexpensive in Cost. Every Recipe has its Photograph.

Issued from the office of The "Bestway" Series, Fleetway House, Farringdon Street, London, E.C.4.

11 Illustration of a housewife from a cookery book, c. 1930

12 Family in Whitechapel, 1930s. Photograph by Edith Tudor Hart (courtesy Wolf Suschitzky)

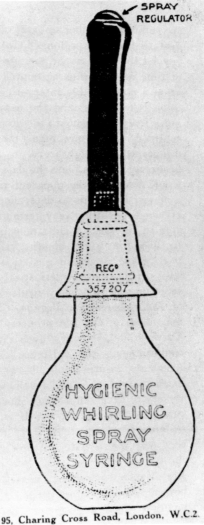

PATENT HYGIENIC SYRINGE.

Recommended by all the leading medical men as absolutely essential to every woman who values cleanliness.

The reason it has achieved and enjoys such world-wide popularity is because it

CLEANSES INSTANTLY.

Unlike other Syringes, it has **Full-Size Bulbs**, and holds the **fullest quantity of water possible.**

When the Bulb is released the liquid is **again drawn into the Bulb.**
It is worth and sold elsewhere at 15/- ; we sell it to you for

8/6

It is only obtainable from us at this low price. For antiseptic Spray Tablets to be used with this Syringe, see page 42

The above patent Spray Syringe will be sent for **8/6** post free from

THE HYGIENIC STORES, LTD.,

95, Charing Cross Road, London, W.C.2.

13 Advertisement for Patent Hygienic Syringe, 1930

14 The police removing WSPU hecklers whilst Lloyd George spoke at Llanystymdwy, September 1912 (courtesy of the Mansell Collection/Museum of London)

15 Women marching from Derby to London, 1930s (courtesy of the National Museum of Labour History)

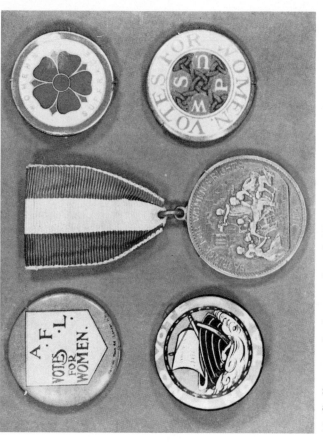

16 Suffragette badges and medallion commemorating the introduction of force feeding for imprisoned suffragettes (courtesy of the Museum of London)

(iii)   The general tidying-up of all the rooms in daily
        use.

The Arrangement of the Daily Work

  (i)   Collect all apparatus and equipment.
 (ii)   Remove all dust and waste water:
        (a) Clean the fire-place and re-lay the fire.
        (b) Clean the washstand or fitted hand-basin.
        (c) Sweep the floor.
        (d) Dust all ledges as high as the upstretched arm
             can reach, and dust all furniture and ornaments.

Note. Beds should be made before starting to sweep the
floor.

(iii)   Rub up all bright surfaces, the polished floor last of
        all.
(iv)   Give the room a general tidying.
 (v)   If the cleaning equipment is not to be used for other
        rooms it can then be put tidily away.

The above list is merely an outline of each day's work. The
detailed stages involved cover a further six whole pages.[29]

During the Second World War, the government and
other official bodies issued many interesting recipe books,
which are worth looking at. People often still have them at
home and Raynes Minns quotes some of these.[30]

Another category of manuals to which I should like to
draw attention is 'childcare'. I have no space to write about
them here – but like household manuals they make fascinating reading.

Women's magazines

The role of women's magazines and how they project particular images of women according to the political and
economic needs of any given period has already been discussed (see above Chapter 2). Magazines show us how women
and definitions of femininity have been 'socially constructed'.
The relationship between these images and the reality of
most women's lives has not always been particularly close –
but nevertheless the magazines are an interesting source.
Women's magazines certainly make good reading. The
articles, stories, advertisements and particularly the

problem page are often quite riveting. But what about their usefulness? The reservations I would point out are firstly, that often the magazines reflect a middle-class lifestyle which was not, of course, enjoyed by most women in Britain and secondly, they are not a tremendously useful source of *local* history: they often portray a sort of 'Mrs Britain', rather than a Scots, Irish, Welsh or English woman. Having said that, I would also like to point out that I think that in some ways they come nearer top the reality of women's lives (particularly middle-class women's lives) than say household manuals. Patricia Branca notes how nineteenth-century manuals always advise cash purchases of domestic appliances, furniture, etc., but that the magazines reveal a great deal of credit buying.[31] Possibly magazines were more in touch with the daily life of British women in the home because of the two-way contact involved in the correspondence pages. Visually too, the magazines are interesting. Magazine illustrations depict, e.g., kitchens, household gadgets, babies' clothes, etc. Often they are the only such source. But, of course, although interesting in themselves we should probably take them no more seriously as depicting middle-class homes than we would contemporary pictures of the huge gadget-packed kitchens depicted in many advertisements today.

The potential market for women's magazines was realized early in the nineteenth century but not fully exploited until the second half of the century. By the twentieth century the number of magazines increased greatly – the real boom time coming in the 1950s. Cynthia White's study of magazines is well worth reading and has a very helpful list of magazines.[32] I suggest a list of interesting nineteenth and twentieth-century magazines in the practical schedule to Chapter 2 but the real problem, which is also discussed in Chapter 2, is the availability of old magazines.

RECORD SOURCES

Not surprisingly there are few documentary sources which throw light on women's home lives. Little survives, or ever existed, which was either written by the women themselves or written by others about them. One is exceptionally lucky if one finds a diary or an account book. Clearly, working-class women had little time for record keeping and the writing of diaries and household accounts was almost exclusively an upper- and middle-class activity. Where diaries do survive they vary enormously in usefulness. Georgiana Elwell's diary, of Wednesbury Forge[33] is mainly limited to such entries as: Sat. Aug. 1st. 1868. 'Mr. Dawes came and played at croquet with Alfred, Carew and me.' I once read the diaries of a lady in mid-Wales, who recorded nothing except the weather for thirty years. On the other hand, there may well be really excellent historical sources tucked away in people's attics and one is far more likely to locate them in private homes than in libraries. A neighbour lent me her mother's household account book cum diary.[34] It begins in 1904 and contains recipes, details of payments to the cook and gives a whole range of glimpses into the life of a well-to-do young married woman. It is noteworthy that all the recipes she recorded, with only one or two exceptions, were for cakes and desserts – not for basic meals. Her charitable activities were chiefly in aid of the Girls' Friendly Society, the Anglican support organization for domestic servants, and her notebook records meetings of the GFS and fund-raising activities for it. It also shows her having hats altered at the milliner's to keep up with fashion and shopping either in person or by mail order from one of the many catalogues which she had sent for.

Two other types of records may be consulted. The Census records have frequently been referred to. A specific use for them in this context would be to note the ages of working mothers and their children and to examine these facts over the period from 1851 to 1881. Did the age at which women went out to work alter? Apparently the older pattern was for women to work when their children were very young, leaving them in the care of childminders and the later pattern is for women to wait until their children are older before going out to work. It would be interesting to see if change occurred in this period and to note regional variations.

Finally, it is worth pointing out record sources on housing. These can be useful as housing seriously affected the quality of people's lives. Both maps, showing housing density, and sometimes individual house plans may be kept in local record offices.

ORAL SOURCES

Obviously oral history is an excellent source for discovering and reconstructing the lives lived by women within the home. It is also in most cases the *only* source. Paul Thompson's, *The Voice of the Past: Oral History*[35] is again an excellent guide. The interviewing of older people can yield good results. Following his model, I think it is a useful idea to begin by questioning older people – women and men – about their home life as children and particularly about their mother's role in the family. There are many, many questions to be asked and the following are intended as a starting point.

Questions to ask regarding childhood

Where did you live? Describe your house. How many rooms were there? What were they used for? Did you share a bedroom? bed? What washing, cooking facilities were there? How many lived in the house? Were there any lodgers? Servants?

Who cleaned? Cooked? Made fires? Made and repaired clothes? Went shopping? Did you have new or second-hand clothes/shoes? What did your father do in the house? – clean, etc.? Did he look after the children at all? How? Did he wash you, read to you, etc.?

What activities did your mother do outside the home? Did she go out in the evenings? Did your father go out in the evenings? Where?

Were your parents strict towards you? Did they punish you? Why? How? Could you, for example, talk at meals? What did they bring you up to regard as important? Did their ideas influence the sort of person you have become?

Then one could turn to the adult life of married women. The questions suggested above on childhood could be added to and easily adapted by rephrasing.

Family Life after Marriage

How did you and your husband manage the budget? Did you

know what your husband earned? Who paid the bills? How did you decide how to allocate your money for various things – e.g. rent, food, clothes?

Returning to the childhood section – adapt the questions on housing, domestic routine and sexual division of labour in the home, and leisure.

Add too questions on parental attitudes towards children. Did you believe there was a right way to bring up children? How? Did you and your husband agree on this? Who helped you, if you were worried about your children? Your mother? Mother-in-law? Did you believe that girls and boys should be brought up differently? Did you think that they should learn different skills, behave differently? Did you expect your daughters and sons to help in the home? How?

If a woman worked outside the home after a marriage, add the following questions. Who looked after your children? Did you think it was good or bad for your children to be looked after by somebody else? Did you pay the person looking after your children?

Finally, not all women whose main sphere of activity was the home were married women. I think the lives of single daughters should also be investigated and appropriate questions put to them. E.g. Why did you remain in your parental home after becoming an adult? To look after a parent? Younger children? Because you could not afford to move out? What domestic work did you do at home? Was it assumed that a single daughter, rather than a single son, should remain at home?

Apart from oral interviews, researchers could also inquire if there are any verses or rhymes concerning house-work. I have come across many concerning washing clothes and ironing. For example,

They that wash on Monday
Have all the week to dry
They that wash on Tuesday
Are not so much awry
They that wash on Wednesday
Are not so much to blame

They that wash on Thursday
Wash for very shame
They that wash on Friday
Wash in sorry need
They that wash on Saturday
Are lazy sluts indeed.

Photographs

Visual material, depicting the interiors of homes and the family within the home is obviously very valuable. It is also unfortunately hard to come by. Some well-to-do families – perhaps with a keen amateur photographer in their number – may have had their photographs taken indoors – but there do not appear to have been many of them. The British take their photographs out of doors – and mainly in very set circumstances i.e. on the beach, on pleasure steamers. It is hardly an accurate reflection of people's lifestyles. (If only people had photographed their bedrooms, their kitchens and the dinners on their plates.)

Still, it is worth digging around for visual evidence. There are some major national photographic collections such as The Radio Times Hulton Picture Library – but that is expensive to use. Local museums would be a better starting point. Lately, too there has been a great deal of interest taken in old photographs and many photograph books have been published about specific localities. One should look at these – although regrettably many concentrate on aspects such as communications, religion and male leisure activities. The family albums of older local women ought to be examined. Most will suffer from the outdoor happy picture syndrome but it is still worth looking. Lots of my family pictures were taken in the back garden – so there are views of the coal shed, outside lavatory and the back of the house.

Museums

Many museums concentrate on aspects of domestic life. Often they have reconstructed rooms or whole houses. Some have displays of domestic implements. Such museums are well worth visiting as they enable one to recapture to a certain degree what life was like for women in the past. But unfortunately I don't think that most of them come far enough up to date. There are many nineteenth-century kitchens but I have not seen a 1930s kitchen in any museum in this country that I have visited. It would certainly make an interesting exhibit – as an exhibition in Frankfurt proved.[36] It took the theme of Women's Everyday Life and The Women's Movement and presented displays on the periods 1890–1918, 1918–1933, 1933–1945, 1945–1960 and finally 1968–1980. Within each period it concentrated on love, beauty, upbringing, household duties, work outside the home, leisure, and the women's movement. A similar exhibition or exhibitions in Britain would I think be very informative.

NOTES

1 A. Clark, *Working Life of Women in the Seventeenth Century*, 1919, reissued London, Routledge & Kegan Paul, 1983; C. Hall, 'The history of the housewife', in E. Malos (ed.), *The Politics of Housework*, London, Allison & Busby, 1980.

2 C. Hall, 'The early formation of Victorian domestic ideology', in S. Burman (ed.), *Fit Work for Women*, London, Croom Helm, 1979; and C. Hall, 'Gender divisions and class formation in the Birmingham middle class 1780–1850' in R. Samuel (ed.), *People's History and Socialist Theory*, London, Routledge & Kegan Paul, 1981.

3 P. Branca, 'Image and reality, the myth of the idle Victorian woman', in M. Hartman and L. W. Banner, (eds), *Clio's Consciousness Raised*, New York, Harper, 1974. Much of Branca's evidence is drawn from Eliza Warren, *How I Managed My House on Two Hundred Pounds a Year*, London, 1865. See also Chapter 2 above.

4 See particularly Chapter 4 in this volume.

5 The most useful of the many books on the family is M. Anderson, *Approaches to the History of the Western Family*, London, Macmillan, 1980. This presents and summarizes all the main research findings on the family.

6 M. Pember Reeves, *Round About a Pound a Week*, London, Virago, 1979.

7 The Pilgrim Trust, *Men Without Work*, Cambridge University Press, 1938.

8 Carnegie United Kingdom Trust, *Disinherited Youth*, Edinburgh, 1943, cited by J. Stevenson, *Social Conditions in Britain between the Wars*, Harmondsworth, Penguin, 1977, p. 261.

9 Stevenson, op. cit.
10 L. Oren, 'The welfare of women in labouring families: England 1860–1950', in Hartman and Banner, op. cit.
11 M. Spring Rice, *Working Class Wives*, London, Virago, 1981.
12 Pember Reeves, op. cit., p. 2.
13 Ibid., pp. 48–9.
14 Ibid., pp. 80–1.
15 Ibid., pp. 113–14.
16 Ibid., pp. 166–8.
17 Spring Rice, op. cit., p. 175.
18 Ibid., p. 59.
19 Ibid., p. 135.
20 Ibid., p. 84.
21 S. S. Ellis, *The Women of England*, London, 1839; *The Mothers of England*, London, 1843; *The Wives of England*, London, 1843; and *The Daughters of England*, London, 1844.
22 Ellis, *The Daughters of England*, London, 1844, p. 11.
23 Ibid., p. 13.
24 Ibid., p. 219. See also Chapter 2 above.
25 A. Atkinson and G. Holroyd, *Practical Cookery*, London, Sixth edn, 1911.
26 M. Swift, *Feed the Brute*, London, Bles, 1925, pp. 7–8.
27 Ibid.
28 A. M. Kaye, *A Student's Handbook of Housewifery*, London, Dent, 1940, pp. 187–93. This book is bound in washable cloth!
29 Ibid., pp. 208–13.
30 R. Minns, *Bombers and Mash*, London, Virago, 1980.
31 P. Branca, *Silent Sisterhood*, London, Croom Helm, 1977, pp. 28–9.
32 Cynthia White, *Women's Magazines 1693–1968*, London, Michael Joseph, 1970.
33 C. J. L. Elwell (ed.), *A Lady of Wednesbury Forge: The Diary of Georgiana Elwell*, Tipton, Black Country Society, 1976.
34 Account and note book of Miss Hinde of Penarth.
35 P. Thompson, *The Voice of the Past: Oral History*, Oxford University Press, 1978.
36 Frauenalltag und Frauenbewegung 1890–1980, Historisches Museum, Frankfurt a. M., West Germany.

Chapter six

Aspects of sexuality

A great deal has been written on the sexuality – or, more precisely lack of sexuality – of the Victorian lady. Strong sexual appetites ill became the Angel in the Home: they were the province of whores and wanton women. Less has been written on the same topic with regard to working-class women. What information is available on this subject must be set in the context of poverty, overcrowded housing, lack of sanitary facilities and large families. But the question of women's sexual desires, regardless of class, is an extremely difficult area to investigate and so cannot be a central issue in a guide to the local sources of women's history. It is necessary for me to confine myself to certain issues where it is possible to conduct local research and to achieve some degree of success.

The areas which I have chosen to concentrate upon are all to a certain extent open to investigation. The three areas, which I deal with here are illegitimacy, birth control and lesbian existence.

ILLEGITIMACY

This area has certain attractions for the researcher since it is a subject which is to some degree quantifiable. There are difficulties, but it is possible to work out the local illegitimacy rate. One should however be wary about jumping to any conclusions about female sexuality from information about local illegitimacy figures. Illegitimacy records by no means reveal a complete picture of extra-marital relationships: we only have evidence of such activity if an illegitimate child was baptized or buried in infancy (in the period before registration i.e. before 1838), or born less than nine months after marriage. Nor can one make generalizations about changes in the illegitimacy rate over a period of years. One can only say with any confidence that it is linked to the general fertility rate.

Peter Laslett's work in this field is very valuable.[1] It enables local findings to be set against national patterns. He shows, for example, that between 1845 and 1921 5.3 per cent of births recorded in England and Wales were illegitimate births and that in the succeeding fifty years this rose to 6.6 per cent. These figures are not particularly high if compared to those of some other societies, but they do mean that considerable numbers of women in Britain bore children out of wedlock. Their history is worth following up. There were considerable local variations. In 1842, for example, Cumberland, Norfolk, Shropshire and Westmorland head the table for illegitimate births, whilst Monmouthshire is near the bottom. Does that mean that people in Monmouthshire were less promiscuous or less fertile or are we left to make guesses about infanticide, contraception and abortion?

Although there are difficulties in assessing the information, I think it is worth investigating. It is possible, from the sources, given below, to calculate the local illegitimacy rate and to work out how many children were born less than nine months after a marriage. One should bear in mind that in some areas a marriage did not take place until the woman had become pregnant, thereby proving her fertility: this was the case in some parts of Wales. It is also very interesting to gauge local reactions to 'unmarried mothers' and again it should be possible, at least in this century, to find out.

BIRTH CONTROL

The study of the local availability of information on and aids to birth control is a vital question in women's history. It is actually far easier to conduct research into this issue for the twentieth century than for the nineteenth. Nevertheless, depending on the local sources, it may be possible to come up with some answers on the earlier century.

There are several useful surveys of nineteenth-century literature on birth control.[2] They note the major works of Malthus, Place, Carlile and Knowlton in the first half of the century. Malthus's *Essay on the Principle of Population*

(1798) was designed to cut the numbers of the working class and so attracted some radical opposition. He recommended that the poor should marry late and practise abstinence. More practical and sympathetic advice came from the radical Francis Place, who in 1823 distributed his notorious hand-bills on contraception, explaining the methods of the sponge, the sheath and withdrawal. One of the most interesting works and the most positive in its advocacy of birth control is Richard Carlile's, *Every Woman's Book or What is Love*, first published in 1825. Carlile considered sexual desires normal and healthy in women. He too advocated the sheath and coitus interruptus, but he favoured the sponge, which placed control in the hands of the woman. A new means of contraception was introduced in England with the publication of Charles Knowlton's, *Fruits of Philosophy* (1834). It was the syringe or douche, made of metal and to be employed with solutions based on alum, sulphate of zinc, sal eratus, vinegar or chloride of soda. Knowlton recommended this on the grounds of cheapness, harmlessness and because it placed control in women's hands, though it was, in fact, far from reliable. One further contraceptive device was apparently in use by the 1840s – the cervical cap. The vulcanization of rubber (1843) enabled the manufacture of fairly cheap and comfortable caps. Thus by 1850 the sponge, douche and cap were all available in Britain and all gave the woman some degree of control over conception.

The second half of the nineteenth century saw the introduction of a new improved diaphragm – the Mensinga diaphragm, or Dutch cap, invented by a Dutch doctor in the 1870s. The same decade, however, witnessed the trial of Annie Besant and Charles Bradlaugh (1877–8) for republishing a cheap edition of Knowlton's, *Fruits of Philosophy*. As Annie Besant pointed out, the publication of the cheap edition meant that working-class women could buy for 6d. what richer women could already purchase for several shillings at W.H. Smith's.

The question remains of how widely birth control was practised. Certainly the birth rate began to fall. This began in 1877 and continued until the 1920s. Certainly, too, contraceptive literature sold in very large numbers. For example, in the years 1876–7 over 165,000 copies of

Knowlton's *Fruits of Philosophy* were sold.[3] Magazines too
carried many advertisements for contraceptive devices,
including abortifacient pills. But yet, it would seem that
birth control was mainly practised by the middle classes.
Family size was by the turn of the century clearly marked by
divisions along class lines.[4] No doubt some better-off working-class families were practising some form of family limitation, but it was the members of the upper professional classes
who showed the greatest drop in fertility. Sheila Rowbotham
wrote that, 'the more effective methods were beyond the
reach of most working class women'.[5] Why should that be?
Part of the answer must be related to the cost of some of these
devices. The following list shows just how expensive some
contraceptives were for a family trying to live on 'Round
about a Pound a Week'.

> The Rendell Pessary – soluble quinine pessary at 2s. per
> doz.
> The Improved Prolapsus Check Pessaries – 3 sizes –
> 2s.3d. ea.
> Messinga Pessary with Spring Rim – 3 sizes – 3s. each.
> The Gem Pessary with Sponge Dome – 5s. each.
> The Spring Unique Pessary with Solid or Inflated Rim
> 1s.6d.
> Inflated Ball Pessary – 3 sizes – 3s.6d. each.
> Contraceptive Sponge – enclosed in a silk net – 1s. each.
> Quinine Compound – 1s.; 2s. per box.
> Vulcanite Syringe – 3s.6d. each.
> Vertical and Reverse Syringe – 5s.6d. each.[6]

One must also take into account the often overcrowded
and insanitary living conditions of the poor. Some of the more
elaborate devices – e.g. the Irrigator, a two pint canister
suspended above the bed – could scarcely practically be used
in working-class homes.

A married couple in mid-Victorian England could expect
5.5 to 6 live births: a couple in the period 1925 to 1929 could
expect 2.2. It was a dramatic change, but yet it was clear that
many couples were using some form of 'pre-industrial' birth
control – i.e. restraint, abstinence or the safe period.[7]
The period from the First World War onwards was to be

important in the spread of artificial methods of birth control. Clearly demand was there. The pathetic letters to the Women's Co-operative Guild, published in 1915, demonstrated the strain of repeated pregnancies on women's health and lives. Letters came from such women as the one whose plight is summarized, 'Wages 16s. to 18s. nine children, one still birth, one miscarriage.'[8] Fear of pregnancy haunted many women. 'I shouldn't mind married life so much if it wasn't for bedtime', was a remark frequently made to Mrs Eyles.[9] The response to public meetings, the vast sales of birth control literature and again the overwhelming number of letters to Marie Stopes testify to great demand for birth control.[10] Throughout the 1920s women in the Labour party fought for party support for birth control.[11]

The name of Marie Stopes stands out in the annals of the twentieth-century birth control movements. A eugenicist, interested in curbing the breeding of the 'C 3 population', she had little real understanding of the lives of working-class women. Yet Stopes, by setting contraception in the context of marriage, made birth control, hitherto linked with promiscuity, a respectable issue. Despite opposition from the church and the medical profession, she opened the first birth control clinic in Holloway, London. (Stopes favoured the cap as a means of contraception.) Within the next three years the clinic gave advice to 5,000 women.[12] The spread of birth control clinics is an important development which took place in the 1920s and 1930s. Later in 1921 the Malthusian League opened a clinic at Walworth.[13] The election of the first Labour government to power in 1924 proved a disappointment to birth controllers who hoped the state would now take responsibility for disseminating contraceptive advice. The campaign within and outside the Labour party was stepped up. Stella Browne and Dora Russell were active in the campaign. Voluntary clinics again felt that responsibility lay with them. In 1924 the Society for the Provision of Birth Control Clinics (actually the Walworth centre) encouraged the setting up of new clinics: the first of these to open outside London was in Wolverhampton in May 1926. Others followed. The fight within the Labour party continued and progressive Labour-controlled councils began to take an interest. In 1924 Brighton Council called upon the government to set up birth control clinics – but not until 1930 did the government partially give way by conceding that existing Maternity and Child Welfare clinics could give birth control instruction to mothers whose health would be injured by further pregnancies (Memorandum 153/MCW). In 1930 all the major birth control organizations, including Stopes's, came together to form the National Birth Control Council and in 1931 this became the National Birth Control Association (NBCA). Stopes did not remain long and was soon off in her independent way again. Memorandum 153/MCW and subsequent government circulars in the 1930s provided local authorities and regional hospital boards with the power to set up birth control clinics themselves or to assist the NBCA in providing voluntary clinics. There was actually no compunction to do so and there were many local disputes on the issue of birth control clinics in the 1930s between those who were demanding facilities and those who were fiercely opposed to them. In fact, the result of government policy and the activities of the NBCA meant that the number of clinics increased from under 20 in the decade 1921–31 to about 60 in the decade 1931–41 and to about 140 in 1951. The co-operation between the State and the NBCA in the 1930s meant that by the outbreak of the Second World War the idea of family planning had been integrated into the machinery of the state. Finally we should note that a fall in population growth in the 1930s and fears of a dwindling population influenced the NBCA to change its name in 1939 to the Family Planning Association.

Provision in Scotland lagged behind England. However, in the mid-1930s two official reports (see below) recommended wider provision of contraceptive advice in Scotland. The NBCA sent Miss Holland to Glasgow in 1936: Mrs Grey took over as Scottish adviser to form branches and clinics. In May 1939 the NBCA organized a deputation to the Scottish Office to urge greater local authority action in giving contraceptive advice. In Scotland – in contrast to England and Wales – private practitioners undertook more maternity and child welfare work. As Audrey Leathard points out, by 1939 six voluntary clinics existed but only five out of a possible fifty-five Scottish authorities had any sort of provision.[14]

I have so far made no mention of abortion. It was illegal for most of our period (up till 1803 it was legal prior to 'quickening') but nevertheless it was resorted to by many women. In nineteenth-century magazines many advertisements claimed 'to remove blockages'. N.E. Himes's study of abortion in 1927 revealed a high number of miscarriages and abortions among working-class women.[15] In 1939 an official surmise of the number of deaths annually attributable to abortion was between 110,000 and 150,000.[16] Local evidence, presented in the fight to set up birth control clinics shows that abortion was widely practised. Abortion was illegal under The Offences against the Person Act. The 1929 Infant Life Preservation Act reaffirmed the illegality of abortion, *except* where it could be proved that an abortion had been performed to save the life of the mother. The Abortion Law Reform Society, founded in 1936, although strongly supported by feminists such as Stella Browne (who believed abortion was a woman's right), argued for a change in the law on the grounds of the high incidence of maternal deaths from illicit abortions.[17] One legal judgment, made in the 1930s, however, is important. A judgment made by Justice MacNaghten in 1938 indicated that it was lawful for a doctor to terminate a pregnancy in order to safeguard a woman's mental health and to prevent her from becoming 'a mental and physical wreck'.[18] This decision left many loopholes and ambiguities in the law, often helping wealthy women procure abortions but of little help to most women, but the whole issue of abortion was not seriously confronted until the 1960s.

LESBIAN EXISTENCE

It is important not to define female sexuality as exclusively heterosexual. There has been, of course, enormous pressure on women, and men, to conform to heterosexuality, but according to Lilian Faderman's study, based on letters, diaries and literary accounts, this has not always been the case.[19] She writes of the 'passionate friendships' and undying fidelity with which some women, mainly middle-class, lived their lives together. According to her work it was only in the second half of the nineteenth century that attitudes towards such relationships changed. Sensational lesbian literature began to appear and women who loved other women were labelled 'true inverts'. With the spread of Freudian ideas in this century lesbianism – or a sustaining relationship between two women – was condemned as deviancy. Faderman's work is fascinating and one of the interesting points she raises relates to the connection between lesbianism and feminism. It would be interesting, if possible, to explore this link.

Much of Faderman's writing concerns literate, often fairly affluent, lesbians. The social pressures and even more economic pressures to conform to heterosexuality must have weighed much more heavily on working-class women, whose main hope of economic survival was marriage. If they remained unmarried they risked losing their jobs if their sexual orientation was known. Precisely because of a fear of social ostracism or of losing a job, many lesbians have remained invisible. It is this invisibility which makes lesbian history hard to track down – but I think it is worth trying, I have chosen the term 'lesbian existence', suggested by Adrienne Rich, as a more accurate term for our purposes than lesbianism.[20] In suggesting that local groups try to investigate this subject, I am suggesting that they try to find out about the *lifestyles* of lesbian women in the past.

The sources in this chapter are arranged somewhat differently than in the other chapters. I have arranged the sources under the three main areas of investigation outlined, i.e. illegitimacy, birth control and lesbian existence. There is some cross-referencing.

ILLEGITIMACY

Secondary sources
P. Laslett, *Family Life and Illicit Love in Earlier Generations*, Cambridge University Press, 1977.

Primary sources

Parish registers

Parish registers, noting baptisms, marriages and deaths have been kept in England and Wales since 1538. They are the prime source of information down to the 1830s. Unfortunately they have not all survived, but where they have, they are an excellent source. Some of them have been printed. Printed registers are listed by A. M. Burke.[21] The original documents may still be kept in the parish church, or in the local or diocesan record office. The wording for illegitimate births varies, but it is usually quite clear. For example,

> 1614. Frendlesse the sonne of Joane Robinsonne base gotten as she sayeth by one John Longe, was baptized first of November. (Edingley, Nottinghamshire).[22]

Often children are simply labelled bastard. At least one parish – Edgmond, Salop – kept a special bastard register and is full of invective against loose living.[23]

Sometimes parish accounts survive giving details of expenses paid for the lying-in of a poor woman who bore an illegitimate child. The parish would be anxious to return her to her home parish, which would have to keep her from the Poor Rate. Finally, it is possible to track down children in a parish who were born less than nine months after their parents' marriage. It is simply a matter of cross-referencing between the births and marriage entries.

Court records

Single women were sometimes driven to infanticide because they would be unable to earn a living if they had also to care for a child. If discovered, women suspected of infanticide would be brought to trial before a court – usually the Assize Court.

It is possible to track down accounts of these trials. Actually they are most easily read in local newspaper accounts, which report fully on Assize trials. The records themselves, as mentioned above, are held for the most part centrally, e.g. in The Public Record Office or for Wales in the National Library of Wales. The court records are much fuller than the newspaper accounts. This example comes from Swansea, Glamorgan. The indictment charged one Sarah Jones, a domestic servant, in June 1872 of:

> Not having the fear of God before her eyes and being moved insidiously by the instigation of the devil, did feloniously wilfully and of her malice aforethought did kill and murder the infant female child of her the said Sarah Jones then recently born of her body of her the said Sarah Jones; Against the peace of Our Lady the Queen.[24]

The witnesses' depositions (statements) include a detailed account given by Sarah's mistress, who suspected that she had borne a child, and an account rendered by a female neighbour, who found the child's body near the railway line. The various statements make it clear that Sarah was going about her work in the house immediately after her confinement. The doctor's evidence proved the child had been born alive and then suffocated.

From the time of Elizabeth I the parish was responsible for the maintenance of bastards. Various attempts were made to shift the burden on to the mother and putative father but the parish often paid in the end. Bearing an illegitimate child was, in fact, a sin. An Act of James I, modified by another of 1810, authorized justices to commit to prison 'a lewd woman who shall have a bastard which shall be chargeable to the parish'.[25] In fact this act was only, understandably, very patchily enforced, but it was sometimes acted upon. The named father would have to give a bond indemnifying the parish from the cost of supporting his child or a recognizance, with security to appear at the next Quarter Sessions Court. If he did not do so, he was put into gaol.

The records of the Court of Quarter Sessions – i.e. rolls and minute books, contain some interesting details. They show attempts to extract maintenance from the father, details of punishment of 'unmarried mothers' in the local house of correction and expenses of her lying-in and removal back to her home parish. Quarter Sessions records are usually held in the local county record office.

Coroners' records
Local record offices may have documents entitled Returns of
Coroners' Inquests. These contain two sorts of relevant information, i.e. the records of the deaths of new-born infants (in
very many cases, illegitimate) and the records of details of
women who died from abortions. The following Welsh
examples illustrate the usefulness of this source. They come
from Swansea, Newbridge, Merthyr and Ogmore. I include
only the most important columns in the table below.

Return of Coroner's inquest

Name of Deceased	Nature of Injury	Verdict	Age	Date of Death	Date of Inquest	Place of Inquest
Swansea						
Newborn male child	found dead	Manslaughter	—	—	18 June 1871	Aberavon
Mary Davies	Sudden	Haemorrhage after procuring an abortion	23	15 Sep 1871	9 Oct 1871	Penclawdd
Newbridge						
Newly born female child	Found on side of River Taff	Wilful murder	—	—	16 Jan 1875	Traveller's Rest Inn
Merthyr						
Child unknown	Drowned	Wilful murder of infant	—	—	7 Dec 1869	White Horse, Cwmbran
Ogmore						
Mary Ann David	Drowned by her mother Catherine David	Wilful murder	20 mth	12 Dec 1872	14 Dec 1872	Prince of Wales Inn, Kenfig Hill[26]

These records contain bare facts and leave us wondering
about the circumstances of the crime and of what happened to
the people who were charged. The answers can often be found
in local newspapers, where details are usually recorded in the
period directly after an inquest.

Government reports
The first to be mentioned in the context of illegitimacy must
be the printed *Reports of the Registrar General on Births*,

Deaths and Marriages. These date from the 1840s and they are available in major libraries.

They are packed with tables giving information – usually county by county – on births, deaths and marriages. The tables dealing with births distinguish the legitimate from the illegitimate. The report covering the year 1865, for example, provided the following information on the northern counties:

County	Children born out of wedlock to every 100 births
Durham	5.4
Northumberland	7.8
Cumberland	11.7
Westmorland	9.6

The London Figure was 4.4.[27]

There are separate reports for Scotland. In 1863, for example, the illegitimacy figures for the main regions of Scotland were:

Scotland	Per cent of illegitimate births
Insular Districts	4.9
Mainland Rural Districts	10.6
Town Districts	9.7

The counties of Banff and Elgin incidentally had illegitimacy rates of over 16 per cent.[28]

The issue of bastards is closely associated with the administration of the Poor Law, which was the subject of government investigations. The *Report of the Royal Commission on the Poor Law* (1834) – XXVIII runs to 22 volumes – but a synopsis has conveniently been published in a single paperback.

The Report was very harsh on unmarried mothers. It quotes many local witnesses, who believed that some women made a living from bearing illegitimate children. Perhaps they did. This extract comes from Lincolnshire.

John Kirkham, Assistant Overseer, Louth,
Lincolnshire, has had six parishes at a time under his
charge. With respect to the women, in the course of my
personal acquaintance with those parishes I have had to
manage, as well as from extensive inquiry, I find there
are numbers in most parishes who have from two to four
children, receiving different sums of money with each
according to the ability of the putative father; so that the
sum the woman receives with the whole of the children,
and what the mother can earn, enables them to live as
comfortably, or indeed more so, than most families in the
neighbourhood. It may be truly said, that the money she
receives is more than sufficient to repay her for the loss
her misconduct has occasioned her, and it really becomes
a source of emolument and is looked upon by others as an
encouragement to vice. Many of those escape
punishment of any sort, and if some of them go to the
house of correction for twelve months, it appears to have
very little effect either upon them or upon the morals of
others.[29]

The commissioners recommended that unmarried mothers
should no longer be sent to gaol and that they should no
longer be removed from the parish. On the other hand, they
placed the full penalties for illegitimacy on the woman: 'If our
recommendations are adopted a bastard will be what
Providence appears to have ordained it should be, a burthen
on its mother, and, where she cannot maintain it, on her
parents.'[30]

Oral sources
To trace the attitude towards 'unmarried mothers' in this
century, the oral interview will be invaluable. I am not pro-
posing that researchers dig up women's painful past experiences by interviewing now elderly unmarried women who
bore children, but almost everyone will know someone who
had an illegitimate child. I recently heard an interview in
S.E. London, conducted by one of a group of women who were
investigating their local past: the respondent told a horror
story of how an unmarried, pregnant girl, whom she knew

well, was treated. The girl was removed to a hospital in another part of the city for her confinement, throughout which nuns chastized her for her wickedness.

Among the questions to ask are, I suggest: What happened to girls who were unmarried and became pregnant? Where were their babies born? What happened to the baby? What did people (you) think of the young woman? The baby? Where did the young woman/baby live? Did the woman later marry? Do you know of any woman who had more than one illegitimate baby?

One woman whom I interviewed in West London, talking of the 1920s and 1930s, said: 'To have a baby if you weren't married, you wouldn't go home. It was a terrible disgrace. And to live with a man was terrible. You got talked about all over the shop. If you wore powder, they said you were no good.'[31]

BIRTH CONTROL

Secondary sources

J. A. and O. Banks, *Feminism and Family Planning in Victorian England*, Liverpool University Press, 1964.

P. Branca, *Silent Sisterhood: Middle Class Women in the Victorian Home*, London, Croom Helm, 1975, esp. Chapter 7.

P. Fryer, *The Birth Controllers*, London, Corgi, 1967.

K. Hindell and M. Simms, *Abortion Law Reformed*, London, Peter Owen, 1971.

P. Knight, 'Women and abortion in Victorian and Edwardian England', *History Workshop*, 4, Autumn 1977.

A. Leathard, *The Fight for Family Planning*, London, Macmillan, 1980.

A. McLaren, 'Women's Work and the regulation of family size: the question of abortion in nineteenth century England', *History Workshop*, 4, Autumn 1977.

A. McLaren, 'Abortion in England 1900–1914', *Victorian Studies*, 20,4, Summer 1977.

J. Peel and M. Potts, *Textbook of Contraceptive Practice*, Cambridge University Press, 1969 (very technical).

G. Weeks, *Sex, Politics and Society*, London, Longman, 1981.

Individual Studies
R. Hall, *Marie Stopes*, London, Virago, 1977.
S. Rowbotham, *A New World for Women: Stella Browne — Socialist Feminist*, London, Pluto, 1977.

Primary material in print
M. Llewelyn Davies, *Maternity Letters from Working Women*, London, Virago, 1978.
R. Hall, *Dear Dr. Stopes: Sex in the 1920's*, Harmondsworth, Penguin, 1981.
N. E. Himes, 'British birth control clinics', *Eugenics Review*, vol, XX, no. 3, 1928, pp. 157–65.
M. Spring Rice, *Working Class Wives: Their Health and Conditions*, London, Virago, 1981.

Articles on specific localities
A. Court, 'The Birmingham Family Planning Association 1927–1955', *Family Planning*, 4, 2, 1955.
C. Tamplin, 'Early days in Newcastle', *Family Planning*, 11.3.1962.

Contemporary Journals
The following are very important.
Birth Control News: The Statesman's Newspaper (1922–46) (BL/Fawcett).
This was the organ of Marie Stopes's Society for Constructive Birth Control. It contains a great deal of local information and provided a record of the development of birth control in Britain. The edition of October 1924 (vol III, no. 6), for example, contained accounts of Tom Cochrane, a Brighton councillor's, motion to urge the government to grant powers to local authorities to make financial provision for the establishment of clinics and of the mayor of Wrexham's advocacy of birth control in his town.
The New Generation (1922–76) (replaced *The Malthusian*; BL). It contains a great deal of useful local information. It is particularly interesting for its record of the activities of Stella Browne, who travelled and spoke widely.[32]
The Woman's Leader (1920–32) (BL/Fawcett).
This is another useful journal, which carefully noted and

monitored developments in the spread of birth control clinics throughout Britain. The extracts given below are dated 31 January 1930 and 20 June 1930.

Local Authorities and Birth Control.

Further information has come through during the past week, concerning the action of Local Authorities in response to the Shoreditch Borough Council's demand for support in its request to the Ministry of Health for leave to provide information on birth control through the medium of the local public health service. Recently we recorded the decision of the Bootle Borough Council and of the Birkenhead Health Committee to support the Shoreditch request. We now learn that the St. Helen's Council has taken similar action.

Congratulations to Warwickshire.

The Warwickshire County Council can be added to the list of those Local Health Authorities who have authorized the medical officers at all maternity centres under the Council to give medical information on birth control to married women. In the report of the County Council, the Public Health Committee in making their recommendations stated that they had received a letter from the Secretary of the Women's Co-operative Guild in the Coventry district enclosing the following resolution: 'That this meeting of the Coventry, Warwick, and Kenilworth District of the Women's Co-operative Guild notes with pleasure that a conference of Public Health Authorities held in London demanded that birth control information be given to all those desirous of obtaining the same. We desire that this information should be available to all married persons at all maternity centres within the City of Coventry and the county areas.' The time is indeed ripe, and it is satisfactory to note attention paid to organized women by their elected representatives.

Other journals well worth consulting include *Labour Woman* (BL), and *The National Council of Women's News* (Fawcett Library). The British Library and the Fawcett Library are the best places to get hold of these journals which are unfortunately not easily available outside London.

Sex manuals

Sex manuals or marriage manuals make interesting reading.
Old ones are usually abundantly available in second-hand
bookshops. Their usefulness is, however, somewhat questionable since it is impossible to estimate how far they
reflected practice or indeed influenced it. Many reveal very
interesting attitudes to female sexuality.

Bernarr Macfadden's, *Womanhood and Marriage* was
published in America in 1918 but was also sold in Britain. He
stated confidently,

> Man's passions are more easily aroused than woman's,
> and more insistent, because it is a man's nature to be
> active and energetic. Woman is by nature, negative and
> passive and for this reason is less easily stirred and can
> more readily control herself.

He went on to prescribe a remedy for 'marital excess' in the
first months of marriage, in the couple occupying separate
beds. He showed no confidence at all in *any* method of birth
control, believing them all to be harmful or ineffectual.[33]

Dr Oster Mann's, *Birth Control: Husband and Wife's
Handbook* (1930) has a distinctly commercial flavour. It is
packed with advertisements, some of which are most mysterious. Under the heading 'A Hint to Ladies' one advertisement
boasts that Dr Reynold's Pills 'never fail to give relief in all
women's complaints'. The pills are recommended as a safe
and sure cure for anaemia, irregularities, etc. They sold at 3/-
a box or 5/- for extra strong.

Oster Mann ran through the techniques of birth control—
always with advice of where appliances could be purchased.
He dismissed withdrawal because of 'its baneful effects on the
nervous system' and was sceptical of the safe period. Quite
rightly, since he gives as the time to avoid intercourse 'six
days before menstruation and nine or ten days afterwards.'
He went on to other methods.

> Dr. Oster Mann recommends his Soluble Quinine
> Pessaries, which are at once harmless and effectual in
> preventing conception. The use of these Soluble
> Pessaries is not at all repulsive to the most refined and

delicate feelings, and they possess distinct advantages when compared with other preventative checks. The sale of Dr. Oster Mann's Soluble Pessaries has increased considerably of late, consequent upon their becoming more generally known. With these Soluble Quinine Pessaries an injection is recommended, although not positively necessary, and need not be done until several hours have elapsed. For this purpose a good English Enema Syringe such as Higginson's, should be used. Those who can afford it should obtain the Hygienic Whirling Spray Syringe, the action of which is double – alternate douche and suction, removing all foreign matter from the vagina and the neck of the womb, but its special advantage is that it can be used in bed without fear of wetting the bed clothes.

When it is decided to use the Enema or Hygienic Whirling Spray Syringe, a reliable injection can be made by using 'Hygeoids', the Antiseptic Tablets, obtained from The Hygienic Stores, Ltd., 95, Charing Cross Road, London, W.C.2.[34]

Another sex manual which I found in a local second-hand shop was Dr Eustace Chesser's *Love Without Fear*.[35] Chesser was a prolific producer of such manuals. His work covers several pages in the British Library catalogue. My copy was the revised 1948 edition. Since the first edition of 1941, it had been reprinted thirteen times. He gives practical advice on sexual intercourse and on birth control – but, although apparently solicitous that women should enjoy sex and alarmed by the fact that 50 per cent of the women in the eastern cantons of Switzerland never experienced orgasm, his advice to women was to fake orgasm. 'Simulation of orgasm is within the power of any intelligent woman.'[36]

All the manuals of the pre-war period which I unearthed condemn masturbation or any homosexual practices.

Advertisements

Many magazines and newspapers ran advertisements for birth control devices and particularly for abortifacient drugs. The medical profession frequently complained about filthy

advertisements which lie on every breakfast table.[37] Many of
the pills, containing lead, skirted around the law by claiming
to treat anaemia and 'irregularities'.

A BOON TO WOMANKIND
'DR. PATTERSON'S'
FAMOUS PILLS
Contain no Irritative or Dangerous Drugs
THE GREAT REMEDY FOR
IRREGULARITIES OF EVERY DESCRIPTION
These Pills were used with unvarying success in the
treatment of all Ailments during Dr. Patterson's 30
years' experience in some of the largest institutions
abroad. They restore to their usual health, when
Pennyroyal and Steel, Pil Cochiac, Bitter Apple,
mixtures, pellets and tablets, etc. fail; they have the
approval of the Medical Profession, and are in daily
use at home and abroad. In all cases of anaemia,
lassitude, melancholy, variable appetite, weakness and
debility of every description they are the safest and most
efficacious medicine known; they may be safely taken
at any time, and their use according to the directions
given with each box, will quickly bring about the desired
effect. The great and constantly increasing sale of these
Pills is not the result of extensive advertising, but of
personal recommendations alone (a sure test of their
merits).
PERSONAL ATTENTION GIVEN TO ALL ORDERS.[38]

Much of this business was mail order and therefore laid
women open to blackmail. The following advertisements
come from a national and a local newspaper:

Widow Welch's female pills; prompt and reliable for
ladies 1/1 or 2/9 per box from all chemists,
(*News of the World*)

and

My special mixture of pills is guaranteed to be the most
reliable remedy known.
(Halifax Evening Courier)[39]

Government reports
Maternal mortality, abortion and changing trends in population became a focus of government attention in the 1920s and 1930s. The 1949 report on population is particularly useful because it surveys the fifty preceding years.

The following list covers England, Wales and Scotland:
J. Campbell, *Maternal Mortality*, London, Ministry of Health, 1924.
J. Campbell, *The Protection of Motherhood*, London, Ministry of Health, 1927.
Interim Report of the Departmental Committee on Maternal Mortality and Morbidity, London, Ministry of Health, 1930.
Final Report of the Departmental Committee on Maternal Mortality and Morbidity, London, Ministry of Health, 1932.
J. Campbell, *High Maternal Mortality in Certain Areas*, London, Ministry of Health, 1932.
C. A. Douglas and P. McKinlay, *Report on Maternal Morbidity and Mortality in Scotland*, Edinburgh, Department of Health for Scotland, 1935.
Report on the Scottish Health Services, Edinburgh, Department of Health for Scotland, 1936 (Cmd 5204).
Report on Investigation into Maternal Mortality and Morbidity, London, Ministry of Health, 1937.
Report of the Interdepartmental Committee on Abortion, London, Ministry of Health and Home Office, 1939.
E. Lewis Faning, *Report on an Enquiry into Family Limitation and its Influence on Human Fertility during the Past Fifty Years*, London, Royal Commission on Population, 1949.

Newspapers
Many national and local newspapers reported fully on birth control controversies and the setting up of clinics. The *Manchester Guardian* reported reactions to the establishment of a clinic in Salford throughout the spring of 1926. The Bishop raged against 'these strange filthy things' and against 'the powers of evil' in the Greengate clinic.[40] A protest meeting was held: this time a local canon opposed birth control on the grounds of the declining numbers of the white races and when reminded that the black man was his brother, he replied, 'But I would ask, do you desire him as a brother in

law?'[41] The next month the supporters of the clinic met and managed to avoid a rough house by only allowing supporters in.[42] In Cardiff, the medical officer spoke of the great demand for contraceptive information and warned that 'an alternative to birth control is being widely practised, namely self-induced abortion'.[43] Struggles to set up clinics in major cities such as Birmingham were fully reported in both national and local newspapers in the early 1930s.

Record sources

The archives of the Family Planning Association contain a wealth of information on birth control availability throughout Britain. The collection is housed in the David Owen Centre, University College, Cardiff. In order to consult the collection it is necessary to obtain permission in writing from The Family Planning Information Service. This collection contains FPA leaflets (stating the case for birth control), Ministry of Health memoranda to local authorities, resolutions of various women's organizations on the subject of birth control and a whole wealth of documentary evidence on struggles to set up clinics. It has especially interesting material for the 1930s.

The following letter issued by the Monmouthshire County Council shows a very unsympathetic attitude.

MONMOUTHSHIRE COUNTY COUNCIL

Dear Sir,

Birth Control

Adverting to your letter of the 14th inst. your District Councillors were of course not aware at the time they passed the resolution that the Public Health Committee have considered the subject matter of your letter on more than one occasion, and as recently as July last similar letters from three District Councils (following upon visits made by Mrs Joyce Daniels, the representative of the National Birth Control Association) were placed before them.

The County Council are acting with entire accordance with the Memoranda issued by the Ministry of Health upon this important question, and in cases where there are medical grounds for giving advice on contraceptive methods, such advice is being tendered to married women who are in attendance at the Council's Centres, but such advice is limited to cases where further pregnancy would be detrimental to health.

Mrs Daniels has been officially informed by the County Medical Officer on at least two occasions that the County Council were carrying out the Memoranda of the Ministry of Health referred to. Apparently this repeated assurance is not sufficient for Mrs Daniels, and what the agitation really amounts to is the establishment of Birth Control clinics for all and sundry.

Apart from the practice mentioned above, the County Council have no power to establish Birth Control Clinics within the Administrative County for supplying indiscriminate advice.

Yours truly,

Thomas Hughes

Clerk to the Council.

W. H. Trump,
Clerk to Rhymney U. D. Council,
   Rhymney.[44]

Eventually, Monmouthshire fell to the birth controllers and a clinic was set up to serve the whole county. The next extract shows how much the new clinic's services were appreciated.

MONMOUTHSHIRE BRANCH

A feature of this clinic is that, although it has to serve for the whole of the county, patients have turned up from remote parts of the area and have been very willing to pay the clinic charges on top of heavy bus fares. They have also been fairly regular in the matter of return visits.

I have had many requests for minor gynaecological ailments to be treated in the clinic, and were we in a position to enlarge the scope of the clinic in this direction, I believe the attendance would greatly increase. One of our most grateful patients is a woman who came down from a little remote village on the top of a mountain. She was over 40, and looked terribly ill and worried. She came asking for Birth Control advice, which our doctor gave her, but it appeared she had been living in a state of dread, believing she had cancer of the womb. Of this fear doctor was able to relieve her mind, and the difference in this patient's mental and physical condition is tremendous.

74 new patients have attended since the clinic was opened, an average of 6 per month, which is all the more satisfactory in view of the fact that we do not get any patients referred from the Health Authorities.[45]

Finally in Merthyr Tydfil the problem was rather different. In 1938 few women were attending the clinic. Part of the explanation was the availabiltiy of contraceptives sold in slot machines in packs of cigarettes and sweets.

The Marie Stopes papers are in The British Library Stopes Collection in the Manuscript Department. The collection is only currently being organized and catalogued.

It is worth inquiring locally, especially if you know the location of clinics, regarding the survival and access to local birth control clinic records.

The main body to consult for information on campaigns to legalize abortion is the Abortion Law Reform Association – ALRA. ALRA was founded in 1936.

Records and publications of women's groups

Several women's organizations worked hard to promote birth control. Among these I would mention The Women's Co-operative Guild. Their archives are held in the British Library of Political Science in the London School of Economics. Prior permission to use this library must always be sought because of lack of space. Women within the Labour party also actively campaigned to achieve party endorsement for birth control and for the spread of clinics. Labour party records, particularly for the 1920s, will give a picture of their activities. Labour party conference reports should be held in major libraries and failing that, they may be consulted at the Labour Party Library.

Oral

Finally, it would be very worthwhile to question older women on the availability of birth control advice in your area. I suggest questions should take the line of local availability rather than questioning respondents about their personal use of birth control – unless the interviewer knows the respondent very well. In that case some of the following questions could be asked: when did you learn about the 'facts of life'? Where? From your mother? Older sisters or brothers? From friends? At school? At work? What sort of wrong information was circulated? How many children did you have? Was that the number you wanted? What contraceptive knowledge did you have? Where did you learn that? Was there a birth control clinic in your area? Was your GP sympathetic to women seeking birth control advice?

Diana Gittins's oral history interviews of women between the wars are interesting to read and are printed in *Oral History*.[46] The following interview was conducted by a friend with her mother-in-law, who lives in Fulham. The interviewee was born in 1902 into a working-class family and married in the early 1920s: she had two children

Q. How did you avoid having more than two children?
A. I turned my face to the wall by making out I was asleep.
Q. You didn't use any birth control at all?
A. No. I simply said NO.
Q. Was this usual? Was this what everybody did in those days if they didn't want a big family?
A. Oh, No. Some of their husbands would beat the life out of them.
Q. But there wasn't any birth control clinic?
A. No, and it was a terrible thing.[47]

Whether facilities were available or not this woman clearly did not know of them and perhaps might not have 'liked to' take advantage of them.

Museum collections

The actual artefacts – and very strange looking some of them are – may be seen in The Marie Stopes Collection in the

Science Museum in London and The Collis Collection at the London School of Economics. The first collection is an open exhibition but in order to gain access to The Collis Collection it is advisable to write first explaining that you wish to see this collection and requesting a day library ticket in order to gain admittance.

LESBIAN SOURCES

Secondary
G. H. Bell (ed.), *The Hamwood Papers of the Ladies of Llangollen and Caroline Hamilton*, London, Macmillan, 1930.
L. Faderman, *Surpassing the Love of Men*, London, Junction, 1981.
E. O. Somerville and M. Ross, *Irish Memories*, New York, Longman, 1917.
N. Nicolson, *Portrait of a Marriage*, London, Atheneum, 1973.
Una Lady Trowbridge, *Life and Death of Radclyffe Hall*, London, Hammond, Hammond & Co., 1961 (copyright date).

Record sources
I can only suggest that investigators contact the Lesbian Archives Collective in Manchester and other feminist archive collections, which are listed at the end of the book.

Newspaper/journals
The only Lesbian journals which I have discovered are all post-1945, e.g. *Arena 3* and *Sappho*. The best hope, therefore, of discovering lesbian history seems to lie with oral history.

Oral sources
It is very important that older lesbians should be interviewed. The life of such women, especially in the provinces, remains hidden. Given the many pressures to conform to 'heterosexual normality' and given the fact that these seem to have been even stronger in the period under consideration, it may not be easy to find women to interview. One needs contacts and it may be a good idea to get in touch with the

local Campaign for Homosexual Equality, CHE: you can probably get a contact address from the newspaper *Gay News*. If older women are willing to be interviewed on this subject some of the questions which it may be useful to pose are as follows: how old were you when you first realized that you were lesbian? Was it easy or hard to meet other lesbians? Was there any lesbian social life? Any clubs, bars, etc.? How did other people react to lesbians, e.g. in school, at work, socially? Would a gay woman lose her job if her lesbianism was known? Did you feel oppressed by society's attitudes towards gay people?

There are clearly a lot more pertinent questions to ask but they may well become impertinent and unless one knows the interviewee quite well one must be cautious in pursuing one's historical curiosity at the expense of other people's feelings. I recorded an interview with one older lesbian. She came from a comfortable London middle-class background, recognized her lesbianism early in life and has been active in various gay organizations since the 1960s. She is a very interesting person and a friend so I was delighted that she agreed to be interviewed. Here are some extracts from the interview.

Olive b. 1916.

Well I discovered it when I was about 14 or 15 when I fell for my head girl at school – convent school – and she understood but she didn't say anything to me. We stayed friends after she left at 18 and went to university but when I was 18 she told me all about it and I was very relieved. I wondered why I hadn't wanted to go out with boy friends like all my school friends had and we started an affair. I felt no guilt whatsoever – we just went into it and it was gorgeous. My mother, who was very, very strict about boy friends – it was amazing in those days women didn't think that sort of thing – she used to invite my friend to come and stay weekends with me and so I had no difficulty whatsoever. If I went home with B. everything was perfect – you see it kept me away from all those nasty boy friends she was worried about.

Q.   Was there any sort of organized gay scene?

A.   The first time I realized that there was a gay scene was after the war. Before the war I don't know. We were happy ourselves and then the war broke out and she went (she was half French) into the French resistance. Unfortunately just before the end of the war she was captured by the Germans, she got pneumonia and she died. For a long while I wasn't interested in anybody else then somebody took me to the Gateways in Chelsea. In those days it was very, very *comme il faut* – everybody wore tweed suits or pin striped suits, either with slacks or with a skirt and a nice white shirt and a tie and an eton crop.

Q.   Were they all women there or was it a mixed club?

A.   Completely women. All females. They had a beautiful three piece orchestra, they had a piano, a violin and a double bass, as far as I remember. Sort of palm court. It was really sweet. You could go there and have tea and for drinks at night and some people danced together but not an awful lot. It was more talking to each other. The younger, daring ones danced together. The atmosphere was very nice, very formal and very nice. There wasn't any backbiting. Nobody was trying to take anybody else's friends away from them. Very, very nice.

Q.   Were people open about being gay?

A.   No. It was very difficult to find out in those days. . . . In the thirties and forties and fifties it was difficult – it was really from the sixties onwards that it became easier and you could recognize people.

Q.   Were there any other clubs?

A.   There were. One in Notting Hill Gate. I went to one before the war in Chelsea. That was very select.

Q.   What sort of people went there?

A.   Middle-class and upper middle-class. Nothing but. Really it was quite a snobbish affair.

Q.   Did being gay ever affect you in your job?

A.   I was fortunate. Apart from the war, when everybody had to work, I didn't go to work until I was well into my thirties.[48]

NOTES

1 P. Laslett, *Family Life and Illicit Love in Earlier Generations*, Cambridge University Press, 1977. See in particular Chapter 3, 'Long-term trends in bastardy'.

2 Note in particular P. Fryer, *The Birth Controllers*, London, Corgi, 1967; A. Leathard, *The Fight for Family Planning*, London, Macmillan, 1980. (Leathard's is a very clear account of twentieth-century development.) See also G. Weeks, *Sex, Politics and Society*, London, Longman, 1981.

3 F. B. Smith, 'Sexuality in Britain 1800–1900', *University of Newcastle (Australia) Historical Journal*, vol. 2, pt 3, 1974, p. 23.

4 G. Weeks, op. cit., p. 45; P. Branca, *Silent Sisterhood: Middle Class Women in the Victorian Home*, London, Croom Helm, 1975, pp. 114–23.

5 S. Rowbotham, *Hidden From History: 300 Years of Women's Oppression and the Fight Against It*, London, Pluto, 1973, p. 76.

6 Branca, op. cit., p. 136. Note that various pessaries came in only three sizes: they now come in many sizes.

7 The following survey is based on Weeks's useful and full account, op. cit. The safe period was incidentally, believed for a long time to be directly between menstrual periods – i.e. it was far from safe.

8 M. Llewelyn Davies, *Maternity: Letters from Working Women*, London, Virago, 1978, pp. 20–1.

9 M. L. Eyles, *The Woman in the Little House*, London, Grant Richards, 1922, p. 129.

10 Weeks, op. cit., p. 187. Marie Stopes's *Married Love*, published in 1918, had been reprinted twenty-two times and sold 400,000 copies by 1923. For a selection of the letters to Marie Stopes, see R. Hall, *Dear Dr. Stopes*, Harmondsworth, Penguin, 1981.

11 Leathard, op. cit., gives a detailed account.

12 Ibid., p. 13.

13 Ibid., p. 15. The whole struggle to set up birth control clinics is very clearly recounted by Leathard and my account draws on it.

14 Ibid., p. 66.

15 N. E. Himes, 'British birth control clinics', *Eugenics Review*, vol. XX, no. 3, 1928, pp. 157–65.

16 Leathard, op. cit., p. 37.

17 On Stella Browne see S. Rowbotham, *A New World for Women: Stella Browne – Socialist Feminist*, London, Pluto, 1977.

18 Leathard, op. cit., pp. 63–4.

19 L. Faderman, *Surpassing the Love of Men*, London, Junction, 1981.

20 A. Rich, *Compulsory Heterosexuality and Lesbian Existence*, London, Onlywomen Press, 1981.

21 A. M. Burke, *Key to Parish Registers*, London, 1908. See also J. West, *Village Records*, London, Macmillan, 1962.
22 Cited W. E. Tate, *The Parish Chest*, Cambridge University Press, 1960, p. 62.
23 Ibid., p. 61.
24 Public Record Office, Assize 72/2.
25 U. R. Q. Henriques, *Before the Welfare State*, London, Longman, 1979. This gives an interesting and clear account.
26 Glamorgan County Record Office, Cardiff. Return of Coroners' Inquests (Swansea, Newbridge, Ogmore, Merthyr Districts), 1869–75.
27 *28th. Annual Report of the Registrar General of Births, Deaths, and Marriages in England*, 1867, p. xiv.
28 *9th. Annual Report of the Registrar General of Births, Deaths and Marriages in Scotland*, 1866, p. v.
29 S. G. and E. O. Checkland, *The Poor Law Report of 1834*, Harmondsworth, Penguin, 1974, p. 262.
30 Ibid., p. 482.
31 Oral Interview. Bella. Tape 17, side 2. Interviewed by Jennifer L. Homer and Eileen Hannaford.
32 See, Rowbotham, *A New World for Women*.
33 B. Macfadden, *Womanhood and Marriage*, New York, Physical Culture Corporation, 1918.
34 Dr Oster Mann, *Birth Control: Husband and Wife's Handbook*, London, 1930, pp. 49–50.
35 E. Chesser, *Love without Fear*, London, Rich & Cowan, 1948.
36 Ibid., p. 82.
37 P. Knight, 'Women and abortion in Victorian and Edwardian England', *History Workshop*, 4, 1977, p. 61.
38 This advertisement is taken from Oster Mann, op. cit., but it appeared very widely.
39 Cited Knight, loc. cit., p. 61. *News of the World*, 7 January 1912, and *Halifax Evening Courier*, 2 January 1912.
40 *Manchester Guardian*, 22 March 1926.
41 Ibid., 14 April 1926.
42 Ibid., 21 May 1926.
43 *Daily Herald*, 21 April 1932.
44 Records of Family Planning Association, Cardiff.
45 Ibid.
46 D. G. Gittins, 'Married life and birth control between the wars', *Oral History*, vol. 3, no. 2, 1975.
47 Oral Interview. Bella. Tape 17, side 2.
48 Oral Interview. Olive. Tape 20, side 1.

Chapter seven

Women and politics

If I were writing about women and politics in present-day Britain I would quite naturally take a broad view of the subject. I would look at women in 'mainstream' politics, i.e. the male-dominated world of the political parties, but I would also automatically look at the area of feminist politics i.e. at the writings and activities of women in the Women's Movement, The National Abortion Campaign, Women's Aid, Rape Crisis, lesbian campaigns and in the anti-nuclear weapons peace movement – particularly at the Women for Life on Earth Movement. In turning to the past it is important that I look for women not only in so-called 'mainstream' politics but in feminist and alternative politics too.

This chapter, like the others in this book, is not concerned with famous names. It is not about the remarkable women who made the breakthrough to become MPs and cabinet ministers. It is about women's political involvement in their own localities and the sources suggested below are local rather than national. I have taken the terms politics and political action to mean not only long campaigns but spontaneous local actions which lasted hours or days rather than months and years. By including short-lived actions and by stretching the conventional usage of the word politics to include feminist politics, I have greatly broadened the spectrum. Now if we look for women who were involved in 'politics', we can be confident that we will find them.

SURVEY

Women have been active in politics throughout the period spanned by this book. Corn riots were common in Britain in the eighteenth and early nineteenth century. These riots, caused by a scarcity of corn and by high prices, frequently involved women: often women were the dominant elements.

In Wales in the 1790s women, 'were the most vocal extreme members of the mob who marched from Llangyfelach to Swansea in February 1793 and from the parish of Llangattock to Beaufort in March 1800.'[1] 1795 has been called, 'the year of . . . the revolt of the housewives.'[2] Similar food riots, dominated by women, had taken place in Dover in 1740, in Taunton 1753 and in London in 1800.[3] In Nottingham in 1812 a spectacular protest against food prices was staged by women:

> The disturbance began by several women in Turncalf alley sticking a halfpenny loaf on the top of a fishing rod after having streaked it with red ochre and tied around it was a shred of black cloth, emblematic it was said of 'bleeding famine decked in sack cloth'.[4]

But women were not moved to action only by food prices. In the general election of 1831 in Merthyr Tydfil, a South Wales iron town, thousands of working-class men and women were moved to insurrection: one of the causes to spark off that mass rising was the heartless actions of the Court of Requests in collecting debts in a period of severe depression.[5] These examples are not isolated incidents.[6] Chartism was a powerful popular movement from the late 1830s in which women were greatly involved. The movement centred around the Great Charter. The first draft included votes for men and women over twenty-one: its other demands were a secret ballot, no property qualifications for MPs, equal constituencies and annual parliaments. It has been estimated that women formed at least 80 political unions and chartist associations between 1837 and 1844.[7] Yet how little local work has been done on these women chartists! These women were active in London, Halifax, Sheffield, Newcastle upon Tyne, Birmingham, Glasgow, Nottingham and elsewhere.

Middle-class women were involved in several political campaigns in the first half of the nineteenth century. They participated in the Anti-Slavery Movement but their activities in this appear to have been restricted to fund-raising.[8] As late as 1853 the Bristol and Clifton Ladies Anti-Slavery Society appealed for a gentleman to organize their public meetings since this was not considered as a suitable activity

for a lady.[9] Middle-class women were also involved in the
Anti-Corn Law League (which strove to abolish the corn laws
that tended to keep prices high), but their activities in this
movement went beyond fund-raising. The female secretary of
the National Bazaar Committee wrote to working men
urging them, 'to stand forth and denounce as unholy, unjust
and cruel all restrictions on the price of food' and assured
them that, 'the ladies are resolved to perform their arduous
part'.[10] Other women campaigned for legal changes in child
custody, divorce and with regard to married women's
property.[11] This activity took place throughout the 1850s and
1860s but it was not until the 1870s that a very clear link
between the political activity of middle-class women and
feminism emerged. This fusion can first be seen in Josephine
Butler's campaign against the Contagious Diseases Acts.

These acts were passed in the 1860s and were aimed at
controlling venereal disease among the armed forces: they
empowered the police to pick up, medically examine and lock
up women suspected of prostitution in port and garrison
towns. Infected women would be put in a 'lock up' whilst those
free from disease had to report for regular checks. Josephine
Butler viewed prostitutes as the victims of the economic
position of women and of the dual standard of morality which
allowed men to sin with impunity, i.e. her thinking, though
firmly rooted in her Christianity, was clearly linked to
feminist thinking. Given the propriety of the times this was
an amazing struggle for respectable women to have taken on.
The campaign led to the defeat of a pro-Acts parliamentary
candidate in Colchester in 1870 and eventually to the aboli-
tion of the Acts in 1886. (The impact of the CD Acts upon
women in two English ports, Plymouth and Southampton,
and the local campaigns against the Acts there have already
been examined.)[12]

By the 1870s many working-class women were becoming
involved in the Trade Union Movement and in socialist
politics (see Chapter 4). By 1874 Emma Paterson had
founded the Women's Protective and Provident League (later
the Women's Trade Union League) with the aim of organiz-
ing and politicizing working women. Women were active in
early socialist parties such as the Social Democratic

Federation (SDF) and the Independent Labour Party (ILP) long before suffrage was achieved. Many other women joined the Co-operative Women's Guild, which after 1889 under the general secretaryship of Margaret Llewelyn Davies became staunchly feminist and supportive of the suffrage campaign. It was also to be very active in campaigning for better living and childcare facilities for working-class women.

But it is the struggle for the vote that commands our attention. The vote was the focus and the prime demand of a great mass movement of women. Unfortunately, historians' interest in the suffrage has concentrated on the activities of the leadership and we are led to believe that the suffrage was predominantly a middle-class movement. Liddington and Norris's model book, *One Hand Tied Behind Us*, which examines the efforts of the working-class radical suffragists in Lancashire, has broken away from the narrow emphasis on the national leadership.[13] Women all over Britain were involved but yet the local histories remain to be written: sadly, they could have been better done twenty or thirty years ago when oral interviews were still a possibility. The story of the campaign for the vote is complex and too long to relate here. Suffice it to say that the main groupings were the National Union of Women's Suffrage Societies (NUWSS), which was a constitutional organization; the Women's Social and Political Union (WSPU), which was the militant branch and which engaged in acts of violence against property; the Women's Freedom League (WFL) split off from the WSPU and encouraged resistance to the payment of various taxes. All these groups had local branches. In Scotland the Scottish Federation of the National Union of Women's Suffrage Societies, established in 1910, embraced all the independent non-militant suffrage organizations outside the WFL. By 1914 the Scottish NUWSS had established 63 societies from Orkney down to the border with England and employed five paid organizers. Both the WSPU and the WFL were strong in Scotland and the militant activities of the former included the bombing of the Royal Observatory in Edinburgh and arson at Kelso race track.

The suffrage campaigners achieved a partial victory in 1918 when married women over thirty were allowed to vote in local government elections and when women over thirty were granted the vote in parliamentary elections. Not until 1928 were all women over twenty-one enfranchised. However, from 1918 onwards we can begin to look in earnest for women in local government politics and in local branches of political parties. Yet just because women were at last enfranchised, this does not mean that we should cease to look for other political activity on the part of women. The tradition of spontaneous direct action continued. During the First World War women in Glasgow, London and elsewhere organized rent strikes (see below). In Merthyr Tydfil in the mid-1930s women, like their militant counterparts a hundred years earlier, rose up and stormed a government department. This time the issue was a proposed dole cut and the women led an attack on the employment exchange: the cut was abandoned. Other non-parliamentary activity on specific issues of importance to women continued and some of these movements are referred to below.

Writing of the history of British feminist activity between the wars, Olive Banks laments the fact that the research simply has not been done but confidently expects, 'the recent interest in feminist studies will produce some of the necessary research before very long' (1981).[14] I hope that much of this research will be local.

At a national level in 1919 the old non-militant NUWSS was renamed the National Union of Societies for Equal Citizenship (NUSEC). This and other pressure groups, such as Viscountess Rhondda's Six Points Group, attempted to ensure that women's rights issues were brought before Parliament. In the 1920s feminists continued to fight for equal suffrage, which was not granted until 1928, and to fight on feminist and welfare issues such as equal guardianship of children, equality in divorce and widows' pensions.[15] All these aims were attained in the 1920s largely through the support of the Labour party. However, the 1920s saw a split in feminist aims caused by dissension on two issues. Firstly, there was the emergence of 'new feminism', which placed special emphasis on the differences between men and women and accentuated the centrality of women's role as wives and mothers. This was scarcely new but it did cause a split in feminist ranks by alienating women like Viscountess Rhondda and Winifred Holtby who simply wanted to remove any existing barriers between the sexes. The 'new feminists', such as Eleanor Rathbone, sought to introduce a system of 'family endowments' which would make married women and their children independent of their husbands. The second major point of division centred on the question of protective legislation. The division on this issue hardened along class lines: whilst middle-class women saw it as a hindrance to a woman's right to work, working-class women largely supported it. Such divisions weakened British feminism and the equal rights wing of the movement seemed to be subsumed within the welfare wing of feminism, which sought better welfare for women and children. When equal suffrage was at last attained NUSEC split into two – along the lines of the existing divisions within the movement, i.e. the National Council for Equal Citizenship, which continued to press for equal rights, and the new body the union of Townswomen's Guilds, the main function of which was educational. The Townswomen's Guild can scarcely be thought of as at all political. They sought to avoid controversy and concentrated on housewifely and consumer issues. Occasionally in the 1930s the Guild flashed back to feminist awareness and participated in such campaigns as that for women police.

There are yet many further points which space prevents me from going into fully but they are all important areas of women's political activity. Then, as now, many women were active in the Peace Movement and were active in local branches of the League of Nations Union and the Women's International League for Peace and Freedom. Many women fought against unemployment. Dora Cox organized a hunger march from South Wales to London in 1934: it was the first march where women marched alongside men and not in a separate women's section. Finally it should also be remembered that women were campaigning throughout this period for birth control and abortion.

QUESTIONS

The following questions may prove a helpful way in to this

topic. What political action were women engaged in in your
community? Is there any evidence for their involvement in
early radical movements and protests? in Chartism? in early
socialist movements? in the suffrage campaign? in pacifist
actions, etc.? (If in the suffrage campaign, to what national
body was the local branch affiliated?) Were women involved
in any political party – Conservative, Liberal, Labour, Com-
munist, etc.? What sort of work did women do in the parties?
Fund-raising? Canvassing? Tea-making, etc.? What issues
involved women most and spurred them to political action?
Issues concerning children? Housing? Employment? Did
women form themselves into any pressure groups on any
specific issue? From your researches you may get the impression that women were not very interested in 'main-stream'
politics. Try to find out in that case why they voted as they
did? Was it husband's influence? Father's influence? Other
factors? See also the questions directed to women in the oral
sources section below.

SECONDARY SOURCES
See also Chapter 4.

General
Olive Banks, *Faces of Feminism: A Study of Feminism as a
Social Movement*, Oxford, Martin Robinson, 1981.
Margaret Stacey and Marian Price, *Women, Power and
Politics*, London, Tavistock, 1981.

Early radical activity
J. O'Brien, *Women's Liberation in Labour History: A Case
Study from Nottingham*, London, Spokesman Pamphlet, no.
24.
Dorothy Thompson, 'Women and nineteenth century radical
politics: a lost dimension', in J. Mitchell and A. Oakley (eds),
The Rights and Wrongs of Women, Harmondsworth,
Penguin, 1976.

Chartism
F. G. Mather (ed.), *Chartism and Society*, London, Bell &
Hyman, 1980.

Dorothy Thompson, *The Early Chartists*, London, Macmillan, 1971.

Later Nineteenth-century and suffrage

Patricia Hollis, *Women in Public: The Women's Movement 1850–1900*, London, George Allen & Unwin, 1979.

Lesley Parker Hume, *The National Union of Women's Suffrage Societies*, New York, Garland, 1982.

Jill Liddington and Jill Norris, *One Hand Tied Behind Us: The Rise of the Women's Suffrage Movement*, London, Virago, 1978.

Andrew Rosen, *Rise Up, Women!*, London, Routledge & Kegan Paul, 1974.

Judith R. Walkowitz and Daniel J. Walkowitz, 'We are not beasts of the field: prostitution and the poor in Plymouth and Southampton under the Contagious Diseases Act', in M. Hartman and L. Banner (eds), *Clio's Consciousness Raised*, New York, Harper & Row, 1974.

BIOGRAPHIES AND AUTOBIOGRAPHIES

Vera Brittain, *Testament of Youth*, London, Virago, 1978.

Vera Brittain, *Testament of Experience*, London, Virago, 1979.

Vera Brittain, *Testament of Friendship*, London, Virago, 1980.

Doris Nield Chew, *Ada Nield Chew: The Life and Writings of a Working Woman*, London, Virago, 1982.

Hannah Mitchell, *The Hard Way Up*, London, Virago, 1977.

Dora Russell, *The Tamarisk Tree*, I, II and III (forthcoming), London, Virago, 1975–.

JOURNALS

Many journals were produced by women's groups in the past – just as they are today, and like so many present-day publications many were not preserved. The further problem with old journals is their availability. The major collections are the British Library and the Fawcett Society Library. Despite the problem of availability some of the suffrage magazines are so interesting and such a good source of local information that they deserve inclusion. The chief ones are:

Common Cause (1909–13); superseded by *Women's Suffrage: the Common Cause of Humanity* (1913–14); superseded by *Common Cause of Humanity* (1914–20); superseded by *Woman's Leader and the Common Cause* (1920–33) (BL/Fawcett).

The Suffragette, organ of WSPU, edited by Christabel Pankhurst (1912–15); superseded by *Britannia* (1915–18) (BL/Fawcett).

The Vote (1909–33), organ of the WFL (BL/Fawcett).

Votes for Women (1907–18), WSPU, edited by Pethwick Lawrences (BL/Fawcett).

Woman's Dreadnought (1914–17); superseded by *Worker's Dreadnought* (1917–24) (BL).

Woman's Franchise (1907–11) (BL/Fawcett).

Woman's Suffrage Journal (1870–90), edited by Lydia Becker (BL/Fawcett).

In order to show the range of material I would like to give just two extracts. *The Suffragette* gave very full coverage to the militant campaign. The edition of 14 February 1913 gave graphic accounts of the attack on the orchid house at Kew, the invasion of Newcastle Town Hall – which was daubed with slogans four feet high – and accounts of telegraph wire cutting. The extract emphasizes the impact of the wire cutting.

TELEGRAPH WIRES CUT.
Glasgow isolated from London.

On Saturday telegraphic communication was entirely cut off between London and Glasgow for several hours, with serious results to the commercial men of the latter city. The destruction of the aerial wires was at first attributed to the gale, but when it was discovered that the underground cables were also out of order, inquiries were instituted, and it was found that fuse-boxes in connection with the underground communication had been blown up. The aerial wires had been cut through with scissors. 'There is no question,' says *The Daily Telegraph*, 'but that the damage was done by Suffragists.

Indeed, at the Glasgow Suffragists' headquarters no denial was given to the allegation.' During market hours Glasgow stockbrokers did not get through a single wire from London.

On the morning of Friday, February 7, it was discovered that between twenty and thirty telephone wires, including some trunk wires, were cut on the public highway near Dumbarton.

A notice was found affixed to a post with the inscription 'Votes for Women' upon it.

Wires Cut in Birmingham.

When the Birmingham and Coventry telegraph departments applied the usual daily tests to wires between the two cities yesterday morning, the discovery was made that communication was broken, and that several telegraph wires between Coventry and Birmingham had been severed, and damage done to the extent of about £10.

It is supposed that the wires were cut with long-handled clippers, such as are used in trimming trees.

The police are making inquiries, but so far they have no clue to the identity of the persons responsible for the damage.

They are satisfied, however, that it is the work of Suffragists, and a woman's footprints have been discovered in the turf immediately below the broken wires.

Votes for Women contains fascinating information from the branches and demonstrates organization on a national scale. To take one example, a mass demonstration was organized in Hyde Park for 21 June 1908. Cheap trains were arranged from all parts of Britain to converge on London. Maps showed the train routes and detailed instructions told people from the regions where they were to be marshalled and gave them their route to Hyde Park. They were all advised of that day's new marching song. It began,

March, women, march! The sun rides high,
Proud summer vaunts it in the sky
Proud let your steps and voices be –
March, women, march to Victory.

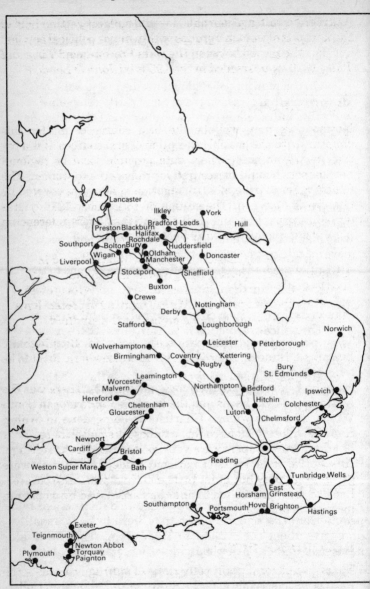

Map of England showing places served by special trains to London, Sunday, June 21 1908 for the Votes for Women Demonstration

Apart from suffrage journals, I would suggest getting hold of the journals of women's groups within major political parties.

For the period between the wars I recommend *Time and Tide* (1920–) superseded in the 1950s by *John O'London*.

NEWSPAPERS

Newspapers may well be the best source of all for this chapter, with the possible exception of oral sources. It is a big task but from the earliest date possible local or regional newspapers should be scoured for references to women. The Glasgow rent strike of 1915, mentioned above, is covered by Glasgow's *Forward*. The edition of 16 October 1915 quotes other newspapers and makes national cross-referencing possible: it quotes the *Daily Sketch* as follows,

> The example of Glasgow's women will be followed in London today. Tooting will give the lead to the metropolis. Northampton has already made its protest against the rent profiteer. We are fighting to protect lives and property – not to make profits for the landlord.

This particular strike also took place in Birmingham, Liverpool, Dundee, Aberdeen, Ayr and elsewhere. It could be followed up.

The Chartists had their own newspapers. There was the *Northern Star* in Leeds and the *Western Vindicator* in South Wales. Work on women Chartists is being done in Wales. Similar investigations could be undertaken elsewhere.

Local newspapers are a very good source for the suffrage. Any outrages or visits of national leaders to an area were given great play but quiet little meetings were also covered. Look to local papers too to find the part played by women in local government.

RECORD SOURCES

There are several main collections of suffrage records – the Fawcett Society Library, the Suffragette Fellowship Collection at the London Museum and the archive department of Manchester Central Library. There are various western

Scottish records in the Mitchell Library in Glasgow and the
records of Sylvia Pankhurst's East London Federation of
Suffragettes is in the Internationaal Instituut for Sociale
Geschiedenis in Amsterdam. Margaret Barrow gives more
details of these collections, except for the Scottish records.[16]
There is an urgent need, however, to track down local records
concerning the suffrage campaign. As Margaret Barrow
writes,

> There is scope for an attempt to be made to trace the
> branch records of various suffrage organizations for
> these records could include undiscovered aspects of the
> movement, for instance, the effect of suffragist or
> suffragette activities in a small community and the way
> in which the activities of individual women were
> received by their families in a closely knit society. Local
> records could also show whether or not branches always
> followed the party line advocated by headquarters,
> particularly with regard to violence.[17]

These records are worth tracking down. I found what remains
of the Cardiff branch records in the Friends' Meeting House:
they are now in Glamorgan Record Office.

The records of the Co-operative Women's Guild from
1890–1944 are in the British Library of Political and
Economic Science. There may well be local branch records
still retained by one-time members.

A collection of papers relating to the Contagious
Diseases campaign is in the Fawcett Library.

If researchers have found evidence of women participating in early disturbances and riots, then they might go on
to check if women were arrested and prosecuted. Court
records may throw light on this. A really big disturbance
might have led not only to a trial at Quarter Sessions or the
Assizes but it may have led to the government sending in
troops. In that case consult the Home Office Records at the
Public Record Office in Kew.

Finally for women's participation in local parties
approach the branch offices of the political parties. Their
participation in local council activities will be recorded in
council records, which may still be at the town hall.

ORAL SOURCES

I have talked to many women who were politically active before the Second World War and I have become aware of the highly active role played by some women. By chance I met a woman who had organized a hunger march from South Wales in the 1930s and another who had organized and arranged for the transfer of children from Spain to Neath in the Spanish Civil War. But not all political action will be quite as impressive and I suggest that researchers should approach women who were involved in local branches of political parties.

Here are some suggested questions to pose: When did you first become interested in politics? Why? Were you influenced by your parents? husband? Did any one issue spark off your interest? Did you join a political party? Which? Why? Was there a separate women's section? How many women were in your local branch? What activities did you take part in? How were women regarded by men in the party? Were your political views known at work? Were you favoured/discriminated against because of them?

PHOTOGRAPHS AND ILLUSTRATIONS

Newspapers and magazines are a good source of photographs and illustrations. Museums too hold old photographs. The National Labour History Museum has photographs of women who were on marches and demonstrations. The People's Palace in Glasgow has photographs relating to the rent strike. It is therefore worth looking for material in local museums and in record offices. Also ask the women whom you interview if they have old photographs.

MISCELLANEA

There are collections of artefacts relating to the suffrage campaign in the Fawcett Library (portraits, postcards, posters, medals); the London Museum (banners, badges, suffragette roll of honour of imprisoned suffragettes, items made in prison and prison cutlery); Manchester Central Library (banners). It is worth looking around museums and asking what they have: they do not put everything on display. Bristol museum recently put on display, in a small exhibition at Blaise Castle, an anti-suffrage inkwell. The People's Palace in Glasgow has a collection of Scottish suffrage 'memorabilia' including WSPU motoring scarves, cups, saucers and teapots, badges, banners and pamphlets.

NOTES

1 D. J. V. Jones, *Before Rebecca: Popular Protests in Wales*, London, Allen Lane, pp. 33–4.
2 J. L. Hammond and B. Hammond, *The Village Labourer 1760–1832* (1911), London, Longman, 1966.
3 J. Stevenson, *Popular Disturbances in England*, London, Longman, 1979, pp. 101–2.
4 J. O'Brien, *Women's Liberation in Labour History: A Case Study from Nottingham*, London, Spokesman Pamphlet no. 24, no date.
5 G. A. Williams, *The Merthyr Rising*, London, Croom Helm, 1978.
6 D. Thompson, 'Women and nineteenth century radical politics: a lost dimension', in J. Mitchell and A. Oakley (eds), *The Rights and Wrongs of Women*, Harmondsworth, Penguin, 1976.
7 F. G. Mather, *Chartism and Society*, London, Bell & Hyman, 1980, p. 114.
8 O. Banks, *Faces of Feminism: A Study of Feminism as a Social Movement*, Oxford, Martin Robinson, 1981, p. 23.
9 Ibid., p. 23.
10 Cited in P. Hollis, *Women in Public: The Women's Movement*, London, George Allen & Unwin, 1979, p. 287.
11 See ibid., pp. 167–96.
12 J. R. and D. J. Walkowitz, 'We are not beasts of the field: prostitution and the poor in Plymouth and Southampton under the Contagious Diseases Acts', in M. Hartman and L. Banner (eds), *Clio's Consciousness Raised*, New York, Harper & Row, 1974, pp. 192–225.
13 J. Liddington and J. Norris, *One Hand Tied Behind Us: The Rise of the Women's Suffrage Movement*, London, Virago, 1978.
14 Banks, op. cit., p. 153.
15 For a survey of these years, see Banks, op. cit.
16 M. Barrow, *Women 1870–1928*, New York, Garland, pp. 47–53.
17 Ibid., p. 247.

Chapter eight

Sharing your findings

This chapter is concerned with the sifting and presentation of material which a group or an individual may have gathered. Having collected a mass of information – in itself an exciting and rewarding task – people sometimes get overwhelmed by the sheer bulk of the material. There is no need for that.

Probably researchers, having read this book, will have decided to concentrate on certain areas of women's lives, though, if people allow themselves enough time, it is quite feasible to cover a broad spectrum. Within each area of investigation it is important to pose some of the questions suggested in each chapter. For example, if a group is looking at women's waged work in a town, then start by simply asking what work women did. Establish the range – make a list, make a clear graph showing the numbers or percentage of women in each occupation. (You can be fairly accurate in the period covered by the census.) Go on to inquire about working conditions, wages, trade union activity, the status of one job compared to another, relationships between men and women at work and in trade unions. Record your information and see what conclusions you reach from it. Questions do not need to be complicated to yield interesting answers. Keep an open mind about what you will find. I have suggested a few methods of approach which may prove helpful, e.g. the theory of women as a reserve army of labour and the influence of the domestic ideology on women's lives. Both are useful approaches but I do not wish to tell people what they will find. Who knows until questions are put and many local answers are found? There is an urgent need for local investigations in order that by gathering specific local information, we can challenge all the tired generalizations about what women did, what women were and what women wanted. It is therefore very important that having gathered information, that information should be shared. I suggest a few ways of presenting material and of ensuring that other people know about the work done. In fact, it is a good idea to think out early on how you wish to present your findings: this decision can influence the type of material you gather.

Groups may like to consider some of the following ideas.

LOCAL RADIO

Approach your local radio station and tell them of your project. They can assist in making a programme on the project. (They can also be useful in advertising any other sort of end product of a women's history investigation and they might also be useful in putting groups in touch with people to interview.)

VIDEO

Video is not such an expensive medium to use providing you have access to equipment. There are many local video workshops throughout the country, so approach them and discuss your work as the subject of a possible video film. There may also be, in big cities, a women's film collective. They too could be approached.

PAMPHLETS

This is a popular way in which local historians make known their findings. It is also a good method of publishing the biographies or autobiographies of older women. If a group decides upon this method they could usefully contact The Federation of Worker Writers and Community Publishers. Its member groups include Bristol Broadsides, East Bowling History Workshop (Bradford) and S.E.1 People's History Group.

CALENDARS

Illustrated calendars showing photographs of local women – at work, at home, enjoying themselves – are another possibility.

LOCAL HISTORY SOCIETY JOURNALS

Contribute articles or reminiscences of older women to local history journals. Consult the editor before you start work. The national journal *History Workshop* has set up local workshops and it would be a good idea to contact *History Workshop* in London to inquire if there is a local branch. The journal may be interested in articles or reports of work in progress.

LECTURES/TALKS

It would be very good if local researchers gave talks or lectures to any other interested organizations in their area.

HISTORY WALKS

One idea of drawing attention to women's history, which has been employed in some big cities (so far London, Birmingham and Manchester) is to organize 'history walks' along a route passing places of interest in the history of women.

EXHIBITIONS

If you are able to collect good visual material or convert factual material into visual modes of expression (e.g. graphs, tables) an exhibition is a good way of sharing your findings. In a group, in the town where I now live, we organized a women's history exhibition. We concentrated on education, waged work (mainly domestic service and shop work), home-life and leisure. We collected photographs, old notices and posters, household manuals and domestic objects (the museum lent us a vacuum cleaner *circa* 1900) and old clothes, displayed on tailors' dummies and group members. We conveyed census information in graph form and, with the permission of the interviewees, made a tape recorder and our tapes available if people wanted to listen.

Groups may think of other ways of making their findings known and of course there is no reason at all to confine yourself to any one method. In fact, by employing a variety of the methods of sharing the research findings you will reach a wider audience.

Finally, it would be most useful if these research findings were preserved. This can be done both locally and nationally. I suggest researchers deposit a record of their work or any of their publications in the local library or record office. Tape recordings could also be deposited in record offices or they could be sent to the Oral History Society, thereby giving wide access to them. Video tapes are probably best deposited in video workshops. Lastly in order that there can be a central place, where a record is kept of all the local research going on, I would urge local groups and individuals to inform the Women's Research and Resources Centre of their project and to provide details of where their findings are stored.

Some useful addresses

Before visiting the places listed below *please write or telephone*

Association of Assistant Mistresses
29 Gordon Square, London WC1N 0PU (01–387 5674)

Association of Head Mistresses
29 Gordon Square, London WC1H 0PU (01–387 1361)

Birmingham Feminist History Group
c/o Janice Winship, Bleak House, 137 Newton Rd, Birmingham 11 (021–7736063)

British Film Institute
127 Charing Cross Road, London WC2H 0EA (01–437 4355)

British Library: Newspaper Library
Colindale Avenue, London NW9 (01–200 5515)

British Library: Reference Division
Department of Printed Books and Department of Manuscripts, Great Russell Street, London WC1B 3DG (01–636 1544)

British Library of Political and Economic Science
London School of Economics, Houghton Street, London WC2A 2AC (01–405 7686)

The Collis Collection
The Archive Department, London School of Economics, 10 Portugal Street, London WC2 (01–405 7686 Ext. 241)

David Owen Centre for Population Growth
Park Place, Cardiff

Department of Education and Science Library
Elizabeth House, York Road, London SE1

Fawcett Library
City of London Polytechnic, Old Castle Street, London
E1 7NT (01–283 1030 Ext. 570)

The Federation of Worker Writers & Community Publishers
c/o 10 Brief Street, London SE5 9RD (01–274 4617)

The Feminist Archive
8 St Saviour's Terrace, Larkhall, Bath, Avon

Girls' Friendly Society
126 Queens Gate, South Kensington, London SW7 5LQ
(01–589 9628)

Greater London Council Record Office
40 Northampton Road, London EC1R 0AB (01–633 6851)

History Workshop Journal
25 Horsell Road, London N5 1XL

Imperial War Museum
Lambeth Road, London SE1 6HZ (01–735 3922)

Internationaal Instituut voor Sociale Geschiedenis
Herengracht 262–266, Amsterdam C, The Netherlands

Labour Party Library
Transport House, Smith Square, London SW1P
(01–834 9434)

Lesbian Archive Collective
Lesbian Link, 61A Bloom Street, Manchester (061 236 6205
or Rochdale 40878)

Liverpool Feminist History Group
c/o Linda Grant, 12 Devonshire Rd, Liverpool 8
(051–728 7849)

London Feminist History Group
c/o Women's Research and Resources Centre

Manchester Central Library
St Peter's Square, Manchester M2 5PD (061–236 9422)

Manchester Feminist History Group
c/o Manchester Area Resource Centre, 61 Bloom Street,
Manchester

The Marie Stopes Collection
Science Museum, Exhibition Road, South Kensington
SW7 2DD (01–589 3456)

Museum of London
150 London Wall, London EC2Y 5HN (01–600 3699)

National Council of Women of Great Britain
36 Lower Sloane Street, London SW1W 8BP (01–730 0619)

National Federation of Women's Institutes
39 Eccleston Street, London SW1W 9NT (01–730 7212)

The National Film Archive
81 Dean Street, London W1V 6AA (01–437 4355)

National Library of Wales
Aberystwyth, Dyfed

The National Museum of Labour History
Limehouse Town Hall, Commercial Road, London E14
(01–515 3229)

National Register of Archives
Quality House, Quality Court, Chancery Lane, London
WC2A 1HP (01–242 1198)

National Union of Teachers
Hamilton House, Mableton Place, London WC1H 9BH
(01–387 6806)

The Other Cinema
79 Wardour Street, Tisbury Court, London W1V
(01–734 8508)

Oral History Society
Department of Sociology, University of Essex, Colchester,
Essex

The People's Palace
Glasgow Green, Glasgow (041–554 0223)

Public Records Office
Chancery Lane, London (01–405 0741)
Ruskin Avenue, Kew, Richmond (01–876 3444)

The Radio Times Hulton Picture Library
35 Marylebone High Street, London W1M 4AA
(01–580 5577)

Sheffield Feminist History Group
c/o Cathy Burke, 72 Clarkegrove Road, Sheffield 10
(0742–681127)

The Trade Union Congress Library
Congress House, 21–28 Great Russell Street, London
WC1B 3LS (01–636 4030)

Welsh Feminist History Group
c/o Department of Arts and Languages, Polytechnic of Wales,
Pontypridd, Mid Glamorgan (0443 405133 Ext. 2774)

Women's Research and Resources Centre
190 Upper Street, London N1 1RQ (01–359 5773)

Index